FOSTERING HABITS OF MIND
IN TODAY'S STUDENTS

FOSTERING HABITS OF MIND IN TODAY'S STUDENTS

A New Approach to Developmental Education

EDITED BY

Jennifer Fletcher, Adela Najarro,
and Hetty Yelland

Foreword by
Emily Lardner

STERLING, VIRGINIA

Published by Stylus Publishing, LLC
22883 Quicksilver Drive
Sterling, Virginia 20166-2102

Library of Congress Cataloging-in-Publication Data
Fletcher, Jennifer, 1972-
Fostering habits of mind in today's students : a new approach to
developmental education / Jenifer Fletcher, Adela Najarro, and
Hetty Yelland.
  pages cm
Includes bibliographical references and index.
ISBN 978-1-62036-179-5 (cloth : alk. paper)
ISBN 978-1-62036-180-1 (pbk. : alk. paper)
ISBN 978-1-62036-181-8 (library networkable e-edition)
ISBN 978-1-62036-182-5 (consumer e-edition)
1. Developmental studies programs. 2. College teaching.
3. Remedial teaching. 4. Education, Higher. I. Najarro, Adela.
II. Yelland, Hetty. III. Title.
LB2331.2.F54 2015
378.125--dc23

                                                    2014029556

13-digit ISBN: 978-1-62036-179-5 (cloth)
13-digit ISBN: 978-1-62036-180-1 (paper)
13-digit ISBN: 978-1-62036-181-8 (library networkable e-edition)
13-digit ISBN: 978-1-62036-182-5 (consumer e-edition)

Printed in the United States of America

All first editions printed on acid-free paper
that meets the American National Standards Institute
Z39-48 Standard.

Bulk Purchases

Quantity discounts are available for use in workshops and for
staff development.
Call 1-800-232-0223

First Edition, 2015

10   9   8   7   6   5   4   3   2   1

This book is dedicated to the memory of Heidi Ramirez, our colleague, collaborator, and friend. Heidi was a Hartnell College English department faculty member and one of the founding members of the Collaborative Alliance for Postsecondary Success (CAPS). We owe a great deal to Heidi for her enthusiasm, intelligence, and commitment to our success and the success of our students.

CONTENTS

FOREWORD

I met the teachers whose work is presented in this book several years ago, at a summer institute organized by the Collaborative Alliance for Postsecondary Success (CAPS). Prior to the meeting, I had immersed myself in documents describing the project and its purpose, and I thought I understood what the project was about. Walking into the room that morning, I realized that while the project was about sharing strategies for helping students develop productive habits of mind, the energy behind the work came from the relationships teachers had and were developing with each other. That day, I was in the presence of a group of teachers who respected and liked each other, were happy to be in each other's company, and wanted to talk about how to build on students' strengths in ways that would help them succeed in math and in writing.

If we want more students to succeed in college, we need to make space and time for faculty to reflect on their practices. CAPS did that. Teachers had the opportunity to spend time together, share their practices, argue about approaches, and compare results. What they had in common was a passion for helping students to succeed, and that energy was palpable in the room that morning. Foreshadowing the strong focus in this book on connecting student learning with specific and thoughtful teaching practices, the CAPS summer institute intertwined faculty-focused goals and student-focused goals.

The faculty-focused goals were intended to apply to not only everyone participating in CAPS but also faculty with whom CAPS participants collaborated. The following faculty-focused goals were named: (a) to support continued professional learning and collaboration within and across institutional and disciplinary contexts, and (b) to examine and apply current scholarship on student success. The following student-focused goals were also named: (a) to promote student retention by continuing to identify practices that build engagement, and (b) to promote student learning by continuing to explore and implement practices that serve vertical and lateral transfer of learning. Building on that foundation, this book demonstrates the power of organizing professional learning across disciplines and institutions, grounded in research on student engagement and success, to make our classrooms places where we practice scholarly teaching for the sake of our students.

In her introduction to this book, "Why Habits of Mind Matter," Jennifer Fletcher describes herself as a graduate student, wildly curious about the processes that lie behind the products—the books—that she is reading. Only when she had the opportunity to work in the shared open space of the British Library's reading room did she have the chance to see scholars at work—"taking notes, turning pages, frowning, and sighing" (1). That revelation, or series of revelations, about how scholars actually do what they do, coupled with her later experiences as a teacher, led Fletcher to conclude that "we can do a better job exposing the hidden brainwork that leads to academic success" (2).

This book does that work, by describing not only the brainwork—the habits of mind—necessary for student success but also the brainwork behind the thoughtful design of dozens of activities and assignments. Echoing the dual goals of that 2011 summer institute, each chapter includes an essay examining current scholarship and connecting it with practice followed by "lesson exemplars" with clearly identified goals that lend themselves to adaptation in a variety of settings.

One gift of this book is that it not only treats teaching as a scholarly matter, in particular the teaching of students in their first year of college, but also assumes teaching is a social practice. The project and these chapters are grounded in hours of collaborative conversations among teachers at three different institutions, from different departments, who all took seriously the charge to examine their collective practices and strengthen them. As a group, they worked to set norms for their professional interactions. They adopted an "assets-based" approach to their work with each other, just as they did in their classes with students. Across their differences, they built a community of practice grounded in a shared commitment to connecting theory and practice, using each to inform the other. As a result, readers have the good fortune to meet different teachers—to hear different voices—all of whom share a commitment to building on students' assets and helping students cultivate productive habits of mind.

Another gift of this book is the way it builds a strong case for focusing on "habits of mind," a phrase that's explained and then developed, with numerous examples of not only students' habits of mind but also our own. Habits of mind—such as engagement, curiosity, metacognition, or transfer of learning, to name some that are the focus of the lessons included here—are ongoing. They are habits, practices, not something we master and move beyond. The lessons in each chapter give teachers many ways to make these invisible practices visible. By making them visible, teachers make these habits of mind discussable, coachable, and available for students to reflect upon and assess.

A final gift of this book is that it admits to the lifelong work of becoming better teachers, together. The very same developmental learning cycle that is traced through these chapters, from discovering assets and creating communities, to developing self-efficacy and transferring learning, applies to groups of teachers, within and across institutions, who commit themselves to learning together how to apply current scholarship on student success in their classrooms. For the vast majority of us who teach in higher education, the challenge of helping students turn access to higher education into a successful series of learning experiences remains a critical one. It's not something we can solve on our own, even if we are terrific instructors, because we are not our students' only teachers. Students need our whole institutions to work better—they need to encounter more teachers, more often, who are as thoughtful and explicit about making the "hidden brainwork" behind academic success visible as are the writers of this book.

Emily Lardner
Director
Washington Center
The Evergreen State College

PREFACE

When the 13 contributors and three editors first met to plan this project, we started with a list of what we *didn't* want our book to be: "boring," "inaccessible and muddled," "overly didactic and impractical," and "dry." Instead, we imagined a resource for busy college teachers that would be "passionate," "stimulating," "practical," and "vibrant"—something we ourselves would enjoy reading. The result is *Fostering Habits of Mind in Today's Students: A New Approach to Developmental Education.*

As developmental education faculty at three Hispanic-serving institutions in California, we were concerned by the way some basic skills programs and "remedial" courses promoted only short term, decontextualized learning—something we knew did not help the first-generation and multilingual college students we served. Instead, we wanted "deeper learning"[1] that would lead to internalized and transferable competencies. We wanted to develop our students' habits of mind.

Through a multicampus grant from the Lumina Foundation's Minority-Serving Institutions–Models of Success program, we collaborated on a collection of lesson exemplars designed to foster students' holistic intellectual growth by targeting such dispositional capacities as engagement, persistence, motivation, curiosity, and self-efficacy. For example, one lesson uses a candid approach to peer review to develop flexibility and openness. Another combines argumentation skills with metacognition. A third addresses students' math anxiety through reflective-writing prompts. As we piloted the lessons in our own classrooms, we found that students who internalize these habits of mind are indeed more likely to trust their efforts, feel connected to their college culture, enjoy their studies, and understand learning as a process.

Our classroom-ready lessons reflect the personal perspectives and unique institutional contexts of their authors, which include tenure-line and adjunct faculty from two community colleges and a four-year university. Chapters follow the arc of a full instructional cycle for a typical developmental education course, beginning with the first introductory days and then moving through the term to the last weeks when students complete the final course projects. You will find an introductory essay linking theory to practice at the start of each chapter.

Our Purpose

Habits of mind are at the heart of any college success story. Those students who persist to degree completion know the cumulative impact of habitual discipline, flexibility, resilience, and creativity on their long-term success. We believe that explicit coaching in habits of mind is important for all learners at all levels of instruction. By making these largely unseen behaviors visible to more students, we seek to increase student retention and success, particularly among our most underserved and underrepresented populations. In doing so, we are responding to the scholarship on student success that repeatedly calls for models of how to formalize instruction in habits of mind.

How to Use This Book

Teachers can read these chapters consecutively or selectively. Read the research-based introductory articles for in-depth discussions on particular habits of mind that apply for significant teaching moments in the semester. You may also find it useful to skip around. Maybe one afternoon you'll read an introductory essay, but on Sunday night when you are looking for a new idea, you'll scan the exemplars for assignments and activities that can be put to immediate use. At the end of each exemplar, you'll find a Quick Start Guide listing the necessary first steps for putting the exemplar into practice in your own classroom.

Our intention is not to add extra responsibilities to college teachers' already full plates. Instead, we want to showcase ways to make procedural knowledge and dispositional capacities visible *while* teaching the academic content of our different subject areas.

Throughout the book, current college faculty share their knowledge about what works in the classroom. We hope you will find lots of helpful ideas for creating a student-centered classroom where habits of mind are cultivated and valued.

Note

1. The National Research Council's report *Education for Life and Work: Developing Transferable Knowledge and Skills in the 21st Century* (Committee on Defining Deeper Learning and 21st Century Skills. Eds. James W. Pellegrino and Margaret L. Hilton. Board on Testing and Assessment and Board on Science Education, Division of Behavioral and Social Sciences and Education. Washington, DC: The National Academies Press, 2012) became an important resource for our work. This project was also influenced by *Framework for Success in Postsecondary Writing*, a 2011 publication by the Council of Writing Program Administrators, the National Council of Teachers of English, and the National Writing Project (Urbana: National Council of Teachers of English, 2011).

ACKNOWLEDGMENTS

Creating this project together was a powerful reminder of why we love to teach. We love to teach because it gives us joy, because we are driven by curiosity, grateful to our mentors, and inspired by our students. This book grew out of that shared sense of passion and responsibility. We are deeply thankful to the many outstanding colleagues, students, and educational leaders who helped to nurture our own habits of mind during this process.

We would first like to acknowledge those faculty who participated in the three-year faculty collaboration among California State University at Monterey Bay (CSUMB), Cabrillo College, and Hartnell College from which this book originated. Our partnership, which we called the Collaborative Alliance for Postsecondary Success (CAPS), was generously funded by a grant from the Lumina Foundation's Minority-Serving Institutions—Models of Success program. The goal of our grant was to improve student retention and success in the developmental math and writing programs at all three institutions through shared expectations and instructional practices.

From Cabrillo College, we thank Ed Braunhut, Mary Buchanan, Brad Krein, Veronica Lundquist, Victor Ramos, Julessa Bass, Lydia Graecyn, Jennifer McGuire, Tina Sander, and Ted Shank.

From CSUMB, we appreciatively thank Lipika Deka, Rachel Esselstein, Hongde Hu, Lorraine O'Shea, Michael Scott, Alysia Walther, Maria Boza, Axil Cricchio, Natasha Oehlman, and Mark Roberts.

From Hartnell College, we are grateful to Jim Butler, Mohammed Hussain, Carolyn Jensen, Greg Perkins, Ken Rand, Sue Sedrak, Patrick Staten, Afshin Tiraie, Olga Blomgren, Sunita Lanka, Heidi Ramirez, Wendy Roscher, and Daphne Young.

A special thank-you to CSUMB student assistant Liliana Castrellon for all her help. Thank you to all the administrators who supported the faculty collaboration, especially Kathy Cruz-Uribe, Suzanne Flannigan, and Renee Kilmer.

Thank you to Dale Oliver of Humboldt State University, Marcy Alancraig of Cabrillo College, and Sugie Goen-Salter of San Francisco

State University for the inspiration they provided by presenting at our summer institutes.

We would also like to thank Leticia Tomas Bustillos, Noel Harmon, Clemencia Cosentino, and Debra Strong for their expert guidance and feedback during the grant implementation.

The Institute for Higher Education Policy provided outstanding faculty development support for our project, as did the Association of American Colleges and Universities's (AAC&U) Give Students a Compass initiative. Sarah Burrows and Alexandra Hartnett at Stylus Publishing deserve recognition for the superb work they've done guiding the book from development to production; we're deeply grateful for their expert help at each stage of the process. Jerrold H. Zar kindly granted us permission to use "Candidate for a Pullet Surprise," first published in 1994 in the *Journal of Irreproducible Results*. We are also grateful to AAC&U's journal *Liberal Education* for permission to use excerpts from Jennifer Fletcher's 2013 article "Critical Habits of Mind: Exposing the Process of Development."

Most of all, we would like to thank our families for their support and patience and Becky Rosenberg for her outstanding leadership, guidance, support, and contributions.

INTRODUCTION

Why Habits of Mind Matter

Jennifer Fletcher

"Success in work and life in the 21st century is associated with cognitive, intrapersonal, and interpersonal competencies that allow individuals to adapt effectively to changing situations rather than to rely solely on well-worn procedures."

—From *Education for Life and Work* (National Research Council 70)

"We rarely talk about passion in education, as if doing so makes the work of teachers seem less serious, more emotional than cognitive, somewhat biased or of lesser import."

—John Hattie (23)

When I first started graduate school, I was an incurable snoop. Deeply curious about the lifestyles of my professors, I looked through the bookcases in their offices, studied the clutter on their desks, and asked personal questions about everything from how they balanced work with family to how many hours they slept at night. Yet I wasn't trying to pry into their private lives; I was simply fascinated by how they did their academic work because I'd never seen professional scholarship in action before. I knew the results, but not the process.

Later, when I had the opportunity to work in the open, shared space of the British Library's reading room, I found myself in an intellectual voyeur's heaven. Here before me were world-renowned researchers, taking notes, turning pages, frowning, and sighing. It was a revelation to me to see in person the struggles I had associated with novices replicated on the faces of experts. In the reading room, I at last saw the photo negative of academic labor—a total inversion of production and product.

1

Too often, our students do not see this master image. In *Clueless in Academe*, Gerald Graff argues that many students (and people in general) feel unnecessarily confused and embarrassed in the world of higher education because it obscures its own processes. Graff claims that "academia reinforces cluelessness by making its ideas, problems, and ways of thinking *look* more opaque, narrowly specialized, and beyond normal capacities than they are or need to be" (1). My own bewilderment by what Graff calls the "mysterious guild secrets" (191) of graduate education convinced me we can do a better job exposing the hidden brainwork that leads to academic success.

One way to do this is by showing our students how habits of mind contribute to deep and transferable learning.

Habits of Mind and College Readiness

Those of us who have been hard at work on college access and success efforts can take comfort from the recent convergence of scholarship that links habits of mind to academic preparation. Competency initiatives such as Liberal Education and America's Promise (AAC&U), California's *Academic Literacy* report (ICAS), or the National Governors Association's (2010) Common Core State Standards all herald the cultivation of broad intellectual practices as an essential part of college- and career-readiness. In 2011, the Council of Writing Program Administrators, National Council of Teachers of English, and National Writing Project jointly published *Framework for Success in Postsecondary Writing*—one of the first documents of its kind to explicitly link habits of mind, learning experiences, and academic skills. For students in developmental or "remedial" classes, these habits of mind are critical; without a sense of intellectual curiosity, motivation, and confidence many learners disengage from academic culture before they have even started their college-level coursework.

> For students in developmental or "remedial" classes, these habits of mind are critical; without a sense of intellectual curiosity, motivation, and confidence many learners disengage from academic culture before they have even started their college-level coursework.

The 15 teachers you'll meet throughout this book's collection of lesson exemplars share a commitment to improving the retention and success of our most vulnerable first-year college students. For the many first-generation, multilingual, low-income, and underrepresented students we serve in our developmental education programs, knowledge of how to thrive academically is at least as important as the content-based learning outcomes on our course syllabi.

We began working together on this project in 2010. Funded by a grant from the Lumina Foundation, our collaboration involved a three-year partnership among two California community colleges and a state university that enabled us to make a deep study of the practices that most directly contribute to students' successful transition to higher education. Thirty developmental math and writing instructors from Cabrillo College, California State University at Monterey Bay (CSUMB), and Hartnell College participated in the grant. All three campuses are Hispanic-serving institutions whose students herald from throughout the "salad bowl" of the Salinas Valley and from up and down California's foggy central coast. This is Steinbeck country. Placement in college-level writing and math classes hovers around 50% for first-time students at the state school and is lower at the two community colleges. Most students work, receive financial aid, and—should they persist until graduation—will be among the first in their families to earn an associate's or bachelor's degree. First-year retention rates for each campus vary from below 50% to a high of 76%.

Many of our students have math or writing anxiety. Most are surprised by the amount of studying required outside of class. Few have regular routines or dedicated spaces for academic work. These are not "deficits" our students bring to college; they are data for making instructional decisions.

Through our faculty collaboration, we discovered that nearly all of us were already trying to do something to strengthen the "soft skills" that didn't appear as learning outcomes on our syllabi, but that we nevertheless knew were critical for our students' success—skills such as the ability to persist during difficult reading or to self-motivate despite a 40-hour workweek.

Our Approach

Although we haven't found a magic bullet, we have found a shared understanding of the intellectual qualities higher education faculty believe most contribute to first-year students' readiness for college coursework. These include engagement, curiosity, motivation, risk taking, and persistence (ICAS 3–5) (CWPA, NCTE, NWP 4–5). Our own experience as college instructors confirms that students who have these foundational dispositions are indeed well poised to continue their growth as scholars. Yet few prebaccalaureate programs directly address the mental attitudes that prepare students for college coursework, presumably because an "attitude" is not a discrete skill. It is generally easier to assess vocabulary knowledge, for instance, than stamina or self-efficacy. Increasingly, however, educational research is helping us understand traits such as motivation as learned behaviors, not innate abilities (Pintrich and Schunk 6–7). What once was often perceived as the "natural" disposition of the academically well prepared, we now recognize as a set of intellectual attitudes that can be deliberately taught and consciously acquired.

> What once was often perceived as the "natural" disposition of the academically well prepared, we now recognize as a set of intellectual attitudes that can be deliberately taught and consciously acquired.

Throughout the book, the lessons focus on modeling and coaching—that is, on making dispositional behaviors explicit and on nurturing learners as they develop their academic identities and confidence. We believe that individual teachers can have a profound impact on their students' lives regardless of their institutional contexts (Wright, Horn, and Sanders 66), and we understand that, as developmental education faculty, we are often the first contact our students have with the world of higher education. Thus, it makes good sense to us to focus on classroom learning experiences that most effectively and supportively induct today's students into academic culture. This belief in the value of developmental education faculty and programs strongly informed our approach.

Even more importantly, we were guided by a deep respect and regard for our students. As we prepared our lessons, we kept in view the faces of those students who diligently filled our classrooms at 8:00 a.m. or 8:00 p.m., who incurred debt to pursue a degree, and who took time away from their jobs and families to learn what we had to teach. We thought of students like Jose, who took a developmental writing class at night. A remarkably dedicated student, Jose insisted on attending his student-teacher conference despite the fact that his wife was in labor at the hospital. Over the next few weeks,

Jose struggled to help care for his newborn son while he continued the class. Jose was not even sure what he wanted to major in, but he was determined to create a better life for his family.

Or students like Jeanette, a military widow and a single mother of two children whose dream was to become a high school English teacher. She took one or two classes at a time at a community college before ultimately transferring to a four-year university.

Or like Ricardo, a first-generation college student with strong ties to his hardworking immigrant parents. He grew over the years from a developmental writing student with a distinct voice within his essays to a transfer student interested in science who won a $20,000 scholarship to attend the University of California, Santa Cruz. Our students have been critical partners in this venture and have profoundly influenced our approach through their stories and feedback.

What Are Habits of Mind?

Since the phrase first became popular among educators in the 1990s, scholars have offered many congruous definitions for *habits of mind*: They are "a fundamental set of behaviors for thoughtful teaching and learning" (Costa and Kallick ix), "foundational dispositions well-prepared students have" that are "essential to successful participation in [academic] culture" (ICAS 13), or "ways of approaching learning that are both intellectual and practical" (CWPA, NCTE, and NWP 1). Reading scholar Sheridan Blau calls them "traits of performative literacy" (19). A 2007 Bill and Melinda Gates Foundation report calls them "academic behaviors" (Conley 16). For higher education faculty, habits of mind are often associated with disciplinary ways of thinking and being. These "core elements of the discipline" (Haynie, Chick, and Gurung 4) include domain-specific methods, values, and interests, such as the practices that shape the intellectual identities and labor of social scientists.

Mathematics educator E. Paul Goldenberg gives a particularly useful explanation: "By 'habits of mind,' we mean ways of thinking that one acquires so well, makes so natural, and incorporates so fully into one's repertoire, that they become mental habits—not only can one draw upon them easily, one is likely to do so" (14). Habits of mind, in other words, are an internalized set of practices essential to critical thinking.

Habits of Mind as Learned Behaviors

Although habits of mind may feel natural, these mental attitudes can be intentionally taught and cultivated, according to much of the current research on student success. For instance, Laurie A. Schreiner's work on thriving concludes that success factors such as engagement, determination, positive perspective, and connectedness are "amenable to change within students" (4), rather than fixed attributes over which instructors have little influence.

Recent scholarship has also drawn attention to the importance of making students *aware* of how habits of mind impact learning. It is not enough to create incidental opportunities for curiosity and engagement; we need to direct students' attention to how an ongoing practice of curiosity and engagement can affect their mind-set. Making alert and strategic use of dispositional assets during critical challenges—for instance, actively calling on one's capacity for persistence, resilience, and flexibility during the stress of midterm exams—sustains long-term academic success and growth. Writing on the dispositional character of proactive knowledge, David Perkins suggests that habits of mind even have something of a predictive quality: "They concern not what people are able to do but what they are *inclined* to do" (9; emphasis added). Proactive knowledge of this kind thus contributes to a mindful approach to learning.

> It is not enough to create incidental opportunities for curiosity and engagement; we need to direct students' attention to how an ongoing practice of curiosity and engagement can affect their mind-set.

A Habit by Any Other Name . . .

To be sure, there is a good deal of crossover between habits of mind and what other scholars and educators have called soft skills, deeper learning, 21st-century skills, college and career readiness, next-generation learning, personality traits, positive values or developmental assets, character education, intrapersonal competencies, critical thinking, cognitive strategies, academic behaviors, and psychological phenomena, among other descriptors. The National Research Council (NRC) notes that these labels are applied to a broad range of skills and capacities, including problem solving, collaboration, effective communication, motivation, persistence, creativity, innovation, and ethics (*Education for Life and Work* 1–2). What these labels and competencies have in common is their distinction from traditional disciplinary academic content and skills, such as the content standards of K–12 education or the typical student learning outcomes on a college course syllabus.

Partly because these intellectual capacities are so broad and abstract, they tend to be slighted in favor of more conspicuous and discrete learning outcomes—a neglect that often obscures the very processes by which students acquire proficiency in academic skills and knowledge. In 2001, these attributes were still sufficiently marginalized for transfer theory scholar Robert E. Haskell to claim that "personality and dispositional characteristics of learners have been largely ignored" (115). Despite this neglect, Haskell continues, few people would argue that teachers *shouldn't* foster the development of attitude, motivation, temperament, and character in their students (115).

This book doesn't offer—or endorse—a definitive list of habits of mind. Thus, you will sometimes encounter intellectual habits discussed as singular qualities (e.g., curiosity or persistence), and other times as specific abilities (e.g., the ability to postpone judgment and tolerate ambiguity).

By offering a collection of lesson exemplars targeting habits of mind, we embrace the challenge of teaching something we all seem to value even if we aren't quite sure how to classify or measure it.

From Theory to Practice

Although we knew that we couldn't simply put "supported, holistic intellectual growth" as an outcome on our syllabi (How will you assess it?), we also knew that this was what we were after in focusing on habits of mind. We further believed that this kind of growth depended on explicit coaching and practice. In *College and Career Ready*, educational policy scholar David T. Conley identifies direct instruction in "academic behaviors," such as "resilience in the face of academic frustrations" (114–15), to be a key principle of successful college preparation programs. Accordingly, we sought ways to give these behaviors a dedicated space in our curriculum.

We also invited our students to share their understandings of habits of mind. One of our students, Sabrina, explained why habits of mind matter to her:

Habits of mind matter because they help students when they don't know how to start a paper, solve an equation or talk out a conflict with friends. They matter because what's taught in school isn't always going to help in real life situations. . . . There's not a class on how to surpass writer's block or how to overcome laziness.

Regardless of how we define or delimit *habits of mind*, if we want more of our students to develop these kinds of intellectual qualities, we need to make them an explicit part of our instructional approach.

The Importance of Modeling and Coaching

Two key practices are behind the strategies in this book: modeling and coaching. Many students need to see habits of mind in action to understand these dispositions as learnable attributes. This kind of transparency is about sharing our passions, not just our expectations. Many students also need explicit support to develop the habits of mind that lead to academic success. Modeling and coaching are thus largely about making the invisible visible. John Bean identifies these two practices as central to the development of students' ability to think critically in disciplinary contexts: "Teachers of critical thinking also need to be mentors and coaches, developing a range of strategies for modeling critical thinking, critiquing student performances, and otherwise guiding students toward the habits of inquiry and argument valued in their disciplines" (xi). By showing our students how qualities of mind such as persistence and flexibility aid us in our disciplinary work, we make visible the link between intellectual process and academic product. For students who face significant obstacles on the pathway to degree completion, instruction in habits of mind must be more than incidental.

> By showing our students how qualities of mind such as persistence and flexibility aid us in our disciplinary work, we make visible the link between intellectual process and academic product.

Explicit support can be as simple as a candid note of encouragement. Consider the following e-mail sent by one of the editors to her first-year students just before spring break:

Hi folks,
As we head into our final week before spring break, please be sure that you are continuing to persist in doing your best work for the

course. Now is the time to make sure you've kept up with all the readings, are regularly reviewing your notes, attending every class, and looking ahead to the next deadline. Stamina is a significant factor in academic success, and midterm season is typically when we all (faculty, too) have to dig deep to be sure we're fulfilling all our obligations.

Intentional instruction in habits of mind can also be more formal and disciplinary specific, as is the case with many of the lesson exemplars you'll find in this book. The point is that we can't assume that all our students will naturally acquire these traits without any direct guidance from us.

A New Approach?

The collection of lessons you'll find in this book might more accurately be described as an old approach made new again. Admittedly, there is nothing revolutionary about extolling the indispensability of habits of mind to intellectual growth. Some 2,000–plus years ago Aristotle was telling his students, "It is not unimportant, then, to acquire one sort of habit or another, right from our youth" and reminding them that "excellence is an art won by training and habituation" (Book II, 4; Book I, 7). In Aristotle's works, habit is closely associated with virtue, both of character and of thought (e.g., scientific knowledge, wisdom, deliberation, and comprehension). This latter form of virtue is close kin to the old idea of habits of mind as proper mental discipline.

A few millenia later, the NRC likewise notes the enduring importance of dispositional virtues—what in *Education for Life and Work* the NRC calls "21st century skills." But it also suggests a critical distinction from times past:

> The committee views 21st century skills as dimensions of human competence that have been valuable for many centuries, rather than skills that are suddenly new, unique, and valuable today. One change from the past may lie in Society's desire that all students now attain levels of mastery—across multiple areas of skill and knowledge—that were previously unnecessary for individual success in education and the workplace. (53)

In addition to our changing socioeconomic context, what we believe is new about this approach is our attempt to formalize habits of mind as an instructional method, particularly in prebaccalaureate-level courses. Fostering habits of mind in developmental education courses means we no longer are exclusively concerned with fixing incoming students' sentence boundary problems or inability to solve for X. In "Cultivating the Habits of Mind for Student Success and Achievement," Laurie Hazard notes the novel challenge faced by today's college faculty: "While it goes without saying that students need strong academic skills to succeed in postsecondary education, it is no longer enough to only support students in tackling the traditional range of skills required for successful academic performance" (45).

We also believe there is something innovative in taking this approach in an educational environment preoccupied with value-added measures and institutional capacity. Cultivating habits of mind is a boutique operation, founded on time-intensive, relationship-centered pedagogies. This is artisan teaching. We see our students as apprentices, not products. As Costa and Kallick caution educators, "The Habits of Mind are not a quick fix" (213).

> Cultivating habits of mind is a boutique operation, founded on time-intensive, relationship-centered pedagogies. This is artisan teaching.

Taking the Whole-Term Approach

Our whole-term approach is an additional departure from many traditional programs. This cyclical, developmental view of the academic term is distinct from the episodic view that regard a course as a sequence of assignments to be completed or topics to be covered.

Why is this instructional shift important? Consider the following comment from a CSUMB first-year student from Salinas, who compared being a college student to being in a rodeo: "You're like a bull rider; you're on top for a while, but then you fall and get dragged until the end." We've conceptualized this book in terms of the unique situational demands of a full instructional cycle precisely so our students don't get dragged until the end. Seeing intellectual growth this way means that we expect our students to experience different cognitive and affective stages over the course of an academic term. Learning, John Hattie concludes from his synthesis of more than 800 meta-analyses of studies related to student achievement, is "a time-worn, slow, and gradual, fits-and-starts kind of process" (2). Many of the habits of mind we most ardently seek to develop in ourselves and our students are dependent on conditional knowledge and situational awareness: flexibility, adaptability, patience, metacognition, and a spirit of transfer, to name a few.

Taking the whole-term approach to instruction also helps us better appreciate our students' unique strengths, as well as their changing emotional and intellectual needs.

Anthony A. Ciccone observes in his foreword to *Exploring More Signature Pedagogies: Approaches to Teaching Disciplinary Habits of Mind*, "A pedagogy grounded in the development of the entire person seems a good model for *any* pedagogy" (xiii). We don't see our students as entering our classes with problems that need to be eliminated by a deadline but rather as novices who require our support as they progress through the next phases of their development. And we expect, as Donna Miller reminds us, that "growth will not occur without error" (52).

The Long View of Developmental Education

In 2000, the NRC concluded from its review of converging scholarship from the fields of developmental psychology, cognitive psychology, and neuroscience, among others, that "development is not merely a biologically driven unfolding process, but also an active process that derives essential information from experience" (*How People Learn* 126). In designing learning experiences that foster habits of mind, we diminish the artificial boundary separating developmental education from baccalaureate-level courses. These dispositions support *all* learners at all stages of their

> In designing learning experiences that foster habits of mind, we diminish the artificial boundary separating developmental education from baccalaureate-level courses.

intellectual journeys, not just those who have been identified through placement tests as not yet ready for college math or writing.

This broader view is changing how we see college success. In " 'They Never Told Me What to Expect, so I Didn't Know What to Do': Defining and Clarifying the Role of a Community College Student," Melinda Mechur Karp and Rachel Hare Bork state, "The fact that even academically proficient students have trouble continuing in college suggests that college readiness encompasses more than just academic skills" and argue that "college success is not only about academic preparation but also dependent upon a host of equally important skills, attitudes, habits, and behaviors" (1).

In place of the anterior orientation of remediation, the forward-looking perspective of the growth mind-set enables developmental education to focus on a multiyear process of intellectual maturation that may begin in prebaccalaureate classes but that extends into general education, the major, and beyond. Our aspirations for our students go beyond retention and degree attainment. What we want for the quirky, surprising, talented individuals who show up to our classrooms year after year won't end when they complete college.

One of my students, a young woman who started college in developmental education, recently asked for help preparing for an interview as part of her application to a teacher education program. I realized, in writing my response to her, that these kinds of graduate interviews primarily function as an assessment of candidates' habits of mind. Here's an excerpt from my e-mail:

> Good questions, Alondra! In general, I would expect that you might be asked about your experience working with young people, your own attitude toward teaching and learning, your subject matter expertise, your ability to collaborate effectively, your reliability, etc. My understanding is that one of the key purposes of the interview is to evaluate the applicant's disposition for teaching. In other words, are you an ethical, respectful, knowledgeable, collaborative, trustworthy, resilient, and enthusiastic person who will provide a safe and inclusive learning environment for students?
> Good luck to you!
> Warm regards,
> Jennifer

Habits of mind help us to not only start our intellectual journey but also continue it throughout our postbaccalaureate lives.

Chapter Descriptions

The six chapters of this book present a progressive instructional cycle that begins by discovering students' assets and ends when students can transfer their learning to new tasks and situations. Taken as a whole, the chapters offer a scaffolded procedure for understanding, supporting, engaging, challenging, and releasing students as they develop the intellectual capacities that lead to impassioned and independent learning. Each chapter includes an essay connecting theory to practice, along with individually authored lesson exemplars targeting key habits of mind. Each lesson exemplar reflects the unique perspective and institutional context of its author. You will notice that key principles of our approach have been featured in shaded boxes throughout this introduction as well as in the essays that begin each chapter. You will also see that each lesson description includes sidebars identifying target habits of mind to show how these dispositions are developed in practice.

> Taken as a whole, the chapters offer a scaffolded procedure for understanding, supporting, engaging, challenging, and releasing students as they develop the intellectual capacities that lead to impassioned and independent learning.

The first two chapters address the preconditions for fostering critical habits of mind: knowing our students and helping those students feel that they are valued and needed members of our communities. Chapter 1, "Discovering Assets," affirms the importance of first identifying students' strengths, interests, and prior knowledge before tailoring instruction to meet the needs of specific populations. This chapter also makes a case for why "deficit-based" approaches to developmental education are counterproductive. Chapter 2, "Creating Communities," provides ways to promote collaboration and "safe-to-risk" classroom environments while orienting students to college culture. Lessons for these two chapters include student inventories such as the "Group Résumé," as well as activities that develop group norms.

Chapter 3, "Engaging Learners," draws on the personal and social assets addressed in the first two chapters to engage students in rigorous academic content, as well as joyous intellectual play. Chapter 4, "Building Confidence," offers ways to deepen students' skills, knowledge, and abilities by relating intellectual growth to a sense of a developing academic self—all while moving students past the threshold of superficial learning. Chapter 5, "Developing Students' Self-Efficacy," suggests ways students' increased confidence can lead to a gradual release of responsibility for learning. Chapter 6, "Promoting Transfer of Learning," offers ways to help students apply their sense of confidence and self-efficacy as learners to new assignments and courses. This last chapter represents the ultimate goal of a habits-of-mind-based approach to teaching: authentic, adaptive, lifelong learning. You'll also find a bonus essay in Appendix A, "Making Cross-Disciplinary, Intersegmental Collaboration Work: The Story behind the Exemplars," describing what you might need to know if you are thinking about adopting this kind of collaborative approach to academic preparation on your own campus.

Through this structure, our project acknowledges that a developmental model of education—particularly for "developmental" students—needs to address more than academic content. We consequently target both academic and affective goals through sustained modeling and coaching, showing *how* we do what we do as scholars and why it's fun, hard work worth getting up for each morning. Many of us as developmental education faculty have found that this approach works for all of our students, and we regularly take the approaches presented here into our transfer-, junior-, and senior-level courses. We have even included some habits-of-mind-based lessons from our colleagues in general education, such as an essay assignment from a science class, to help make this point. By fostering the development of habits of mind, we believe we are providing the best possible environment for the mastery of disciplinary knowledge and skills.

Works Cited

AAC&U (Association of American Colleges and Universities). *College Learning for the New Global Century: A Report from the National Leadership Council for Liberal Education & America's Promise*. Washington, DC: AAC&U, 2007. Print.

Aristotle. *Rhetoric*. Trans. W. Rhys Roberts. New York: McGraw-Hill, 1984. Print.

Bean, John C. *Engaging Ideas: The Professor's Guide to Integrating Writing, Critical Thinking, and Active Learning in the Classroom*. San Francisco: Jossey-Bass, 2001. Print.

Blau, S. "Performative Literacy: The Habits of Mind of Highly Literate Readers." *Voices from the Middle* 10.3 (2003): 18–22. Print.

Ciccone, Anthony A. Preface. *Exploring More Signature Pedagogies: Approaches to Teaching Disciplinary Habits of Mind*. Sterling: Stylus, 2012. Print.

Conley, David T. *Redefining College Readiness*. Vol. 3. Eugene: Educational Policy Improvement Center, 2007. Print.

Conley, D. T. *College and Career Ready: Helping All Students Succeed beyond High School*. San Francisco: Jossey-Bass, 2010. Print.

Costa, A. L., and B. Kallick. Preface. *Habits of Mind across the Curriculum: Practical and Creative Strategies for Teachers*. Ed. A. L. Costa and B. Kallick. Alexandria: ASCD, 2009. ix–xiv. Print.

CWPA, NCTE, and NWP (Council of Writing Program Administrators, National Council of Teachers of English, and National Writing Project). *Framework for Success in Postsecondary Writing*. Berkeley: National Writing Project, 2011. Print.

Goldenberg, E. P. " 'Habits of Mind' as an Organizer for the Curriculum." *Journal of Education* 178.1 (1996): 13–34. Print.

Graff, G. *Clueless in Academe: How Schooling Obscures the Life of the Mind.* New Haven: Yale University Press, 2003. Print.

Haskell, Robert E. *Transfer of Learning: Cognition, Instruction, and Reasoning.* San Diego: Academic Press, 2001. Print.

Hattie, John. *Visible Learning: A Synthesis of Over 800 Meta-analyses Relating to Achievement.* London: Routledge, 2009. Print.

Haynie, Aeron, Nancy L. Chick, and Regan A. R. Gurung. "Signature Pedagogies in the Liberal Arts and Beyond." *Exploring More Signature Pedagogies: Approaches to Teaching Disciplinary Habits of Mind.* Sterling: Stylus, 2012. Print.

Hazard, Laurie. "Cultivating the Habits of Mind for Student Success and Achievement." *Research & Teaching in Developmental Education* 29.2 (2013): 45–48. Retrieved 20 Feb. 2014.

ICAS (Intersegmental Committee of Academic Senates). *Academic Literacy: A Statement of Competencies Expected of Students Entering California's Public Colleges and Universities.* Sacramento: ICAS, 2002. Print.

Karp, Melinda M., & Bork, Rachel H. " 'They Never Told Me What to Expect, so I Didn't Know What to Do'. Defining and Clarifying the Role of a Community college Student." Community College Research Center Working Paper No. 47. Teachers College, Columbia University.

Miller, Donna L. "Got It Wrong? Think Again . . . and Again." *Phi Delta Kappan* 94.5 (2013): 50–52. Retrieved 20 Mar. 2014.

National Research Council, Commission on Behavioral and Social Sciences and Education. *How People Learn: Brain, Mind, Experience, and School.* Expanded ed. Washington, DC: National Academy Press, 2000. Print.

National Research Council. *Education for Life and Work: Developing Transferrable Knowledge and Skills in the 21st Century.* Washington, DC: National Academy Press, 2012. Print.

NGACBP & CCSO (National Governors Association Center for Best Practices and Council of Chief State School Officers). *Common Core State Standards for English Language Arts & Literacy in History/Social Studies, Science, and Technological Subjects.* Washington, DC: NGACBP & CCSO, 2010. Web. Retrieved 15 Mar. 2014. <www.corestandards.org/read-the-standards>

Perkins, David. "Beyond Understanding." *Threshold Concepts within the Disciplines.* Ed. Ray Land, Jan H. F. Meyer, and Jan Smith. Rotterdam: Sense Publishers, 2008. 3–20. Print.

Pintrich, Paul R., and Dale H. Schunk. *Motivation in Education: Theory, Research, and Applications.* 2nd ed. Upper Saddle River: Merrill Prentice Hall, 2002. Print.

Schreiner, Laurie A. "The 'Thriving Quotient': A New Vision for Student Success." *About Campus* 15.2 (2010): 2–10. Web. Retrieved 7 Apr. 2013.

Wright, S. Paul, Sandra P. Horn, and William L. Sanders. "Teacher and Classroom Context Effects on Student Achievement: Implications for Teacher Evaluation." *Journal of Personnel Evaluation in Education* 11 (1997): 57–67. Web. 7 July 2012.

DISCOVERING ASSETS

Hetty Yelland

"Students are not only intellectual, but also social and emotional beings. And they are still developing the full range of intellectual, social, and emotional skills. While we cannot control the developmental process, we can shape the intellectual, social, emotional, and physical aspects of classroom climate in developmentally appropriate ways."

—"Theory and Research-Based Principles of Learning"

Discovering assets within the classroom is about taking the focus off of what students may lack and putting the focus on the rich, intrinsic value each individual contributes. This is not to say that the semester's curriculum contains no tests, no argumentative essays, and no grades. However, a classroom environment that begins by focusing on assets, rather than deficits, lays a foundation for creating a culture of both trust and high standards. As Janet Newbury states in "Reconsidering Relational Practice":

> Asset-based . . . development is not about viewing the world through rose-colored glasses. It is, however, about making sure we don't only focus on what is going wrong. If we learn from what is going well, then we can mobilize these strengths, increasing their positive impact and . . . existing assets can be better appreciated and utilized. (2)

Rather than a defective student who has come to our

> Discovering assets within the classroom is about taking the focus off of what students may lack and putting the focus on the rich, intrinsic value each individual contributes.

classroom to be "fixed," it is important to approach the 21st-century learner as an asset.

Too often, students in developmental education are regarded as problems to be eliminated—or outsourced to other institutions. In conversations decrying the cost of remediation, in particular, we encounter frequent complaints about the expense and inefficiency of providing support to students who "should" have already met minimum standards of academic preparation. According to Complete College America's report *Remediation: Higher Education's Bridge to Nowhere*, remedial courses have "wasted so many resources" (4). Even within the classroom, basic skills students can be unfairly judged for being unfamiliar with academic culture and curricula. In addressing habits of mind through an assets-based approach to learning, we are challenging this negative framework, meeting students where they are, and taking the long view of intellectual growth.

This critical shift lays the foundation for success at each new beginning throughout a semester (the first day of class or the start of each new project) because students are never really starting from square one. They already know something about the course they are taking, and from the outset, they also bring their own perspectives, individual characteristics, and past experiences. In "Why Teach Habits of Mind?" Shari Tishman states, "Abilities [as well as] passions, motivation, sensitivities, and values all play a role in bringing intelligence to life. The habits of mind express a character-centered view of intelligence that honors . . . individual differences" (43).

> In addressing habits of mind through an assets-based approach to learning, we are challenging this negative framework, meeting students where they are, and taking the long view of intellectual growth.

An excellent example of this is demonstrated by one Cabrillo College composition instructor who uses Play-Doh. Each student is given a picture of a different object, such as a rubber ducky or a rocket ship, and asked to duplicate the image as a small sculpture at the beginning of class. One student may have a lot of artistic talent. However, another may be good at asking for help. Another student may get creative with an abstract interpretation, while yet another may demonstrate his negotiating power in order to obtain most of the available yellow clay. It quickly becomes clear who is good at what and that everyone is good at something.

Moreover, these interactions are not just tricks to get students to participate, but the beginning of ongoing and growing relationships throughout the semester between the students and the instructor and among the students themselves. Assets-based instruction also fosters another relationship: that between the student and learning. As in all relationships, one that is two-way is healthier and more enriching. The deficit model tells the student that she is lacking in some way and needs to be filled with knowledge. The assets-based model, in contrast, creates reciprocation. The student grows by learning new material and being exposed to new ideas. In turn, the instructor, the class, and the field of study itself are then enriched by the student bringing her unique set of experiences and talents to fruition.

Assets-based teaching and activities may at times overlap with community building, but the two are distinct. Community building fosters identification as a team or unified group. However, the most successful communities are made up of growing, progressing individuals who bring different skills and interests together in support of each other. Thus, discovering assets should precede and then run parallel with community building by highlighting each individual's ability and growth.

Historical Context

The study and practice of emphasizing students' assets grew out of the democratization of higher education in the 1960s and 1970s, which is beautifully detailed within the "Historical Overview" found in George Otte and Rebecca Williams Mlynarczyk's *Basic Writing*. With open enrollment into community colleges, classrooms began filling with nontraditional, ethnically and economically diverse college students unfamiliar with campus culture or expectations. Basic skills curriculum had to be made and remade by faculty—mostly middle-class intellectuals—who, at least initially, had felt overwhelmed by their new students' lack of preparation for college work. In particular, it was and is all too easy to see basic-writing students "as less prepared, less acclimated, and less literate," but "these descriptions had a subtext: the definition had to be diagnosis; the description had to be a prescription" (142–43). As Otte and Mlynarczyk point out, colleges and universities had always been struggling with the underprepared among those admitted. However, the large numbers of basic skills students entering the system at one time forced institutes of higher education to take notice of underperforming students and, consequently, to notice their own failures to adequately provide opportunities for student success across the boundaries of race, class, and gender.

> The study and practice of emphasizing students' assets grew out of the democratization of higher education in the 1960s and 1970s, which is beautifully detailed within the "Historical Overview" found in George Otte and Rebecca Williams Mlynarczyk's *Basic Writing*.

Fortunately, strong faculty voices and leadership, such as those provided by Mina Shaughnessy, stepped forward with not only innovative instructional ideas and pedagogical writings, but also respect for the experiences and cultures of those being taught. As *Basic Writing* attests, "For Shaughnessy, blaming the students for supposed deficiencies was feckless and unjust; errors and other nonstandard features were the result of social inequities, not personal failings" (8). In 1977, Shaughnessy wrote in her groundbreaking work *Errors and Expectations*, "Colleges must be prepared to make more than a graceless and begrudging accommodation to this unpreparedness, opening their doors with one hand and then leading students into an endless corridor of remedial anterooms with the other" (293). From the beginning, basic skills has been aware of itself as not simply academic theory nor pedagogical practice, but as a kind of political movement. Shaughnessy predicted, "As we move closer to this goal [of greater student success] . . . we will be . . . moving deeper into the realizations of a democracy" (294).

Forty years later, higher education is again becoming more elusive to those seeking the American dream. When once colleges and universities were opening doors, now they are closing them and/or offering only limited chances for success. Tuition is going up, financial aid is going down, student loans saddle new graduates with large debts, competition for admission into four-year universities is rising, and restrictions are being put on how many times a student may attempt to take a community college course.

It is very easy to focus on the negative instead of assets. However, it is important for instructors to realize and remember that there is a tradition of inclusiveness and assets-based teaching within the developmental college classroom. The report *Academic Literacy: A Statement of Competencies Expected of Students Entering California's Public*

Colleges and Universities, published by the Intersegmental Committee of the Academic Senates, echoes Shaughnessy's legacy when it states, "We affirm the role of California's schools in enhancing democracy, and we believe that literary skills serve as a foundation for greater equity" (2). Despite political and fiscal challenges to the educational system as a whole, new approaches to developmental education offer renewed hope to 21st-century students and new vigor to those who teach them.

Habits of Mind

The implementation of student learning outcomes as a way to improve instruction and student learning has been one recent method used to promote students' success. In addition, pedagogy that explores the development of habits of mind to facilitate successful learning is also gaining ground as a parallel and equally important instructional tool to implement within the classroom. This is an exciting development for assets based instruction. The Council of Writing Program Administrators, National Council of Teachers of English, and National Writing Project's 2011 Framework for Success in Postsecondary Writing focuses on eight habits of mind: curiosity, openness, engagement, creativity, persistence, responsibility, flexibility, and metacognition (1). In regard to discovering assets, each student comes into the class with his or her strengths.

It is true that one student may be, for example, more creative than another as a result of natural disposition and/or life experiences. Nonetheless, at the onset of each class activity—be it molding Play-Doh or writing a research essay—each individual student has his or her own natural and learned abilities. Everyone does not have to be the same. A student who has been made aware of her strengths is in a better position to use them to perform optimally on any given task. Thus, students can learn from a stance of empowerment. This means that all eight habits of mind apply to discovering assets because each student brings his or her own skill sets to the class and each student is capable of improving upon any of these skills over time.

The three habits of mind that correspond with assets-based instruction—from the teaching point of view—are metacognition, openness, and persistence. Students all have their own strengths to discover. However, the instructor helps the students become aware of what they do well, creates an environment in which students feel comfortable sharing their strengths, and provides opportunities for students to reassess their strengths as they improve and learn throughout the semester.

> The instructor helps the students become aware of what they do well, creates an environment in which students feel comfortable sharing their strengths, and provides opportunities for students to reassess their strengths as they improve and learn throughout the semester.

Metacognitive activities, for example, allow students to take note of not only their initial strengths but also their improvement and readiness to take on new tasks. In Ken Rand's lesson exemplar "Writing in the Math Class" (see chapter 6), students are encouraged to reflect on their feelings about math: some reporting feelings of confidence and more students acknowledging emotional anxiety about math. Either way, through class discussion and activities, students are encouraged to see their initial feelings without self-judgment and to view these emotions as simply a starting point and subject to change. Students are challenged to "unlearn" the deficit way of thinking and to give themselves—and math—a chance to improve. Throughout the semester, the assets-based approach takes on a cyclical nature. After the initial introduction of the class, each new project is an opportunity for students to reflect on their ongoing growth. Within assets-based instruction, metacognition takes place in various activities. However, the focus will always be positive: on what the student can do, self-made goals about what the student feels ready to try, and what the student already knows about a subject.

Assets-based instruction also promotes the habits of mind of openness and persistence. Openness creates an environment in which it is easier for students to attempt unfamiliar subject matter. As college instructors, we would never try to introduce a new writing curriculum into our department without the buy-in of our colleagues. Then why do we sometimes feel we can forgo creating buy-in with our students? For example, in the lesson exemplar included in this chapter entitled "Reflecting Home Culture," Najarro encourages college instructors to build composition classes around a theme that will interest their specific class population. The challenge of learning college-level reading and writing skills can be made less daunting if the subject matter is interesting and somewhat familiar to students. Certainly, students are going to react with less frustration and opposition after there has been an invitation for them to bring their ideas and strengths to the table. This can also be achieved by activities such as providing options for doing an assignment in a way that relies on their own personal

Assets-based instruction also promotes the habits of mind of openness and persistence.

strengths or by having students actively participate in creating some of the curriculum for the class based on what interests them.

From this empowering foundation students are more likely to persist when the class becomes more challenging because they know to focus on methods that work for them. Each student is not capable in a vague, nebulous way. Each knows specifically what traits he or she can draw on to overcome obstacles and solve problems. A closer look at the way assets-based instruction unfolds throughout the semester will help illustrate how these three noncognitive skills give 21st-century students a better chance at college success.

Breaking the Ice

Icebreaker activities are generally associated with community building; however, most icebreakers also promote discovering assets. Individuals consider what they have to offer within this new environment and they also consider what others around them have to offer, always in the optimistic and casual tone set by the activity. The anxiety of the situation is relieved by playful or creative context. The pressure is off because things are not being presented as serious, and the unspoken rule is to focus only on the positive.

Icebreakers are often thought of as games or highly interactive, but in reality these types of activities run along a spectrum from the more outrageous to the more subtle. For example, one Hartnell College math instructor uses clicker technology to give an anonymous survey the first day of class. He includes a variety of questions about math anxiety, education, and experience, as well as silly personal questions. He shows film clips, plays music, and even prides himself on a little dance he does for the class. Students are being expertly lulled into relaxing all their fears around math. The subtext is: "You can do college math. You don't have to be a certain way. Just be yourself."

The subtext is: "You can do college math. You don't have to be a certain way. Just be yourself."

Usually icebreakers take place on the first day or during the first week of class; however, a wider application holds the promise of helping improve overall student success. Dominique Chlup and Tracy Collins's "Breaking the Ice: Using Ice-Breakers and Re-Energizers with Adult Learners," one of the few peer-reviewed articles published on this topic, asserts that these sorts of assets-based teaching methodologies "contribute to improved student participation, increased student persistence, and ultimately enhanced student learning" (34).

Certainly there are advantages to a more broad use of icebreakers throughout the semester. Chlup and Collins discuss both icebreakers and what they term *re-energizers*:

> It is our contention that icebreakers are not one-time events to be used solely on the first day of class. In fact, we both use both icebreakers and re-energizers as needed at various times throughout a course. Re-energizers can be used when energy is low and class morale is lagging, when everyone is not participating, or after a break to refocus a group. (35)

These methods can also be effective at the beginning of a group project. Group members can interact only with each other, or the group can become a team that competes with other groups in the class. For example, students could compete in a scavenger hunt before having to write a group essay together. This would not only promote cohesion, but also provide group members with valuable information about each other's strengths and leadership skills before the graded assignment begins. The best attributes the group members can offer have been highlighted.

Some instructors choose to have a formal discussion to debrief what positive attributes students discovered about themselves and others by participating in the icebreaker activity, but often the debriefing aspect is skipped. Either way, the goal of icebreakers for students is to end by feeling good about the class and, most important, themselves.

Reflective Activities

Another way that assets-based teaching can be applied to a course's curriculum is through the use of reflective activities, usually done in writing. Reflections are excellent ways for students to reassess their skills and habits of mind throughout the semester. They can work as a first-day-of-school activity but work just as well at the start, middle, and end of each assignment. Students may be required to do a freewrite, a journal entry, or a more formal writing assignment. Usually these activities are private between the instructor and the student. However, if students are warned ahead of time, these reflections can be posted on an online discussion board, peer reviewed, or shared using another method.

The purpose of reflective activities in discovering assets is for students to consciously think about what they do well and what they already know. As the semester progresses from one assignment to the next, reflective activities allow students to notice how much they have learned and improved their skills.

One short and informal reflective activity is the six-word story. Like Hemingway's famous six-word short story, "For sale. Baby shoes. Never worn," students are challenged to write their life story in six words or less on a small poster board or large index card (12 × 4 inches, which can be purchased at teachers' supply stores). Stories are shared with the class, and the stories are posted on the wall of the classroom. Variations of this activity can be adapted. For instance, instead of telling a story, students can be asked to give themselves a six-word pep talk for halfway through the semester. The cards are put away for a few weeks and forgotten, but they are brought out again later in the semester so the students can be surprised and inspired by their own words.

Sugie Goen from San Francisco State University uses the KWL+ technique, probably the best example of assets-based reflective writing. As detailed in her and Helen Gillotte-Tropp's "Integrating Reading and Writing: A Response to the Basic Writing 'Crisis,'" the K stands for what students know about the topic. So both reading and writing are based on accessing prior knowledge. Students can start with what they already know, and that is good enough. The W stands for what students would like to know, and students are encouraged to create their own focused thesis out of the topic. L is for the learning that takes place while the student is reading and writing about the topic, and the + stands for what a student would still like to learn about this topic when the assignment is done (99). The entirety of this process is brilliantly assets-based. Students are starting from where they are, not at a deficit. They decide for themselves what direction they want to go, and at the conclusion of a project, they end on a positive note. Students reflect on what new questions or skills remain to be explored, instead of fixating on the grade or what they did wrong in an essay. They end by focusing on the positive and their assets.

Providing Student-Centered Options

Assets-based instruction also offers multiple student options through-out the semester, and there are so many ways to do this that show off students' strengths. We want them to do well, and we want them to show us their best work. Choices help.

For example, a psychology instructor who teaches human sexu-ality at Hartnell lets the students anonymously write any question about sex on an index card on the first day of class. Throughout the semester, she randomly picks a couple of cards to read, answer, and discuss. Students feel that the curriculum is geared toward what they want to learn, so that the habit of mind openness is both reinforced by the class structure and used as a foundation to build community and engagement as the semester progresses.

A variation of this activity that can be adapted to any class is called "fuzzy/clear." Students write two sentences, one on each side of index cards. On one side, students write one thing about the class that is clear to them or one thing they feel they are doing well. On the other side, students share what is unclear, confusing, not yet mas-tered, or fuzzy to them at the moment. This activity can be done periodically or every day as a warm-up. Either way, it is a method that allows students to acknowledge what they are doing well (to discover their assets), while being empowered to direct the learning and review within the classroom.

Both of these activities are assets based and student centered, and there are so many similar options for instructors to employ within the classroom. Some may be student generated. What do the students want to learn or review? What do they want to study? Students can even collaborate on class rules and grading rubrics. However, small changes that are still student centered but not student generated can be just as effective, such as allowing students the option to revise some or all essays or providing a small list of essay test questions from which students can choose to write. In *Engaging Ideas*, John Bean gives students the option of replacing one or two formal assignments with more creative responses (107). In all these cases, students are able to have some choice about what will work best for their present skill set and interests.

The purpose of student-centered options within assets-based instruction is not to lose control of a class, but to inspire a student's best work. Torenbeek, Jansen, and Hofman concluded in their 2011 study entitled "Predicting First-Year Achievement by Pedagogy and Skill Development in the First Weeks at University" that incoming freshmen who took courses that were taught from a student-centered approach were more successful than those who did not: "We found a direct positive

> Providing options within assets-based instruction helps students turn in their best work.

effect of the pedagogical approach on first-year study success. This supports our hypothesis that in a learning environment in which students are actively involved, the subject matter is more deeply processed, leading to better academic performance" (664). Students don't want to get bad grades, and as instructors, we don't want to read piles of confused, uninspired, or poorly written material. Providing options within assets-based instruction helps students turn in their best work. Both the instructor and the student win.

Challenges to an Assets-Based Approach

The main challenge to an assets-based approach is time. Semesters usually feel somewhat rushed as far as covering all the required material for a course. "How can I add anything else?" is an almost universal lament.

As college instructors, we are always striving to retain more students in our classes, to help more of these students succeed, and to ensure that our students transfer the knowledge they have gained into other courses and life situations. Just as in our personal lives, our daily to-do list can sometimes overwhelm our life goals, but the challenge is to think in terms of how efficient and multilayered our curriculum can become. That also can sound somewhat daunting, so another way to think of it is that by updating and adding fun activities to a course's curriculum, we create the potential to enliven and refresh. Instead of doing variations of the same old thing, adding a new layer to an existing activity can make it more interesting for the instructor and more productive for the students at the same time.

Adding more assets-based activities to a course does not entail a major revision of the existing curriculum. Some—not all—current assignments, activities, and even lectures can be enhanced to promote discovering assets generally and metacognition, openness, and persistence more specifically. If an instructor wants to go over the syllabus the first day of class and does not feel there is time for an icebreaker another day, then an interactive way of going over the syllabus can be created. For an essay project, add a before-and-after reflective freewrite that can be done as a warm-up or even as homework. Moreover, student options create better work that results in less time grading and explaining corrections. Therefore, the investment of time is worthwhile if doing so promotes student success, enlivens classes for both instructors and students, and results in better student work.

One last point about assets-based instruction and time. Often these types of activities work best if they are done quickly: an ice-breaker that takes one class period, a 10-minute freewrite, or a quick fuzzy/clear. Trying to extend these assignments into something lengthy tends to raise the level of seriousness, making students less participatory and more anxious.

Instructor feedback can be another challenge to assets-based instruction. We spend time drawing out our students, but a bad grade or a paper marked up even in friendly green ink can send them back into their shells. The careful use of low-stakes writing and formative assessments in conjunction with assets-based activities can, nonetheless, provide chances to learn through mistakes and practice. In "High Stakes and Low Stakes in Assigning and Responding to Writing," Peter Elbow famously states,

> Writing can be used informally, even casually, and in a nonevalu-ative setting. In truth, if we are looking for the best possible low stakes arena for language—for using language to learn, explore, take risks, or communicate with ourselves and not have our lan-guage be evaluated—writing is much better than speech. (6)

Indeed, Hartnell College instructor Ken Rand, who assigns a lot of low-stakes writing in his math classes, loves to say how well students can write when they know that they are not being evaluated.

Additionally, formative assessments provide chances for students to learn through practice. Online platforms, in particular, can pro-vide an easy way to offer formative assessments. Usually colleges do not require a class to be fully online to use the resources. On these platforms, students can take quizzes and tests multiple times, and the system can often self-record the highest score. Therefore, if an instructor is testing his students' vocabulary for terms pertaining to essay writing, such as *thesis* or *citation*, students can take the test sev-eral times at home using their notes. As a result, even initial wrong answers can be turned into an asset: an opportunity to review and learn from one's materials. Summative assessments, such as argumen-tative essays, still maintain the classes' high standards and ensure stu-dent learning outcomes have been met throughout the semester, but students are not held to these standards when an activity has just been introduced or it is their first time trying out a new skill.

Conclusion

The little engine that could did not just say "I think I can" one time, nor did he chant his mantra only for the first and easiest mile of the journey. No, he said it all the way to the summit and down again to his destination. "I think I can" changed only slightly into "I knew I could!"

That is what discovering assets is all about. Students have different abilities and histories, and they do not need to be the same. They have come to our classes to learn, but the surprise is the instructor and the field of study itself grow from each student's contribution. Part of our job as instructors is to help our students discover what their individual strengths are, so that they too can say, "I knew I could!"

> Part of our job as instructors is to help our students discover what their individual strengths are, so that they too can say, "I knew I could!"

Works Cited

Bean, John. *Engaging Ideas: The Professor's Guide to Integrating Writing, Critical Thinking, and Active Learning in the Classroom*. San Francisco: Jossey-Bass, 2001. Print.

Chlup, Dominique, and Tracy Collins. "Breaking the Ice: Using Ice-Breakers and Re-Energizers with Adult Learners." *Adult Learning* (Fall 2012): 34–39. MasterFile Complete. Web. 23 Jan. 2014.

Complete College America. *Remediation: Higher Education's Bridge to Nowhere*. April 2012. Web. 15 Dec. 2015.

Council of Writing Program Administrators, National Council of Teachers of English, and National Writing Project. *Framework for Success in Postsecondary Writing*. Urbana: National Council of Teachers of English, 2011. Print.

Elbow, Peter. "High Stakes and Low Stakes in Assigning and Responding to Writing." *New Directions for Teaching and Learning* (Spring 1997): 5–13. MasterFile Complete. Web. 23 Jan. 2014.

Goen, Sugie, and Helen Gillotte-Tropp. "Integrating Reading and Writing: A Response to the Basic Writing 'Crisis.' " *Journal of Basic Writing* 22.2 (2003): 90–113. MasterFile Complete. Web. 23 Jan. 2014.

ICAS (Intersegmental Committee of the Academic Senates of the California Community Colleges, the California State University, and the University of California). *Academic Literacy: A Statement of Competencies Expected of Students Entering California's Public Colleges and Universities.* Sacramento: ICAS, 2002. Print.

Newbury, Janet. "Creating Community: Reconsidering Relational Practice." *Relational Child and Youth Care Practice* 25.3 (Fall 2012): 6–20. Academic Search Complete. Web. 23 Jan. 2014.

Otte, George, and Rebecca Williams Mlynarczyk. *Basic Writing*. West Lafayette: Parlor P, 2010. Print.

Shaughnessy, Mina. *Errors and Expectations: A Guide for the Teacher of Basic Writing*. New York: Oxford UP, 1977. Print.

"Theory and Research-Based Principles of Learning." Eberly Center for Teaching Excellence and Educational Innovation, Carnegie Mellon, 2007. Web. 10 Sept. 2014. <www.cmu.edu/teaching/>

Tishman, Shari. "Why Teach Habits of Mind?" *Discovering and Exploring Habits of Mind*. Ed. Arthur Costa and Bena Kallick. Alexandria: Association for Supervision and Curriculum Development, 2000. 41–51. Print.

Torenbeek, M., E. P. W. A. Jansen, and W. H. A. Hofman. "Predicting First-Year Achievement by Pedagogy and Skill Development in the First Weeks at University." *Teaching in Higher Education* 16.6 (Dec. 2011): 655–68. MasterFile Complete. Web. 28 Jan. 2014.

Superpower Essay by Lydia Graecyn

Activity: writing the first essay of the semester

Learning Outcomes: discover assets and build confidence

Habits of Mind: metacognition, openness, and persistence

Toby can fix anything with moving parts, such as an engine, a bicycle, or a CD player. Alejandra can make anyone relax, whether a friend is studying for a test, getting ready for court, or preparing for minor surgery. Avery has a green thumb and can resurrect even the most tortured of house plants. Daniel can turn the sobs of frustrated, snotty-nosed, red-faced babies into bubbles of light laughter. Silas always manages to convince the highway patrol officer that he doesn't really want to give him a ticket. Juliet bakes the best cupcakes. Jasmine can unclog any toilet.

I discovered my students had these amazing abilities early on in the semester when I asked them to write an essay about their real-life superpowers. Asking students to carefully consider their talents, abilities, and skills as their very own superpowers invites them to engage in metacognition. Recognizing their assets creates openness on the part of the student because people want acknowledgment for what they do well. This assignment also supports persistence because students work on completing a project that showcases a personal, positive attribute.

I introduce this essay by saying to the students, "Everyone has a superpower, including you!" I then clarify that I do not mean the kind that one gets from a radioactive mutant spider bite, an encounter with beings from outer space, or a fortunate accident in one's cellular code. Neither do I mean the supernatural abilities we read about in comic books or the uncanny traits that belong to heroes in action movies. I'm not suggesting that we are all endowed with the magic you could ask for from a genie such as the ability to fly, turn invisible, or start fires with your mind. When I say "superpower," I am talking about the great things that we already do, the skill we already have, the amazing gift we are already the best at giving. In fact, it often takes some work, such as freewriting, for students to recognize their superpower because when they are so good at doing something and so comfortable with it they might not even think of it as a superpower at all. Often, they might think of their ability as just being themselves; however, if we can get students to think about it, they might come to recognize how special their ability really is.

metacognition

Some students will respond with skepticism to my assertion that indeed each of them has a superpower, so I am always ready with plenty of examples: my friend Antonia loves to travel, and she has been to more than 40 countries on six continents. Often, she makes new friends, and often these new friends want to share food with her as a gesture of hospitality. Antonia has the ability to eat the most unfamiliar foods—things we and she would find disgusting—without making a horrible face or throwing up. In Thailand, tarantula is a rare and special dessert. When the little girl of her host family excitedly offered Antonia the giant, roasted spider, Antonia smiled and ate it up! I could not do that. The ability to eat something we think disgusting certainly qualifies as a superpower!

I also know a man named Jeff who has an interesting superpower. He possesses some special quality that makes other people deeply trust him instantly. Once he was checking out at the grocery store when he realized he had left his wallet at home. The checkout clerk gave Jeff the groceries and a receipt and told him to come back later and pay the bill. Another time Jeff was running down the street late for the bus, and a young woman who had never seen him before pulled over and offered to give him a ride. Jeff's superpower also has a disadvantage. He appears so trustworthy that sometimes people tell Jeff their deep dark secrets, but sometimes he would really rather not know.

I then invite my students to begin thinking about their specific superpowers by freewriting on the topic. I suggest they write about their skills and talents. I ask them what they are known for in their group of friends. They might choose to consider what role they play in their family dynamic. Once they've identified one or more superpowers, I ask them to provide details and to write about the first time they discovered or used their superpower(s), the advantages, the disadvantages, and how the superpower(s) could help them and/or their community in the future. If they write about multiple superpowers, this is also a good time for them to choose one to focus on with plenty of examples of that superpower in action and many specific details. Next, we work on developing the topic into a clear, focused, interesting essay. Every writer will also have the opportunity for peer workshopping.

creativity

Most students enjoy identifying and bragging about their superpower. Occasionally, however, a student will need help discovering what to write about. Alma thought she had nothing even to freewrite about. We often enjoy the things we do well, so I asked her to simply write about activities she liked doing. Alma liked to watch TV, listen to music, and hang out with friends, but what she liked best was shopping. I asked her to explore in writing what in particular she liked about it. She came up with a list that included bringing home pretty things, getting to make her own choices, and finding deals. I asked her probing questions about each of these. When she began to talk about finding great deals, her face lit up. I knew we had discovered something she could write about as her superpower. *openness*

Lenora had a more difficult time finding her superpower to write about. She didn't seem very enthusiastic about anything in her life, so I drew on my classroom observations of her to help her find a direction. Lenora seemed shy in class discussions, but I noticed she did speak in small groups. Could her superpower be the ability to listen well before forming an opinion? Was she able to make sure that everyone had an equal opportunity to speak? Did she somehow support others or give them confidence? Was she able to make others think she was paying attention when in fact she was actually plotting out a great adventure? I showed her that I genuinely believed she had a superpower, and that I really did want to know all about it. I think that my persistence convinced her to keep trying, and she did write an essay she felt proud of.

Ideal for the beginning of the semester, "The Superpower Essay" allows students to develop writing skills while focusing on a subject that recognizes their assets and encourages self-esteem. Although the writing process itself may present challenges, the topic continually reminds students of their capabilities, value, and gifts. This assignment can then set the tone for the entire semester. During workshops, students are more open to constructive criticism because it comes balanced with an acknowledgment and celebration of an area in which the student already excels. Perhaps Angela could benefit from working to better organize her paragraphs, but I want her with me when it's time to pick the perfect watermelon. *openness and self-confidence*

Quick Start Guide

1. Before class, spend some time freewriting and becoming aware of your own superpower and the superpowers of people you know. For inspiration, you may also want to watch Stan Lee's *Superhumans* or a "People Are Awesome" compilation on YouTube.

2. Tell the class about the superpowers of people you know, and/or use the examples from this lesson.

3. Allow time for students to freewrite on their own superpowers.

4. Check in with students and make sure everyone has a topic for his or her essay. Help guide students who need it.

5. Assign the essay.

6. Workshop the essay in class, perhaps allowing students to share their superpowers with the class as a whole.

7. Provide plenty of recognition of students' talents and skills as well as constructive ideas about where to focus their attention to improve their writing.

Reflecting Home Culture by Adela Najarro

> Activity: selecting a course theme and placing the book order
>
> Learning Outcomes: write essays and articulate reading responses in various genres
>
> Habits of Mind: curiosity, engagement, and persistence

It's Book Order Time!

In the middle of grading the second round of papers, maybe the third, arrives the call to place the book order for the following semester. If you're like me, so many times you just repeat the order. But if you're also like me, you know that a different text might work better. If there is one thing we should do when ordering books, it is to consider the students sitting in our classes. We all know our disciplines; we all know the myriad details and objectives we need to teach; we all know, in a comp class anyway, how many revised pages each student must produce. Why not tailor our assignments along a theme that reflects students' lives, interests, challenges, and the world in which they live?

When the content of a composition course centers on a theme, students not only learn the nuts and bolts of college-level writing, but also gain the depth and knowledge that comes with investigating a topic for a sustained period of time. I also advocate selecting a theme that ties into the students' home culture and locale. Students are more likely to write an interesting paper if the topic matters to them, and the topic will more likely matter if it relates to their lives, culture, and direct experience. Even though "The Lives and Times of Ancient engagement Greeks" may appeal to the historian in us, it's vastly distant from the lives students currently lead. When we don't have to fight and coerce students to engage with the material, we make our jobs easier. When the book orders arrive, that's the right time to begin a grand switch into theme-based teaching that correlates to the students' home culture.

What Is Your Student Population?

When picking a theme, it's possible to start with the demographics of your institution. Who attends your school, and what are the major social justice issues students encounter? Currently, I teach at Cabrillo College and we are designated as a Hispanic-serving institution (HSI) because our Latino/a student population is greater than 25%.

Accordingly, the theme for my composition classes is a version of the U.S. Latino/a experience, and a topic that always arises is whether or not racial prejudice and discrimination still exist in our nation. In class, we discuss this highly sensitive topic with reservation, tact, and openness   patience. There are many silences and moments of deep thinking. Even though students do admit they have experienced put-downs for being Mexican and they can see that Santa Cruz County is racially segregated into neighborhoods—for example, the population in Watsonville is predominantly Mexican whereas the neighboring town of Aptos is predominantly White—they desire to find a location of hope where racial inequality is seen as a truth, not as an insurmountable barrier. It is in the essays where their true voices shine through. Over and over, I have students writing about how they faced racial bullying in grade school—on all ends of the spectrum, Latino kids and White. It's in the papers where they bring their experience of society and its injustices and begin to contemplate the big picture of what our racial history entails. They do this deep critical thinking while they learn to organize an essay, write thesis statements, use transitions, and incorporate sources using MLA format!

A composition class structured on a theme allows the instructor to teach course content and college-level writing, while also developing the habits of mind students need for college success. A theme that relates to a student's life and home culture, such as the U.S. Latino/a experience in an HSI, automatically begins in the midst of student experience and knowledge. Students then build on what they know through course readings and college-level research practices. Their curiosity is sparked because they seek to answer questions that relate to their own experience; searching college databases now matters. Students are engaged with research, reading and writing because they are completing their own stories through these activities. In addition, students persist and complete assignments because this is vital work, not only for them but also for the class and for their lives, culture, and communities.

Something to Consider

A theme needs to be large enough to encompass an entire semester's worth of inquiry: Think of it as the thesis statement for your class! It also helps to pick controversial and timely topics. My course themes always focus on some aspect of social justice. The more fire in classroom discussions, the more energized and powerful the writing in students' essays. And, of course, in order to make a theme-based course work, the instructor has to enjoy it too! But choosing solely our interests can lead to disaster—even though the theme may matters to us, it may not matter to the students. So beware.

Throughout my teaching career at the college level, I have come across numerous theme-based composition classes devised by my colleagues that inspired both the students and the instructor. Examples include exploring human sexuality, vampires in literature, gender roles in society, war and peace, the U.S. Latino/a experience, the immigrant experience, growing up, U.S. Japanese internment during World War II, genocide, and images of Africa. There are so many *curiosity* avenues by which to structure theme-based composition courses so that as students learn the standards required for college-level writing they also explore issues that matter deeply to their lives. Connecting their home culture to academic culture validates students because they begin to see themselves as part of the university. They begin to belong and to engage in a discourse that is more important than a sentence fragment. And in so doing, they learn how to avoid sentence fragments because what they are writing matters.

Once a theme has been determined, the next step is to formulate a syllabus. I have a few pointers that make the task go a bit more smoothly. The first step is to calculate the number of weeks of instruction and then subtract two. Always leave the first week to get going and the last week to catch up! The second step is to divide the number of weeks of instruction by the number of papers that you normally assign. These should become subthemes or units for the course. For example, when it is customary to have four essays during a semester, four subthemes or units would work. Let's say your theme is "Gender Roles in Society." Your subthemes might be the roles of women, the roles of men, changes in the 20th century, and gender in the media. For each subtheme, it is important to choose at least one reading selection that begins the discussion. So, basically, you develop one theme with four subthemes, four reading selections, four papers, and four whatever you feel is important. Structuring a syllabus in this manner gets the job done and done well. You teach what you need to teach, you have engaging conversations, and students have real reasons to write, real reasons to learn proper grammar and mechanics, and a real desire to effectively express ideas that are important to them.

Quick Start Guide

1. Follow your bliss! Pick a course theme based on what you love and want to spend a semester discussing, but be sure to take into account the interests, lives, and concerns of your students.
2. Consider the following questions: Who are your students? What issues do they confront? What will matter to them? Will your theme have a broad tie-in with many different types of students?
3. Once you have chosen a course theme, do the math. Divide the weeks of the semester by the number of papers you will teach. This will give you the number of "units" to teach.
4. Apply subthemes and composition course objectives to each unit. For example, for the course theme of the U.S. Latino/a experience, the first paper could focus on paragraph development and exemplification while concentrating on the subtheme of exploring the various terms by which Latinos identify: *Mexican American, Chicano/a, Latino/a, Mexican, American, Cuban*, and so on.
5. Find at least one college-level article to support each unit. Either choose a composition reader that contains these articles or make a course reader through your campus duplications center.
6. Get ready to discuss, argue, mediate, write, read, and have a truly vibrant semester!

Book Building by Adela Najarro

Activity: journal writing

Learning Outcomes: self-management, self-awareness, and collaboration on a team project

Habits of Mind: metacognition, curiosity, self-regulation, creativity, and transfer of learning

We're in the first week of the semester. The syllabus has been handed out, the first assignment has started, and the work begins. When I tell students that college papers at the junior and senior level are typically 10 pages or longer, they all stare at me in disbelief. I let them know how lucky they are that I have set the acceptable page range as four to eight pages while offering extra credit for anyone who reaches 10 pages! Students do an incredible amount of academic writing in any composition course, so to prevent students from getting burned out by the pressures and expectations of academic writing, I assign journal writing. The culminating activity is a class anthology and a book publication party.

intellectual stamina

Creating an anthology is one of the final projects in my college composition classes. As part of my teaching style, I use the freshman comp experience as not only a way for students to learn the structures and demands of academic writing, but also an opportunity for students to develop a stake in their own writing abilities. Besides academic essays, students are required to maintain a weekly journal where they can write in any form of their choosing. They can use their journal as a starting point for their essays; as a place to comment and reflect on course readings; as a location to draft personal writings expressing their hopes and desires; or as an opportunity to write poems, stories, song lyrics, or any other form of writing. The idea behind the journal is to counterpoint academic writing with writing of their own choosing; by writing in a journal, students can begin to develop the concept that writing is integral to a vibrant and inquisitive mind.

curiosity and reflection

Regarding habits of mind, this activity requires students to become metacognitively aware of their role as a writer and participant in academia, which at times means more than simply writing a paper for the teacher. Instead, students realize how writing communicates ideas, thoughts, analyses, and, yes, even feelings about the human experience. They become active, curious, self-regulated participants in academic discourse and structures, and it is hoped that this habit of mind transfers and grows as they continue into other courses and their college experience.

A Semester-Long Project That Begins with the Syllabus

Planning is key for the success of the anthology project. It is paramount to announce and delineate the parameters of the project by assigning weekly journal writing that is part of the course grade. Without grades, unfortunately, too many students will not complete enough journals from which to glean a good selection for the anthology. Central to the project is that students write and write a lot. At first, there may be a bit of grumbling, but once students are writing consistently every week, they begin to open up and eventually they create a gem they are willing to publish and share with the world. This is huge. And scary. So it is necessary to assign a grade to journal writing so that the majority of students will write in their journal responsibility   from the beginning of the semester to the end.

I usually assign students to write in their journal every class meeting. Assigning the journal as part of the regular "homework" routine for the class seems to work in that students generate enough text from which to make a choice for the anthology while not overburdening them with busywork or overburdening myself with grading.

I have graded journals in two ways: on paper and through an online classroom management system, Blackboard. With both methods, I tie grading each essay with the due date. For example, if I assign three essays, I'll collect journals three times; if I assign four essays, I'll collect journals four times. Each time an essay is due, I also specify that a certain number of journal entries are due. If I'm working with paper, students type out the number of required entries and number each one. I simply count how many they have done and grade by the number of entries completed. All entries completed earns an A, 80% earns a B, and so on. (If a point system is used for grade tabulation, points can be assigned for the number of entries completed.) The same process is used with the online grading system, but here I simply have to review the number of entries posted online and use the system's grading protocols.

I'm sure you've noticed that I don't read the journals. Oh, no! Oh, yes! Part of the journal process is for students to develop their own relationship with writing without judgment from authority— independence   that is, the instructor. As part of the journal process, I make it clear to students that I will not read their journal entries unless they specifically invite me to do so in an e-mail or in the journal title or header. When students take this option, I then engage in a dialogue with them and whatever they have chosen to share with me. I will read the journal entry and respond without judgment while reaching out to the student from the heart.

Setting up the journal-writing process requires explanation and discussion during the first weeks of the semester but then becomes automatic and falls to the background. In the final weeks of the semester, I ask students to select three to four pieces that they might want to include in the class anthology; at this point I make it clear that they can choose journal entries or excerpts from essays they have written during the semester, because not everyone is a born creative writer. The class has been organized into groups since the beginning of the semester, so I instrcut the students in each group get together and share and review each other's possible journal entries. Each student receives feedback from his or her peers as to which selection is the strongest. This time is also used to gather editing and revision ideas. I allow one class period for the students to complete their chapter, but groups rarely finish in one session, so it becomes the group's responsibility to meet outside of class in order to finalize their chapter. If meeting outside of class all at once is too much, then much of the collaborative work can be accomplished through e-mail or document sharing on the Internet.

Finally, there is the task of collecting each chapter, and setting the document into book format. Luckily, my local printer requires only a PDF and completes the pagination work as part of its printing services. Another option is to organize the formatting of the book as an extra-credit activity for a group of students or perhaps as a project for a digital media class. The anthology can also be published online, which would then encourage the use of illustrations and color. Whether the anthology is published in hard copy or on the Internet depends on your strengths as an instructor. Ultimately, what matters is that the students' work gets published and they share their voices with the world.

Nerves, Tears, and Lasting Memories

By the time we're in the final third of the semester, students have been working outside of class in small groups to edit their chapter in our class anthology. They have reviewed the journal entries and graded essays they have written and chosen their selection for the anthology. Collaboratively, each group has written an introduction to their chapter, and each student has edited his or her selection for the book. Then there is the book publication party, where all are requested to don their finest, invite friends and family, and read their first publication.

At each book publication party, at least one student has cried. One young woman wrote a nonfiction story about her removal from her home by Child Protective Services as a child. She chose to write about this incident as a way to own her life and to reaffirm the centrality of her family. Though she cried while reading the memoir, she did not stop reading it. When she finished, the other members of her group stood up, and they all hugged. Another time, a student wrote a memoir about how hard his mother worked as a janitor to provide their family with all they needed and how it made him proud to be her son. The mother was the one crying that time. Other students read poems they have written or parts of their research papers. Each student and guest leaves with a copy of the book, and they all sign each other's copies. Along with completing coursework, academic essays, and class discussions, students learn what it means to write something that matters. Their writing matters to each one of them, as well as to their friends and family, and it makes a difference to the students because they feel firsthand the power of written language. And they also see how academic books reflection and   are organized and written while editing a piece of their own writing metacognition   to the level of publication.

Quick Start Guide

1. Make sure to assign journals on your syllabus as a graded item that counts toward the final grade.
2. Assign approximately two journal entries per week.
3. Collect journals with every essay. Don't read the journals; just count how many are completed in order to assign a grade or points.
4. Form small groups in which students share a selection of their journals or excerpts from essays so that they can make the final selections and edit those pieces.
5. Have each small group write an introduction for their chapter.
6. Take the chapters to a printer or place them online.
7. Celebrate with a book publication party.

Opening-Week Activities by Ken Rand

> Activities: various assignments and homework appropriate for the first week of class
>
> Learning Outcomes: self-management, self-awareness, and the development of a cohesive classroom environment
>
> Habits of Mind: metacognition, critical thinking, engagement, motivation, and confidence

Although I am a mathematics instructor, I firmly believe that all of the activities I describe here can be adapted to any class on any level. Basically, you could say that they are, in a sense, generic. I recently organized and held a college conference that took up an entire Saturday where these and other activities were shown to both full- and part-time faculty from across all subject areas. The response was overwhelmingly positive.

Activity #1: Unlearn?

In the 1990s there was a film about college life called *Higher Learning*. Among the many subplots is the story line that "racism" is a "learned" concept. At the end of the movie, the word *unlearn* appears on the screen, and from what I remember it was large enough to take up almost the entire screen, thereby making it a powerful message. For some reason that on-screen message stuck with me, and I began to realize that in order for me to be successful as a math instructor it was extremely important for me to get my students to "unlearn" many of the bad habits and misinformation that they have unfortunately acquired from previous math courses.

How to Start

On opening day of all my classes I give a PowerPoint presentation that is basically an introduction to the class. I start the slide show with a slide that has only the word *unlearn* on it. This word is already on the screen when students enter my room. I show this slide three separate times during the presentation, thereby making it obvious that this word is important. Usually, shortly after I have completed the entire slide show and before I get a chance to talk about "unlearn," a student will ask, "What does unlearn mean?" or "What is it that you want us to unlearn?" In the few rare instances when no one asks this question

I will actually state, "I am waiting for a question." It doesn't take long for this question to be asked.

The Assignment

I ask my students to answer the following three questions in the form of a writing homework assignment (and this is Homework #2, which is a minimum of 50 words):

1. What do you think the word *unlearn* means?
2. Why do you think it is shown on the screen three times?
3. Exactly what is it that you think I want you to unlearn?

Before I collect the homework assignment during the next class session, I ask my students to take out the homework assignment and read it to the other students in their small group (in my classroom all of my students sit in groups of three; this is mandatory). To help them get started I ask that the individuals of each group choose the letter *x, y,* or *z*. I then ask the "x" students to raise their hand and I tell them that they are to go first and read their assignment answers to their table partners, and then the "y" students go next, and so on. If any students are absent, I will ask a student (or students) to move into groups of three. I then ask that each table answer the three assigned questions. Next I ask for any volunteers to read out loud their table's answer to the entire class. I do not comment except to tell them that they are all correct or very close.

The next step is for me to tell my students "my" definition of *unlearn*, which is that I want them to consider the possibility that what they have learned before in algebra might have been confusing for them. I ask the entire class, "How many of you have taken algebra before either in high school or in college?" Usually about 90% to 100% of the students raise their hand. Then I ask them, "Well . . . if you really learned the material before would you be here?" This question always elicits the anticipated response of "no." I tell them that I want this to be the last time they take this course and that I want them to "unlearn" as much as they can, to be open to new and perhaps easier methods that will greatly increase their "understanding" of the material, and to avoid the common practice of "memorizing" information and facts.

reflection and openness

After the discussion I collect the homework assignment, and that night I read the responses (correcting spelling and minor grammar mistakes in the process). I do not grade these assignments except as a completed homework assignment; however, I do hand the papers back to the students during the next class with either a check or check-plus at the top.

Instant Engagement!

Again, this is an opening-week activity in my classes that not only allows me to connect with my students but also allows them to connect with each other. It also helps them to realize that they are not in my class just to copy notes from a board. As is evident by the fact that this assignment has nothing to do with math, they realize that what I want them to do is to learn how to "think." By the second day of class they are actively engaging with each other by sharing their responses. They are learning how to collaborate and come to a collective conclusion.

engagement and collaboration

Challenges

One challenge, as incredible as it may seem, is that not all students do the homework assignment. However, they quickly learn that in my class they are in the minority and that they are missing out on the fun. While the students are collaborating and sharing I walk around the room as an observer just to see how they are working as a team, and, at the same time, I quickly find out who did and who did not do the assignment. A lot of students are not used to nor are they comfortable with working as a team, especially if they do not know the other students at their table. Nonetheless, students quickly start to see the benefits of having someone to help them understand and complete the work that is required.

Another challenge is that not all students "get it." Unlearning is not an easy process. But, I am persistent and I continually remind them that they are making the same mistakes because they have not yet bought into the concept of "unlearn."

Activity #2: E-mail me!

On the first day of class I ask my students to e-mail me and tell me a little about themselves, their family, and their hopes and plans for the future. Just recently I developed a PowToon presentation showing this assignment, with the theme music of *Mission: Impossible* in the background. This assignment is a minimum of twenty-five words, and students have until the end of the week to complete it. I also send an e-mail back to every student with a specific response to whatever the student wrote in his or her e-mail to me. This assignment helps me begin a "connection" with my students, and I believe it lets them know that I am interested in their lives, not just in how they do on a math test. Again, I do not grade or correct this assignment, but I do give my students credit for having completed Homework #1. I also announce in class that a short response such as "Hi, Mr. Rand . . . here is Homework #1" is not acceptable as a college-level assignment.

Challenges and Results

Some students have strange e-mail addresses. Under normal circumstances, I would probably delete a message coming from an unusual address without reading it, so I ask my students to write "Homework #1" and their section number in the subject line so that I at least know the e-mail is legitimate.

Another challenge is that reading the e-mails can be an emotional experience. Some of the students' stories about their backgrounds, their hopes and dreams, and their struggles and obstacles are both heartbreaking and inspiring.

A special note: I just recently decreased the time allowed for this assignment to two days. To my surprise, there was a significant increase in the number of students completing this assignment on time.

Activity #3: Why Are You Taking This Class?

This is an "in-class" assignment (also on the first day) in which I ask my students in my PowerPoint presentation to respond to the following questions on an index card:

1. Do you work?
2. How many hours/week do you work?
3. How many units are you taking this semester?
4. What was your last math class? When was it?
5. List three things you like to do.
6. On the back of the card, tell me why you are taking this class at this particular time in your life.

Connecting with Students Can Be Fun

I have some fun with this assignment in a number of ways. First of all, the last slide on the PowerPoint presentation shows my own Top 10 list of reasons for students taking my class; I show this before they get a chance to write down their own reason(s). This list is meant to be humorous—it's a take on David Letterman's Top 10 lists—and includes items such as "The person in front of me during registration was cute and they enrolled in your class so that's how I got here," or "I have failed algebra seven times before and you are the only instructor I haven't tried yet" (not too funny, but it usually gets the loudest laugh), or "I don't know how I got here—the last thing I remember is passing out in the bathroom."

The next day I continue the fun by reading back to the class some of the comments and reasons from the students. There is almost always one comment from a student that goes something like, "My mom took you, so that's why I'm taking you too." After the laughter subsides, I tell my students, "Can you imagine if I teach long enough that someone someday may eventually write, 'My grandmother took you so that's why I am taking you'?" Some students actually confess, "This really is the fourth time I'm taking this class, and you are the only instructor I haven't tried and this course is the only one keeping me from graduating." I have also gotten the response, "I am taking you again because you are the best instructor I ever had." And to that I responded, "I want to thank my son Kevin for writing this on his card."

Connecting and Engaging

One of the reasons for this assignment is to assist me in connecting with my students and establishing a rapport with them. It also gives me a lot of information about the individual reasons students are taking my class. I also believe that answering "Why am I taking this class?" gets many students to reflect and refocus on their goals for the future.

motivation

What the Instructor Needs

All you need are enough index cards for the class. If index cards are not available, simply have the students use their own paper. And, you also need a sense of humor.

Activity #4: Survivor

Survivor is a game that I borrowed from the Math Jam program at Pasadena City College. It was originally designed as a game to review a specific topic, but I have adapted it as a game for my students to get to know me not as an instructor, but as a person.

How to Play

I have already prepared (as a PowerPoint) a list of about 20 different facts about myself and my family. Each fact has a corresponding "false" fact. The students need to choose which one is true and which one is a lie.

engagement

The game starts by asking all students in the class to stand up and go to the closest empty aisle near their desk. In my class there are three rows of tables, so basically I have students standing in two aisles, one on the left and one on the right. I show the first slide with one fact about me on the left and another fact on the right. One of them is true and the other is false. I tell the students that they have one minute to choose the true statement and then move to the corresponding aisle (either left or right). If they happen to already be on the side they wish to choose, then they don't have to move. For example, the first slide may have the following statements:

Mr. Rand was once a professional singer.	Mr. Rand was once a professional dancer.

After the students have made their choices and moved to the left or right aisle, the wrong statement drops from the screen and the students who chose the wrong answer (aisle) have to sit down. I continue the slide show until only one or two students remain standing. I hand out prizes to the winners (graph paper, coupons, etc.).

Results

First of all, this activity is an incredible amount of fun, and second, my students get to know more about me (and my family), and my connection with my students continues to grow. I continually play this game throughout the semester, but I make the questions topic oriented and use it mostly as a review before a test. When I use it as a review I have the students play as a team (table team) so that they can help each other review for the test in a relaxed and nonthreatening atmosphere.

Activity #5: Obstacles to Success

It is an easy and dangerous trap for us as instructors to allow ourselves to think that every student who does poorly is doing so because he or she is a lazy procrastinator. Quite often students come into our classes with a whole set of obstacles that unless removed or at least addressed will cause them to perform poorly in class.

How to Start

This assignment begins as a class survey that I created on polleverywhere.com. I ask the class to text me a response to "What is the biggest obstacle to your success in this class?" Their responses appear on the screen with the inevitable myriad of reasons, ranging from problems with transportation to family issues, health issues, and, yes, even laziness. With class participation we make a master list on the board of all of these obstacles and other factors hindering success, and the students are asked to copy this list into their notes.

Their assignment is as follows (minimum of 50 words):

1. Choose three obstacles on the list that pertain directly to your performance in this class.
2. Write "why" each one is an obstacle.
3. Choose three obstacles on the list that you think may affect the performance of some of your classmates.
4. Write "why" you think each one is an obstacle.

Results

The next day in class students are asked to take turns sharing their obstacles with their tablemates. They are also asked to help offer their classmates possible solutions to their obstacles.

Something fascinating happens each time I give this assignment, especially after the sharing session. I often find students giving each other phone numbers and e-mail addresses, and I even see other students offering rides to students who have transportation problems.

Benefits

Students need to know that they are not alone when it comes to their obstacles. They quickly learn that other students have the same or similar obstacles and that many obstacles can be overcome with extra effort and the caring of others.

Activity #6: *Higher Learning* Film Clip

As I mentioned before, I use "unlearn" from John Singleton's 1995 movie *Higher Learning* to stimulate reflection and critical thinking. Well, there is also an 8-minute movie scene from that movie that I like to show in class to stimulate and provoke thought and a subsequent writing assignment.

In this movie clip, Laurence Fishburne, as a political science professor, is holding student-teacher conferences in his office. The first student is a young coed who apparently has written an inadequate paper. After he offers her some constructive criticism and a possible alternative topic, she says, "That is a great topic for me to write about." The professor becomes frustrated and tells the student, "You are not here to simply regurgitate facts and information that I give to you. . . . I am looking for evidence of original thought."

The second student is a school athlete who seems to have a problem with how easy it is for White students to do well in school. The professor offers him a hypothetical situation. He says, "Suppose you are at a track meet and there is another runner who is bigger, stronger, and faster than you. Do you leave the track?" The student responds, "Hell no." The professor then asks, "What do you do?" to which the student replies, "I run faster."

The assignment is as follows (minimum of 50 words):

1. What message is the professor trying to get across to the young coed?
2. Does she appear to get the message? How do you know?
3. What message is the professor trying to get across to the track star?
4. Does he appear to get the message? How do you know?
5. What message am I trying to get across to you? Do you get it?

After collecting and reading each paper I have a discussion with the class in order to make sure they "get it."

Results

I know this sounds corny but I have actually had a number of students come up to me in class after I've shown this movie clip to thank me and tell me that this experience is going to change who they are as a student. It doesn't get any more rewarding than that.

The intent and purpose of the movie clip is obvious and so are its metaphors. Students, even though they are in a "math" class, begin (again) to reflect on the hopes, dreams, and goals they have for themselves pertaining to the present and to what they want for themselves after college.

Activity #7: Math-O (Word-O, Hist-O, etc.)

This game is, of course, modeled after bingo. It is used primarily as a review for a test.

How to Play

The instructor needs to prepare 24 review questions. I have these questions on 24 slides in a PowerPoint presentation. Each student is given a 5 × 5 Math-O game sheet consisting of 24 empty boxes and a middle box designated a "Free" space. Students are asked to number the empty boxes from 1 to 24, but they must do this randomly. By doing this randomly no student will have the same game sheet. A question will appear on the screen with a random number, let's say #14. Each student must then write the answer to this question in box #14 on their game sheet. I then ask that each student copy that problem on a separate sheet of paper so that we can go over it later during the "review" process. Even though each student has his or her own game card, I let them get help from other people at the table if needed.

When someone completes five boxes in a row they are supposed to shout out "Math-O." If their responses are correct, then their entire table is declared the winner. I give a variety of different prizes such as "the winning team is exempt from the next 10-point quiz." I then continue the game with the purpose of preparing the entire class for all of the types of questions on the next test. The students are focused on having fun and trying to win prizes, but I'm getting them to practice for the test.

Challenges

Students need to be given a time limit to answer the questions; otherwise, the game will take too long. In case time runs out during the review process (after the game), I have a worksheet that has all of the questions and answers (and work) so that the students can study them for the next test.

Results

Besides being a lot of fun, this activity is a great way to review for a test. I do not purposely give surprise questions on a test. I want my students to know what they are responsible for learning in a specific chapter. This game gives them an accurate preview of the type of questions they can expect on their test. I almost always include some challenge questions on all of my tests with the hope of separating the B students from the A students, but these questions are usually just challenging variations of questions they have seen during the review.

A lot of my college's English instructors and history instructors have already adapted this game to their courses with great results. I am still waiting for the psychology department to try it and perhaps call the game "Psych-O."

Summary

By now you might be thinking, "Does this instructor ever teach math?" My major goal in all of the activities and assignments I have provided here as well as my philosophy of teaching is simply to get my students to "think" and reflect on why they are in college. I also strongly believe in collaborative learning. My responsibility as a college instructor is not just to teach them math but to teach them how to become better students and that working together as a team can produce positive results.

metacognition and transfer of learning

Though most of these assignments are writing assignments, it is continually surprising to me how well students are able to articulate their thoughts when they know they are not being graded on their spelling or grammar.

By the way, over my 27 years of teaching at Hartnell, my overall retention rate is 87%, and 93% of those students pass my class with a C or better.

All of the activities I have provided, including the games and videos, can be found on my college website (No1professor.webs.com) in the file that says "Engagement Conference."

Quick Start Guide

1. Pick one fun activity you would like to try in your class.
2. Make preparations to try this new activity. Will it be on the first day of class next semester or is it an activity you can use to review for an upcoming test?
3. Have fun getting to know your students and letting them get to know you!

2

CREATING COMMUNITIES

Adela Najarro

> "Another advantage of collaborative learning is the practice it gives in leadership, group
> interaction, and public speaking. Collaborative learning is particularly effective at
> increasing the leadership skills of female students and for getting male students used to
> turning to women for help in pressure situations. Finally, collaborative learning takes
> advantage of the rich diversity of students at many of today's colleges and universities."
>
> —John C. Bean (*Engaging Ideas* 166)

It is in the second, third, and fourth weeks, while gathering what students bring to the classroom and discovering the uniqueness of each individual on our course roster, when we can create a student-centered classroom with activities that foster a community of learners. Chapter 1's focus on discovering assets goes hand in hand with the subject of this chapter: creating student-centered classrooms where communities of learners interact with and support each other. Imagine the student who has driven an hour from a remote farm community to begin his college education in your class. Imagine that girl who didn't think her family could afford to send her to college but who is grateful for the scholarship that has paid for this semester's tuition. Imagine that 18-year-old who figures going to college is better than working at Taco Bell. The reasons students end up in our classes are as varied as the students themselves, but one thing they all have in common is fear of the unknown. No student knows what will happen in your class. No one knows the changes that will occur cognitively, socially, and experientially in this semester of college. Not one of the students knows how welcome and engaged he or she will come to feel in your class once a community of learners has been established.

Human beings are communal creatures. In the college classroom we can capitalize on this basic human attribute to engage students in the specific subject matter of our disciplines and courses by creating a learning environment where a sense of community is practiced. Classroom cohesion can be established in any course through activities that lead to students getting to know each other, to bonding with each other, and to working collaboratively with course materials. We can create a community of learners in any classroom through a student-centered, assets-based approach that incorporates vibrant and varied group learning activities, and other pedagogical methods, such as those discussed in the first chapter and throughout this book. This chapter discusses building a community of learners in any discipline and classroom, along with the companion idea of the formal learning community, and presents a case study of the Puente Project.

Creating Communities

Definitions are in order. A *community of learners* arises from a student-centered classroom environment where the instructor facilitates instruction through various engaging pedagogical approaches ranging from the use of games to small groups, minilectures, collaborative projects, research, presentations, and so on. The list of possibilities is endless and available for instructor review through many sources. In tandem, a *formal learning community* has a particular definition: a cohort of students who enroll in two or more linked courses for at least one semester. In this chapter, a *community of learners* refers to the structures and activities that any instructor, in any course, in any discipline can enact in order to create a student-centered classroom where students support and engage one another, and a *formal learning community* refers to a cohort of two or more linked courses. The activities that occur in either type of community are very similar: assets gathering; games; group work and projects; scaffolding; assignments that engage a student's home culture; and, of course, teaching habits of mind

> In this chapter, a *community of learners* refers to the structures and activities that any instructor, in any course, in any discipline can enact in order to create a student-centered classroom where students support and engage one another, and a *formal learning community* refers to a cohort of two or more linked courses.

that lead to college success. My fellow editors and I believe that it is paramount to create a community within each classroom among students and the instructor so that teaching becomes a collaborative activity where all learn and all are engaged.

In any classroom, a community of learners can be established. This involves assets gathering, as noted in our first chapter, but while getting to know students, we can foster students getting to know each other. This can happen through many avenues, including games or small-group work. Usually, the activities involve getting students out of their seats and moving around. Chart paper can be placed around the room with questions written at the top and then students walk around the room and write their answers. The questions can ask for basic information, such as a favorite band, or they can focus on the day's reading selection, such as requesting students to note one detail about characters in a story. The options are unlimited and require only that students write while moving around. There are many sources, including this book, where instructors can find ideas and resources that will help them to create a community of learners in their classroom. One major source is Skip Downing's *On Course* textbook, which is supported by a website that includes myriad activities to supplement the text or to use in a stand-alone fashion after tailoring to specific course needs. Downing has developed his insights concerning effective classroom practices into a national movement that includes a national conference, public workshops, institutional workshops, and a free newsletter and website filled with ideas for best practices in the classroom (see http://oncourseworkshop.com for more information).

John C. Bean's *Engaging Ideas: The Professor's Guide to Integrating Writing, Critical Thinking, and Active Learning in the Classroom* is a one-stop shop for everything an instructor needs to create a vibrant classroom environment where all students learn college-level course content while engaging in critical thinking. In my first years teaching at the college level, I read and reread Bean's book in order to fully understand, test, revise, and use the many different types of activities that Bean suggests. My particular favorites explain many ways to facilitate small-group work and interactions, and then the final section of the book on marking and grading student papers—invaluable! Besides these, there are so many avenues by which to explore developing a student-centered classroom into a community of learners. Bean includes a section on writing assignment guidelines, one on reading challenging texts, and another on small-group activities.

Building Communities of Learners

One of the most important ways to help students feel supported early in a course is to give them a sense of belonging. We want them to feel "at home" in their academic lives; to know that they are valued participants in our classes; to enjoy being connected to their campus community; and to flourish, rather than merely cope. In her description of what it means to "thrive" academically, educational researcher Laurie Schreiner links this critical sense of community support to degree attainment: "Thriving college students not only are academically successful, they also experience a sense of community and a level of psychological well-being that contributes to their persistence to graduation and allows them to gain maximum benefit from being in college" (4).

In many ways, building a community of learners is to a large extent about planning for the nerve-jangling, brain-frying messy middle of the instructional cycle, which is further discussed in chapter 4. But here, at the beginning of the semester, we can establish a community of learners, so that students have a network of supportive peers and hopefully will develop the practice of meeting with instructors and tutors. These communities become the insurance policy for students when the inevitable illnesses, breakups, and car troubles lying in wait around midterms arrive. Though they face problems, with a community of learners supporting each other students find the persistence and self-management to navigate these problems. The first time a student visits office hours shouldn't be during a crisis. Neither should students wait until midterms before they ask questions in class, form a study group, join a club, or use academic support services such as tutoring and counseling centers.

> One of the most important ways to help students feel supported early in a course is to give them a sense of belonging.

In "Making Excellence Inclusive: An Evolving Framework for Student Success," the Association of American Colleges & Universities (AAC&U) identifies supportive learning environments and communities as essential to the intellectual and social development of diverse student populations. As the framework notes, making excellence inclusive requires "attention to the cultural differences learners bring to educational experiences, and how that diversity can enhance the enterprise" and "a welcoming community that engages all of its diversity in the service of student and organizational learning" (Albertine and McNair 3). Both provide rich opportunities for faculty to model qualities such as the ability to experiment with new ideas, see other points of view, and challenge their own beliefs while mentoring the development of these dispositions in their students. For example, two of the lesson exemplars in this chapter—my own "Forming *Familias*" and Tina Sander's "Building a Supportive Community in the Classroom"—demonstrate ways that instructors can draw on students' prior experiences to foster learning environments that aim to be both "inclusive and affirming" (Kuh et al. 8).

In a supportive community of learners, modeling and mentoring intellectual growth additionally occurs through the instructor's testimony as a colearner who has "been there" and through the coaching and encouragement provided to the students. Every semester, I pull out my story about being a "good" student in college but getting Ds and Cs in my World Literature class. It was by meeting with the instructor that I realized I didn't understand how to write a college-level essay, so I proceeded to enroll in every college composition course the university offered. I enjoy telling students that that is how I became an English professor—because I was failing my first literature class! Of course, this story is also one of persistence. I refused to give up and went in search of the answers I needed. Then I ask students to seek me out also, to ask questions, to collect and gather each other's phone numbers and e-mail addresses, to get to know each other. Together we can make a difference. The trademarks of a student-centered classroom apply to all disciplines, and each of us can create a community of learners in our classrooms. These pedagogical practices are so effective that numerous formal learning communities have been established.

The Formal Learning Community

Though practiced in many forms, a formal learning community typically involves a cohort of students who take two or more linked classes in the same semester. In a formal learning community, courses are also thematically linked and support each other in terms of assignments and meeting student needs. In "Building Learning Communities in Nonresidential Campuses," Richard Raymond reports that his university, University of Arkansas at Little Rock, linked a composition course, a speech and communications course, and an anthropology course; all instructors collaborated on devising course syllabi so that students progressed thematically at the same pace in all three classes (271–72). As Raymond mentions in his article, the success of a formal learning community requires campuswide support beginning with student recruitment; scheduling; faculty collaboration; administrative support; and, of course, extra funding to cover expenses, from a recruitment presentation with pizza to paying faculty to collaborate and meet on a regular basis. Once the administrative support exists, a formal learning community can take off and foster student success.

The establishment of learning communities is at the forefront of the institutional practices at Cabrillo College. The variety and range of formal learning communities at Cabrillo College are meant to meet the needs of a diverse student population because the college is a Hispanic-serving institution (HSI). Each semester, Cabrillo has numerous formal learning communities in place, including during summer session. Our summer formal learning community is the Summer Migrant Program (SMP), which is a collaboration between the Pajaro Valley Unified School District's Migrant Education Program and the college. In this formal learning community, students attend summer school and can use the units either to fulfill high school graduation requirements or as a way to get a jump start on the college experience. In the SMP, students take a writing course, a reading course, and a counseling and guidance course. The themes of these courses are the U.S. Latino/a experience and navigating academia.

Two other formal learning communities at Cabrillo are ACE and STARS. Diego Navarro established the Academy for College Excellence, or ACE, as a way for students to gain the habits of mind and skills necessary for college success in one semester. Students attend a two-week session that sets the stage for the entire ACE experience, and then they enroll in a full-time load that may include courses in math, English, social justice, dance, and business. Faculty meet on a weekly basis to discuss curriculum and student progress. Students conduct primary research on social justice issues relevant to their community. This award-winning program has now expanded to other campuses and is set to positively affect how colleges offer instruction throughout the nation (see http://academyforcollege excellence.org for more information).

As a variation of the first-year experience, Cabrillo hosts STARS. A STARS cohort is a two-semester experience beginning in the fall. Students in the cohort take English, math, and a seminar. They also may enroll in a summer bridge program, and the program provides tutoring and supplemental instruction opportunities. The purpose of this formal learning community is to support students during their first year at college by participating in a cohort of like-minded students and through receiving additional support services. At Cabrillo College, we have administrative support and faculty buy-in to run a variety of formal learning communities; I have worked with the Puente Project for the past decade.

Case Study: The Puente Project

The Puente Project was first established in 1981 at Chabot College, a California Community College near Oakland. Felix Galaviz, an academic counselor, and Pat McGrath, an English instructor, identified that although Latino/a students were enrolling in college, the transfer and graduation rates needed to improve. After poring through numerous enrollment, completion, persistence, graduation, and transfer rates, they were able to identify two key areas where Latino/a students faltered: the understanding of academic culture and college-level composition. Puente began as a formal learning community pairing an introduction to college course with a composition course, both thematically focused on the experience of Hispanics in the United States. Currently, Puente is open for all students, and the thematic parameters match student demographics so that each Puente cohort can engage with the sociological makeup that exists on their college campus and within each cohort. At Cabrillo College, an HSI, the Puente cohort is thematically unified on the theme of exploring the U.S. Latino/a experience.

In addition, Puente is more than a pairing of classes. Puente also includes extracurricular activities and a mentorship component. The extracurricular activities allow students to bond and to begin self-identifying as college students. Many times, underserved students experience the college environment as uninviting alien territory. By participating in a series of extracurricular activities, students begin to see themselves as college students who are welcomed and supported while being exposed to the norms expected of college-educated professionals in the United States. Another integral aspect is the mentor component. Each year, every individual Puente student is matched with a mentor from the community who is a college graduate. These professionals volunteer their time with the goal of reaching out to a student. Through the extracurricular activities and the mentor, students begin to visualize a future where they are college graduates and successful professionals who care about and give back to their community.

The Puente Project model combines English composition instruction, personal development, academic counseling, and mentorship with extracurricular activities. All aspects of Puente are thematically focused on the student's home culture and identity depending on each cohort's demographics. At Cabrillo, we focus on the experience of the U.S. Latino/a because that is the demographic of the cohorts and because Cabrillo is an HSI. In accordance, the composition course incorporates contemporary Latino/a literature while exploring culturally relevant writing topics such as immigration or race and identity. The counseling and guidance class teaches students how to navigate academic culture while respecting and valuing home cultural values. Our mentors are Latino/a themselves or seek to help and advance the Latino/a community in the area. An example of how Puente addresses home and cultural values is our *Noche de familia*, when family members are invited to campus in order to meet the instructors and other students in the Puente cohort for that year—the idea being that because the Latino/a family is central to the culture, by having families welcome and understand their child's college aspirations, they will offer help and support throughout the freshman-year experience. We also host a popcorn and movie night during the spring semester during which we show a movie relevant to the Latino/a experience, such as *Under the Same Moon* or *A Better Life*. All of these activities envelop the students and help them to develop an identity as Latino/a college students who have the knowledge and skills to transfer, graduate, and return to their community as leaders and mentors.

One of the best aspects of working in a formal learning community as an instructor is that the training and collaboration with other instructors has made me a better teacher overall. Each new English or counseling instructor must attend a Puente Summer Institute (PSI) where over the course of a week the Puente concept inside and outside of the classroom is reviewed. After the PSI, every semester there is a two-day Puente conference where, once again, the Puente English instructor and counselor stay up-to-date on pedagogical teaching methods and the ideas of how to best

> One of the best aspects of working in a formal learning community as an instructor is that the training and collaboration with other instructors has made me a better teacher overall.

work with each Puente cohort. There are plenty of successful strategies and much information to learn from at each semester's training sessions as a result of the Puente Project enjoying more than 30 years of success training educators.

Student Stories

Creating a community of learners or participating in a formal learning community involves collaboration and group work. One of my favorite projects that I do each semester as part of the Puente Project involves creating a class book (fully explained in chapter 1's "Book Building" exemplar). Students choose one piece of writing to publish and then in groups they write an introduction to their chapter. The purpose of this assignment is to have students understand the structure of academic writing at the book level, to successfully collaborate on a team project, to write the introduction to a book chapter, and to edit writing for publication. In addition, this final project serves as an exercise in metacognition. I ask each "*familia*," or group, to state how participating in Puente, a formal learning community, has affected their academic progress. Here are a few sample paragraphs:

> Being in Puente gave us an opportunity to meet new people, to grow as [people] and set a guideline to follow to achieve our goals. We as a *familia* are proud of our Mexican origin and feel powerful to know that we can succeed and prove [to] others that we are capable of achieving greatness. While being college students we have matured as individuals and have learned how to manage our time and be responsible. We have encountered many roadblocks along the way such as discrimination, economical struggles and some internal hardships. ("Local Gummie Bears")

> Puente gives us a lot of opportunities and helps us to choose a better future for ourselves. Puente has a lot of activities that are made to teach us about life and college. One of the best things that we like about Puente is that we get to visit different universities and we get to see which one we like best. ("Fantastic Five")

> We want to transfer and graduate from a four-year college because we want to encourage our family and community to continue their education in order to have a better future. Sometimes it is hard for us to take care of our brothers, or work, and still have to come to

school, but we don't give up and we still come to class and do well. On the other hand, we have also succeeded because the first step we did was come to college. Also we come to class and we do all the work that we have to do because we want to be remembered as another number of Latinos that have graduated from college. We also want Latinos to know that if we graduate from college, they can also do it. As a *familia*, we have found Puente to be a good environment, and a supportive learning community. ("*Nuestra familia*")

Puente has been the foundation of support for us because it supports us Latinas. Puente has helped us build a bridge over the current of the struggle and oppression that we go through in order to be successful. It has helped us and supported us when we didn't believe in ourselves. We found that we were coming from similar situations and all went through discrimination in being Latinos. ("Sirens")

Our experience with the Puente Program was remarkable. We were all glad we joined this program because even though we talked to each other we weren't as close as we are now. We are truly a *familia* now. The Puente Program helped us all in starting our college life and helping us to set up a path. Thanks to our instructors that have the patience to work with each and every Puente student. Dr. Adela and Rudy have managed to keep us going and reminded us not to give up that easily, that life is hard but it will all pay off in the end. ("Santa Cruz Penguins")

The Puente Program has taught us how to be responsible and proactive when it comes to our academic success and also helped us establish ourselves here at Cabrillo. For example, Puente serves as a good bridge from high school to college and helps students transfer to a four year college and also understand things like knowing what classes to take for our major and financial aid. The program also helps introduce a *familia*, or a group of other Puente students, and helps them find that sense of friendship and common goals where one can ask for help for one another. We learned how it's important to have a *familia* when one is starting off in college because one has that sense of motivation when everyone has the same goal, which is to transfer and obtain a university degree. ("*El Orgullo de Atzlan*")

Conclusion

From the moment we plan our syllabus to the last minutes of the final exam we can build a community of learners in our classrooms. Lydia Graecyn in "Pass as a Class" presents a creative icebreaker that, through a fun game, leads students to depend on each other and to work collaboratively. Tina Sander in "Building a Supportive Community in the Classroom" offers a range of games and group activities that will help any class become student centered. My exemplar, "Forming *Familias*," explains the process that I use to form semester-long groups for my Puente Project cohort. The resources for creating communities of learners are in this volume, they can be found by dropping in on a colleague and by talking shop in our offices, and they exist in workshops and on websites. All we have to do is imagine. Imagine a class where students won't stop talking, discussing, thinking, writing, and collaborating. Imagine teaching this way forever.

Works Cited

Academy for College Excellence. N.p., n.d. Web. 26 Apr. 2014.

Albertine, Susan, and Tia McNair. "Making Excellence Inclusive: An Evolving Framework for Student Success." Washington, DC: AAC&U, 2011. Web.

Bean, John C. *Engaging Ideas: The Professor's Guide to Integrating Writing, Critical Thinking, and Active Learning in the Classroom*. 2nd ed. San Francisco: Jossey-Bass, 2011. Print.

Downing, Skip. "On Course Workshop—Helping Colleges Improve Student Success and Retention." On Course Workshop. N.p., n.d. Web. 26 Apr. 2014.

"*El Orgullo de Atzlan*." *Nuestra Vidas Writing Project*. 2nd ed. Ed. Adela Najarro. Aptos: Cabrillo College, 2013. 48–50. Print.

"Fantastic Five." *Nuestra Vidas Writing Project*. Ed. Adela Najarro. Aptos: Cabrillo College, 2013. 59–60. Print.

Kuh, George D., et al. *Student Success in College: Creating Conditions That Matter*. San Francisco: Jossey-Bass, 2005. Print.

"Local Gummie Bears." *Nuestra Vidas Writing Project*. Ed. Adela Najarro. Aptos: Cabrillo College, 2013. 73–74. Print.

"*Nuestra familia*." *Nuestra Vidas Writing Project*. Ed. Adela Najarro. Aptos: Cabrillo College, 2013. 36–38. Print.

Raymond, Richard. "Building Learning Communities in Nonresidential Campuses." *Teaching English in the Two-Year College* 26.4 (1999): 393–405. Print.

"Santa Cruz Penguins." *Nuestra Vidas Writing Project*. 2nd ed. Ed. Adela Najarro. Aptos: Cabrillo College, 2013. 17–18. Print.

Schreiner, Laurie A. "The 'Thriving Quotient': A New Vision for Student Success." *About Campus* 15.2 (2010): 2–10.

"Sirens." *Nuestra Vidas Writing Project*. 2nd ed. Ed. Adela Najarro. Aptos: Cabrillo College, 2013. 5–7. Print.

Pass as a Class by Lydia Graecyn

Activity: group-building game

Learning Outcomes: self-awareness, group cohesion, and the development of a community of learners

Habits of Mind: openness, engagement, creativity, persistence, and flexibility

A Latina, a Surfer, and a Grandma Walk into a Classroom . . .

A 19-year-old Latina with high, thin, penciled-on eyebrows and a sharply outlined mouth carries a sparkly pink backpack into the classroom, slides into a third-row desk, and adjusts her earbuds. Stumbling in the door, a little out of breath, a 35-year-old male with damp, sun-bleached hair and traces of pasty sunscreen on his face asks if he's in the right place. A woman with short, tight gray curls walks to the front of the class, selects a center seat, gets out a pen and paper, and settles her reading glasses on the end of her short, square nose. Students keep arriving, a few in pairs, but mostly solo, until each of the 30 desks has a new face sitting at it. The students look at each other, silently assessing. They look at me, silently waiting.

How do I begin to encourage this diverse group of individual students to become a cohesive community of learners? Over time, these students will learn that they hold many goals in common besides just successfully completing our class. They will discover the interests, experiences, and skills they share as well as those they don't. They will discover the support they need and the support they can give. I hope they will discover the value of belonging to a community of learners. I want them to see themselves not as lone individuals but as an interdependent tribe on an adventure of academic proportions.

"Pass as a Class" begins the process of community building through interactive play. To successfully reach the goal, students must be open to playing the game. The goal can be reached only if each student completely engages. Individually and as a group students must use their creativity to develop a winning strategy. Reaching the goal will not automatically happen. The group will discover that many strategies fail and that they can reach the desired outcome only through persistence. Lastly, they must be flexible enough to accept input from each other and adapt to changes in the game.

Go Ahead, Drop the Ball!

On the first or second day of class, I tell the students that I know their secret: The real reason they come to school is so they can play their beloved icebreaker games. They simply cannot get enough! Usually, students respond by groaning, rolling their eyes, and shifting uncomfortably in their chairs. Feeling embarrassment together is not the best way to bond, and they expect a repeat of so many forced, awkward, and artificial get-to-know-one-another interactions. I acknowledge my own dislike of icebreaker games and promise this will be fun. They don't believe me.

Nevertheless, the students listen, suspiciously. While the students are still seated, I give the first two instructions: I tell them that I want us to create as much open space in the middle of the classroom as possible by pushing the furniture to the edges of the classroom, quickly and quietly, and that as soon as they finish, they should stand in a circle. By letting them know beforehand that I want them to make a standing circle, aimless milling about is avoided.

As they move their desks, I lead the students who have finished first in some simple stretching both to loosen everyone up and to fill the time as everyone comes to the circle. Next, I show them a ball and explain the game: "Say your name and toss the ball to another student until each student has had a turn. That's it. You don't have to remember the name of who gave you the ball or whom you give the ball to." Sometimes, the students can't believe it's so simple. They

openness   have to remain open to the activity to stay with it. I demonstrate and practice with them. Then I step out of the circle and let them complete the task, which they do.

All of the students must engage for the class to play the game. It won't work if any one individual isn't ready to receive the ball or

engagement   hesitates too long in passing it. The first time through, a few students fumble with the ball and even with their own names. Just having everyone's attention can be unsettling, and I am careful to give encouragement and reassurance, leading them to the habit of mind of persistence. Once the class passes the ball through all the students with relatively little difficulty, I add a twist.

I reveal the goal of the game: To get the ball around to everyone as quickly as possible with each person saying his or her name. I get my timer ready and say, "Go!" At first, the students pass the ball just as they did before only a little faster. I read their time, usually about two minutes, and tell them, "That's a good try, but I've seen faster." The students repeat the game just as they did before but going as fast as they absolutely can. "That's better," I tell them, "but I've seen faster."

Usually the students will grumble and mumble comments to each other, ranging from "I can't do it any faster" to "How can we do it faster?" I give encouragement, but no suggestions, even if they ask. I have confidence that they can figure it out themselves. Usually, students try making a smaller, tighter circle, but that doesn't improve their time significantly. Eventually, they start asking me productive questions. Do they have to stand in a circle? No. Do they have to toss the ball? No. Do they need to pass the ball in a particular order? No. All they need to do is make sure that each student gets the ball and says his or her name.

On their own, students develop and experiment with several strategies. I've seen students organize two parallel lines facing each other and pass the ball back and forth quickly. I'll say, "Pretty good, but I know you can do it faster!" Some groups have formed one long line and passed the ball straight along it. I'll comment, "That's fast, but I know you can beat that time." Often they try to hold the ball in the middle and have everyone reach in and touch the ball. It's hard to get everyone to fit, but some groups will go to extreme acrobatic lengths to make this work. I tell them, "You're really committed to making it work!" One group essentially built a ramp from the tallest to the shortest student, held their arms out, and let the ball roll down. I let them know, "Great thinking! But I know you can do it even faster." Devising any of these solutions requires creativity; moving from one strategy to another requires flexibility; and the willingness to try again after they hear, "I know you can do it even faster," depends on persistence.

The most commonly successful strategy involves one student standing in the center of the circle while holding the ball at arm's length. The other students each put an arm out toward the center and say their names while the student in the center spins. Ta-da! Two seconds. "Congratulations! I knew you could do it faster."

[margin note] flexibility

[margin note] creativity, flexibility, and persistence

High Fives All Around the Classroom

The game ends with cheers, high fives, and sighs of relief. The students smile as they find a chair and plop down, a little out of breath. They weren't expecting to engage so actively. They weren't expecting to get so silly or work with such focus. They feel a sense of pride and think maybe this class is going to be a little different. They have successfully met a challenge as a group and taken their first step toward becoming a community. They have learned they can have fun together, and they have begun to learn that their success is in part interdependent.

Teacher Gets Schooled

Although a physical activity, "Pass as a Class" includes all students regardless of ability or physical limitations (it even works for those of us who are just plain clumsy and uncoordinated!). I had the opportunity to learn just how well this activity can work for everyone, and at the same time I learned a valuable lesson about working with students with disabilities.

Justin, my student and teacher in this exercise, has cerebral palsy and requires crutches to help him stand and walk. Previously, I had not considered that "Pass as a Class" might propose a challenge for differently abled people. I wanted to use this activity to begin to create an inclusive community. How was Justin going to catch a ball when he needed to hold on to his crutches to stand? I felt a sense of panic when I looked at Justin. How could he participate? My mind began to race and problem solve. When it was time to form a standing circle, I decided to bring my large, comfy teaching chair over for Justin to sit in.

As I approached, Justin waved me off, saying "I've got it." He unhooked the metal crutch from his left forearm and moved it under his right armpit. Then he twisted slightly and leaned all his weight onto his right side, freeing up his left. Of course, in daily life Justin faced and managed to adapt to much more challenging situations than the one this exercise presented. He did not need my help. He knew better than I did what he could and couldn't do and what he needed.

self-efficacy and flexibility

I was impressed by his metacognition and was reminded that this habit of mind is something that I want to foster in all my students. As teachers, we are trained to see where a student needs improvement and then to devise a strategy to facilitate that growth. Justin reminded me that students often have a better idea of what will work for them than I do. In respect to differently abled students specifically, he taught me to let them set their own boundaries, which they are far better at assessing than I am. He also reminded me that while

metacognition

I want to be aware of my students' needs, I also want to encourage their engagement in finding their own solutions.

In many ways, Justin had already mastered the habits of mind of openness, engagement, creativity, persistence, and flexibility because doing so was the key to his full participation in daily life. He became a great ally in helping other students to develop these traits.

Other Issues to Consider

If a student absolutely cannot physically participate, he or she can be the timer. In addition, at some point in the exercise, some students may begin to feel discouraged. Remember to offer plenty of enthusiastic encouragement and support. This activity aims to create a community in which they will do this for each other, and eventually for themselves, but they are not there yet! The teacher's modeling remains key in not only setting the tone for the semester but also supporting the students' development of persistence. Carefully monitor for, acknowledge, and praise any instance of a student encouraging or supporting another. We want to nurture that sprouting seed.

Quick Start Guide

1. Push chairs and desks to the edges of the classroom creating as much open space as possible. (Students can do the "Pass as a Class" activity outside, but I recommend using the classroom. This can be the first step in building positive associations with the space they will inhabit most as a class.)
2. Invite everyone to form a circle.
3. Gather everyone's attention.
4. Invite the students to do a few simple stretches. Model this for them.
5. Explain the game: Each student says his or her name and passes the ball to the next student until each student has had a turn.
6. Explain the goal: Get the ball to each student as quickly as possible with each person saying his or her name.
7. Model an example.
8. Toss the ball and let the fun and learning begin!

Building a Supportive Community in the Classroom by Tina Sander

Activity: various games and assignments that build community and establish a student-centered classroom

Learning Outcomes: self-awareness, self-management, and the ability to collaborate and work with others

Habits of Mind: engagement, motivation, and persistence

I have found that building a community of learners in the classroom is vital to student participation, retention, and success. Students are more willing to help each other and to speak up in class if they know each other. Students are more likely to stick with their education if they have friends in the class, and their rates of success are higher if they enjoy the course and their classmates. I provide here various activities that you can do in the beginning of the semester to help build up a community of learners within your classroom. You can also adapt these activities for later in the semester in order to continue the community building.

The objective of these activities is to foster a positive, safe, encouraging classroom atmosphere. Engagement, motivation, and persistence are habits of mind that are developed as students learn more about each other by learning about their personal lives and thoughts, and as they cheer each other on by sharing their backgrounds, goals, and needs.

Activity 1: Truth and Lies

This is a simple activity that I often use on the first day that gets students talking and writing. I start by writing on the board five sentences about myself. Usually three are true and two are false. I explain to the students that this activity has four purposes. The first is to allow them to get personal with me and find out information that lets them see me as a person, rather than just their teacher. The second is to dust the cobwebs out of their minds as they start to think critically about questions they devise while considering my answers as they try to find out the lies. The third is to use the questioning and answering process as a strategy for writing more than one page in response to a specific writing task. And the fourth is to have the students identify each sentence's specific grammatical pattern and use that pattern in sentences that they write about themselves.

I have the students write their own sentences with a certain amount of truths and lies. As an added challenge and to prepare them for writing classes, I also introduce either subordinate clauses (pretransfer-level composition) or verbal modifiers (college-level composition) depending on which class I am teaching. Each sentence that I have written on the board will include one of the grammatical structures, and I ask the students to identify the pattern in the sentences. When students write their own sentences, they must mimic these styles of sentences in order to practice making more complex sentences. Their first essay will then also have a requirement of having at least two sentences following this kind of pattern.

curiosity

Here are some examples:

Pre-College-Level Composition Class
Truth and Lies: Develop your critical thinking skills. Analyze these sentences and my presentation of them. Devise and ask questions to help you determine which are true and which are not. Afterward, you will devise your own sentence with truths and lies.

1. I speak German, English, and Spanish because I was born in Germany and lived in Spain and Ecuador.
2. Because I bike to work most every day, I am usually energized and ready to go.
3. Although I am a triplet, I am not identical to my sisters.
4. While I have worked at Cabrillo since 2007, I have also worked at the Santa Cruz Adult School since 2001.
5. Because I have a baby daughter, I don't have as much time as I used to.

College-Level Composition Class
Truth and Lies: Develop your critical thinking skills. Analyze these sentences and my presentation of them. Devise and ask questions to help you determine which are true and which are not. Afterward, you will devise your own sentence with truths and lies.

1. Born and raised in Germany, I speak German, English, and Spanish.
2. Watching the sun peek over the clouds, I biked to school this morning.

3. Being a triplet, I am neither the oldest nor the youngest in my family.
4. Biking in the mountains, climbing the walls at the gym, and doing yoga, I like to stay active.
5. Having visited Peru, Egypt, Mexico, Thailand, and many places in Europe, I appreciate other cultures and ways of doing things.

Activity 2: Group Résumé

Another activity involves students forming groups of three or four and completing a résumé about themselves and about the class based on the syllabus and their needs. This activity lets the students get to know each other and also lets me know more about them, their understanding of the class, and their experience with college and writing. Each group gets one résumé to complete as a group. The first part of the résumé involves questions about the students and their backgrounds. The second part involves questions related to the syllabus, class, or an essay assignment. After students have time to discuss the answers in groups, we share the answers as a class, and we make our class rules. Variation: This activity can also be adapted for particular essays, so that students review assignment requirements in a small-group format.

The first part of the résumé is always personal questions and the second part relates to the syllabus, class, or a particular essay assignment. For personal questions, I ask students to write down the full name of each student in the group, have them add together the number of years everyone in the group has attended school, and total the number of essays they have written as a group. Then there are some random questions asking for things such as the total number of siblings, the total number of countries visited, or the total number of pizzas consumed in one week. About the syllabus, class, or essay assignment, the group must write down three things that they want to achieve, the name of the text and its main idea, how grades are calculated, and any other questions about the syllabus, class, or assignment that they may have.

I have also found it useful at the start of the semester to ask students to come up with their idea of the perfect classroom and what rules we might need to make this happen. I have students write down three or four rules that they think are essential for our class, and then to discuss them in their small groups. When each group presents their résumé, we also make sure to discuss which rules we would like to adapt as a whole classroom.

engagement
and
collaboration

Activity 3: Sides—New or Experienced Students

This activity is a quick one to get students moving, to introduce themselves to each other, and to learn about success at Cabrillo. I ask the students to go to one side of the room if they have taken classes at Cabrillo before or to the other side if this is their first class at Cabrillo. Then the students who have taken classes at Cabrillo before find a partner on their side of the room and they discuss what helped them succeed in the classes. The students at the other side, the ones who are new to Cabrillo, find a partner on their side and think of questions that they have about Cabrillo. After a few minutes of mingling, it is time to share questions and advice. The new students ask their questions, which the other side answers, and then the students with experience share their recipe for success. Variation: This activity can also be done later with students categorized by experience with college-level writing classes versus no college-level writing classes or even with experience with particular essays or writing styles.

Activity 4: Classmate Bingo

This is a mingle activity that can also be done at the beginning of the semester in order for students to get to know each other. I have bingo cards like the example in Figure 2.1 that I distribute to the students. On the card they will have statements about their classmates.

curiosity

Students then circulate to find people who have done the various things. They have a few minutes to talk to each person about the activity. Each time they find someone who has done one of the activities, they write the name of the person in the corresponding box. The first person to get a bingo wins a prize or extra-credit points and has to share his or her answers. Variation: Instead of bingo, you can have students fill out the entire card by finding someone for each of the statements or you can see how many they can find in a certain amount of time. This bingo card can also be adapted and used later in the semester for essay topics with descriptors such as "knows something about pollution," "has read an article about domestic abuse," "has voted," or "has used quotes successfully before."

Figure 2.1. Example bingo card for "Classmate Bingo."

FIND SOMEONE WHO . . .

Has taken English 255.	Has taken English 100 before.	Has taken a college-level English class.	Has taken a class at a different college. Which one?	Has never taken a college-level class before.
Has traveled to at least 10 other countries.	Has traveled to at least five countries.	Has traveled outside of the United States.	Has seen at least 10 states in the United States.	Has never traveled outside of the United States.
Has published a piece of writing.	Has won an award for writing.	Has earned an A in a writing class.	Has earned an A on an essay.	Enjoys writing.
Has at least four siblings.	Has parents who are still married.	Is the youngest child in the family.	Is the oldest child in the family.	Is an only child.
Has done something exciting.	Has done something scary.	Has helped someone else.	Has been lucky.	Has done something challenging.

Successes and Challenges

These activities can be done with all levels of English classes, and they can easily be adapted for classes of other disciplines. These activities also really help students bond and get to know each other in a context that still relates to the class. Some of these activities can be difficult for students who are physically challenged, and a cluttered classroom can limit all students because clutter impedes movement.

Quick Start Guide

1. Be flexible! Have students use "corners" instead of "sides" so they have four choices instead of two.
2. Introduce new concepts and get students up and moving around by modifying these activities in countless ways. All that is required is your imagination and a problem-solving mindset. Each of these activities can work in your classroom with your students; just plug in your content and go!

Forming *Familias* by Adela Najarro

Activity: creating groups within the college classroom

Learning Outcomes: interdependence and the ability to cooperatively work with others

Habits of Mind: engagement, creativity, and awareness of self and others

They Walk In

During the first week of class, students choose their seats. Some slide to the back left corner and slump down into their hoodies. Three high school friends, excited about their first college class, but scared about what's coming, sit together in the middle of the room but a little off to the side. A young man determined to turn his life around by succeeding in college takes his place front row center. And there they stay. Not interacting. Cemented into their first-day fears and expectations.

Forming "*familias*" is the Puente Project way of forming small groups. The Puente Project is a formal learning community supporting underserved students who desire to transfer to four-year colleges and universities that currently exists in over 60 California Community Colleges. I have been the English instructor for Puente at Cabrillo College for numerous years. The "*familia*" idea is the same as that of establishing permanent small groups in a classroom. The concept of breaking students into small groups is a common pedagogical tool extensively used throughout K–12 and college classrooms. With Puente, because many of our students are Latinos/as, the idea of labeling small groups "*familias*" creates an immediate understanding of the group's purpose: to support and encourage all in the group to reach their goals, and to be happy. We all know through our own experiences as students and instructors that engagement arises when connections to the instructor, fellow students, and course materials are developed and maintained throughout a semester. I might even   engagement go so far as to say that my most engaging and memorable classes were those that I was happy to attend!

Setting up groups in the college classroom allows each student to participate to a greater extent than in the lecture format. Engagement builds because no one can hide in the back of the room or pretend to take notes when a question is asked. Group work allows each student to participate, engage, and find his or her own comfort zone. Forming *familias* creates stable groups within the classroom where students feel welcome, at home, and can interact with each other while learning course content. But do groups really work? Isn't it necessary to instruct students with all the information that the course requires?

Teaching my first American literature class as a graduate student, I tested out whether or not breaking into small groups would work at the college level. I prepared an extensive lecture, while also breaking down the same material into questions that needed to be answered by students working in small groups. I divided the class into random groups, assigned each group a discussion question, and then re-formed the groups as a whole class to review what the students came up with. By the end of the class, all of my major points and examples in my lecture had been brought up by students, along with other points that I had not even considered. From then on, I was sold: Groups are the way to go in a college classroom.

Forming *Familias*

There are many ways to establish groups within a classroom, and groups can be permanent or they can be set up just for one class activity. Using groups moves instruction from a lecture format to a student-centered style. Always, the responsibility for learning rests within the student, but our job as instructors is to consider methods by which we can promote learning in a more effective manner. The content will get taught; you just have to trust the students! That's the hard part.

For effective group work to happen in a classroom, the instructor needs to know exactly what the desired learning outcomes will be. Before placing a lesson in the small-group format, it is necessary to know what students should accomplish. Once the learning outcomes have been identified, it is possible to break them down into smaller pieces that student groups can work on. For example, when discussing a text, it is necessary to ascertain beforehand the main points that students need to understand. It is then these main points that are assigned to various groups as their project for that activity. So the type of group one runs in a class depends on the desired learning outcomes. Group work can be done in pairs, triads, quatrains, and even larger groupings. However, in my experience, concentration and participation wanes when there are more than six students in a group. If there are so many possibilities, how do we form groups in our classrooms?

Let me return to the *familia* style that is used in the Puente Project. The purpose of *familias* is to foster learning within the classroom, but also to have students develop an interactive network of other like-minded students whom they can call on when the semester ends. The *familia* style establishes permanent semester-long student groups. The benefit of this type of grouping is that students get to know each other well, begin to trust one another, and have connections with like-minded students outside of class.   interdependence

To establish *familias*, I begin the first day of class with introductory activities that get students up and out of their seats interacting with one another. Through various games and activities, I have students introduce themselves to people they don't know. We do a lot of icebreakers. Then, during the following weeks, I have students work in pairs and random groups of three, four, and five. I have them make charts answer questions, and take quizzes together. For the first two or three weeks of class, I have students get up out of their seats and work with new people. By the third or fourth week, we have all gotten to know each other, sort of. We are ready to set up permanent *familias*.

At this point, I announce to students that we will form *familias*, and I ask them to write down the names of four other students whom they would like in their *familia*. I guarantee that they will be placed with at least one person from that list. I also give the option for students not to write down names and simply state that they will be fine with whoever is in their group. I collect the *familia* request sheets, and then go home and create magic—I hope. I have found that allowing "friends" to stay together works best when they are paired with another set of "friends" they may not know. This way each *familia* is   openness
new but has a familiar feel. It is also possible to pair high achievers with those who may need more academic support. To have successful groups, it is important to match personalities; that's why it takes nearly a month before permanent *familias* can be formed.

To launch permanent *familias*, the first group project is to develop a group identity. Each *familia* is required to come up with a group name and then to make a poster with that name where each member posts a bio along with a picture. Each *familia* presents their group and poster to the class. These posters are then placed on the classroom walls for all to see. Eventually, they will fall off the walls, but the process of making them is what matters. It is also necessary to mandate a seating chart where each *familia* is assigned its "area" in the room. This helps maintain *familia* unity because every class session the students interact in their groups, even if it's just to say hello. Establishing *familias* also helps with taking attendance, passing back work, getting assignments to students who have missed class, and other administrative duties. I have made folders for each *familia* where they turn in their work. I grade one folder at a time, and then return the folder to the group. This is just a small detail that makes the class easier for me as an instructor.

Establishing *familias* works great, but so do other forms of groups. As previously stated, group work depends on the learning outcomes. Working in pairs is best for a quick check during a lecture. It is possible to deliver information in a lecture style, then stop and ask the class a question that the students need to discuss in pairs. Pairs also are great for exchanging writing and grammar review. For example, after explaining sentence fragments, students can repair fragments in pairs and that way practice with each other the concept that has just been covered. Groups of three, four, and five are great for discussion questions. You can break up your lecture into questions that each group has to answer and then explain to the whole class. When I plan my class, I usually allow for a "group activity." I just place that as something that needs to happen every class—and it does whether it's pairs, triads, or larger groups.

Quick Start Guide

1. Plan plenty of icebreakers for the first few class sessions.
2. Incorporate random group work in pairs, triads, and larger groups the first few weeks of the semester.
3. At week three or four, ask students to select four students whom they would like in their permanent group or to state that they can work in any group assigned.
4. Make up the groups ensuring that each student is placed with one person requested on his or her list.
5. Have the groups make a group collage with a picture and descriptive paragraph for each member of the group. Also ask them to come up with a name and place that on the poster.
6. Set up a seating chart so that each group sits together for each class.
7. Plan group activities each class session for the rest of the semester.
8. Be prepared for lots of talking, interaction, and participation!

3

ENGAGING LEARNERS

Jennifer Fletcher and Hetty Yelland

"What you are in love with, what seizes your imagination, will affect everything. It will decide what will get you out of bed in the morning, what you will do with your evenings . . . what you read, whom you know, what breaks your heart, and what amazes you with joy and gratitude. Fall in love, stay in love, and it will decide everything."

—Fr. Pedro Arrupe, SJ (*Finding God in All Things* 100)

To be engaged means to be connected, committed, and involved. Seasoned college instructors know there is a special window of opportunity for securing students' commitment to learning early in each academic term. We call it "the honeymoon period," and we work hard during this opportune moment to capture our students' interest and trust. This is the time when our most vulnerable students are still making up their minds about the level of commitment they're going to make to the class and to each other. After the honeymoon is over, uncommitted students all too often disappear from our rosters. One community college survey, for instance, found that many of the reasons students give for dropping classes early in the term relate to the management of commitments, including schedule conflicts, new jobs, home obligations, and the coursework itself (Mery 1). Such data tell us that many students respond to the difficulties of academic life by disengaging.

We can fortify students for the challenges to come by providing a critical combination of emotional and intellectual engagement during the early stages of the instructional cycle. Now is the time for strengthening learning communities, for gaining the goodwill and resolve of our students, and for creating safe-to-risk learning environments. It's also the time for inquiry-based learning that sparks students' curiosity and creativity. By strategically addressing students' emotional and intellectual needs, we cultivate the habits of mind that lead to sustained academic effort and long-term growth.

> We can fortify students for the challenges to come by providing a critical combination of emotional and intellectual engagement during the early stages of the instructional cycle.

What Do We Mean by Engagement?

In contrast to narrow views of engagement as "on-task" behavior, engagement as a habit of mind has far more to do with how learners approach their own intellectual growth than with what instructors do to keep students busy. For the authors of CWPA, NCTE, and NWP's *Framework for Success in Postsecondary Writing*, engagement is "a sense of investment and involvement in learning" (1). The idea of investment as a component of intellectual engagement is important. Students need to have some skin in the game in order to justify their involvement. Seen in this light, engaging classroom activities are not simply those that students see as fun but rather are those they see as meaningful. Elizabeth F. Barkley, author of *Student Engagement Techniques: A Handbook for College Faculty*, is quick to point out this distinction: "Engaging students doesn't mean they're being entertained. It means they are thinking" (xii). Laurie A. Schreiner makes a related observation about the difference between involved learning and perfunctory behaviors in her discussion of academic thriving: "Showing up for class and reading the assignment does not equate to psychological engagement in learning" (4). In a blog she wrote for her first-year writing course, a freshman at California State University at Monterey Bay (CSUMB) similarly notes the links among engagement, effort, and deeper learning: "I think the most successful way to be an engaged learner is to always take extra steps to making sure you understand the content. It may take longer but it's essential."

While students bear ultimate responsibility for developing an engaged disposition toward learning, we believe instructors can foster this development through learning experiences that exemplify and nurture learners' personal investment and involvement in their intellectual growth. Indeed, in *Student Success in College:*

Creating Conditions That Matter, George D. Kuh and his coauthors see student engagement as a shared obligation. They identify two key components of engagement that contribute to student success: the amount of time and effort students put into their academic lives and the learning opportunities and services institutions provide to enhance participation in academic life (Kuh et al. 9). Instructors may have limited influence over student effort, but we can control the kinds of learning experiences we offer in our classrooms.

Among the recommended practices the National Research Council (NRC) links to deep and transferable learning, two speak directly to the responsibilities teachers have for designing engaging learning experiences:

- "Engaging learners in challenging tasks, while also supporting them with guidance, feedback, and encouragement to reflect on their own learning process and the status of their understanding" (*Education for Life and Work* 181).
- "Priming student motivation by connecting topics to students' personal lives and interests, engaging students in collaborative problem solving, and drawing attention to the knowledge and skills students are developing, rather than grades or scores" (181).

Both are critical practices for retaining at-risk learners early in the instructional cycle. In the next section, let's look at how these recommendations can be applied in a college classroom.

Classroom Example

In Olga Blomgren's classes at Hartnell College and CSUMB, student engagement techniques are a key means of promoting academic rigor and student ownership of learning. You'll find two of Olga's lesson exemplars in chapters 5 and 6, but a quick look into her classroom here provides a compelling example of student engagement as "the product of motivation and active learning" (Barkley 6).

It's a Thursday evening in late winter, and Olga's students are hard at work finalizing preparations for their group presentations. The class is filled with energy and humor. Olga takes time to check in with individual students, asking how their day is going and following up on situations or concerns they've previously shared with her. Students freely joke with one another without taking time or attention from the evening's business. Their task this night is to identify and explain the key claims and evidence in an article on gender roles their group has been assigned while engaging their audience of peers in a collective interpretation of the text. As the "teachers" of this class, the student facilitators are responsible for planning, organizing, directing, and monitoring the learning experiences—a level of engagement that fosters both advanced literacy practices and academic habits of mind.

The presentations start. Students smile, nod, and continue to be animated and expressive both in small groups and when interacting as a whole class, easily transitioning between a more formal "presentation" style of communication and relaxed, informal speech. They are respectful when posing and responding to questions. At each stage of the process, Olga offers guidance and encouragement. For instance, she follows up the presenters' or audience members' comments by asking probing questions that help students clarify and elaborate on their ideas. She also challenges students to justify their "instructional" choices. "Why did you choose that quotation?" she asks one group. She also encourages one of the other students to extend her thinking beyond her initial conclusions: "You're right that the writer uses this strategy; so what's the effect?"

When one group stops a little short in its analysis, Olga models a paraphrase of a source for the class after eliciting progressively more sophisticated responses from the presenters: "What does the writer mean there? Can you explain that a little? What is she trying to show with this evidence?" She continues to serve as a coach throughout the activity, providing additional prompts and reminders as necessary while still allowing the presenters to fully inhabit the leadership role they were assigned. The class closes with a reflective summary.

Take-Away Learning

Olga's engagement techniques had clearly laid the groundwork for a highly successful student-led class session. Her students did indeed become their peers' teachers, achieving a level of autonomy and leadership more common in upper-division classes than in first-year courses.

This lesson affirms the principles of modeling and coaching as powerful means of promoting student engagement:

1. Modeling: Many students need to see habits of mind in practice to understand how these dispositional capacities help in problem solving, critical thinking, decision making, social development, and goal attainment.
2. Coaching: Many students need ongoing and explicit support as they work to internalize and apply habits of mind.

Modeling and coaching require dedicated classroom time not typically allocated in traditional approaches to college instruction. However, when we view habits of mind as learned attributes rather than as fixed abilities, we're more willing to make this preparatory investment because we believe we can impact student effort and resilience. Current scholarship justifies this approach. The NRC reports that "recent research indicates that intrapersonal skills and dispositions, such as motivation and self regulation, support deeper learning and that these valuable skills can be taught and learned" (*Education for Work and Life* 99). Ultimately, the payoff of increasing our students' dispositional capacities is greater academic knowledge and skill attainment.

> Ultimately, the payoff of increasing our students' dispositional capacities is greater academic knowledge and skill attainment.

Engaging Students Through Intellectual Play

While our overarching goal is the kind of engagement Barkley and Schreiner describe—exemplified by the preceding classroom model—our assets-based approach encourages us to welcome a variety of opening gambits toward deep learning. We can't engage students who don't come to class. Thus, some activities that might at first seem to be all about having fun can turn out to be important gateway engagement techniques.

When we engage students' curiosity through intellectual play, we open the door to enduring interests and practices. A really good question, for example, can sucker students into taking personal and academic risks despite their best defenses. So can a purposeful classroom game. Sharing the pleasures of inquiry and discovery with students is one of the best ways to connect them to not only the learning community but also their own inner intellectual.

Inquiry-based academic fun has several payoffs. It makes visible why we, as academics, do the work we do: because we enjoy it! Modeling our own pleasure in intellectual labor (and play) makes clear to students that thriving in an academic life has a great deal to do with the extent to which we appreciate its intrinsic rewards. Creating opportunities for students to experience this same pleasure is an important part of mentoring developing scholars. Students who are fully engrossed in a game, such as Hetty Yelland's innovative adaptation of Scrabble to teach academic vocabulary (see page 91), show all the signs of engaged learning identified by Bresó, Schaufeli, and Salanova in their quasi-experimental study on self-efficacy: high energy level, enthusiasm, dedication, pride, and absorption (341). Furthermore, such total absorption in play has the added benefit of breaking down students' emotional defenses, and, as Bresó et al. note, "the lower the levels of anxiety, stress, and fatigue are, the higher the levels of self-efficacy will be" (340). Play thus becomes a low-stakes processing strategy to promote greater risk-taking, autonomy, and engagement—ultimately leading to deeper and more meaningful learning.

> Modeling our own pleasure in intellectual labor (and play) makes clear to students that thriving in an academic life has a great deal to do with the extent to which we appreciate its intrinsic rewards.

There are so many good classroom examples to share. Daphne Young, who teaches writing at Hartnell College, Cabrillo College, and CSUMB, uses a bingo-type game (Word-O) to help students study for vocabulary tests. The competition is low stakes. Someone may officially win, but no one loses. Everyone has had a chance to review important material.

Kinesthetic learners' needs are often ignored within higher education settings, so "fun" activities that require students to get up out of their seats can help engage students with a more active learning style. Heidi Ramirez, a former Hartnell College writing instructor, would have students read about different types of dishonesty and then have them make up skits in small groups about each type of lie discussed within the text. Maria Boza, whose exemplar is included in this chapter, has her students participate in a lively, structured debate.

Math instructor Ken Rand uses lots of games during his Math Academy. This is a math review and prep seminar that Hartnell College offers prior to the start of each semester. Students are in the classroom for two weeks, six hours a day, studying math—a strain on attention spans. Rand prides himself on providing T-shirts that read: Eat, Sleep, Math! The trick is that learning and review continue during the games. Whether they are running a relay or doing a *Jeopardy!*-type competition, math is involved. So the students can simultaneously take a break and continue learning.

Engagement as a Habit of Mind

More and more over time, students need to take responsibility for approaching assignments in ways that are personally interesting and intellectually challenging. John Bean's perennially useful book *Engaging Ideas: The Professor's Guide to Integrating Writing, Critical Thinking, and Active Learning in the Classroom* makes the important point that "critical thinking—and indeed all significant learning—originates In the learner's engagement with problems" (xi). Therefore, for the students' own good as well

> More and more over time, students need to take responsibility for approaching assignments in ways that are personally interesting and intellectually challenging.

as the instructor's sanity, every moment of every day cannot and should not be an entertaining show or fun activity.

As in a writing class, some of the topics are more interesting to a particular student than others. One writing topic or reading may naturally lend itself to a large portion of the class whereas students may have to make more of an effort to find other topics and texts compelling. Student complaints are teaching moments. For example, students who say they can't write a good essay because they don't care about the topic need to be informed that finding a way to connect to and care about all topics is part of the assignment. To finish the assignment, engagement is required. But again, the instructor does not refrain from helping students make this connection. The goal is for the "fun" to continue, but on a new level. As Bain states,

> To take a deep approach means to take control of your own education, to decide that you want to understand, to create something new, to search for the meaning that lies behind the text, to realize that words on a page are mere symbols, and that behind those symbols lies a meaning that has a connection with a thousand other aspects of life and with your own development. (38)

Students become more and more engaged in intellectual curiosity over time and, thus, ready to gain confidence, self-efficacy, and self-awareness about the transfer of knowledge. These aspects of engagement are our students' obligation.

First-year CSUMB student Karen, who says she is "itching to do something and to get involved," demonstrates her developing self-efficacy and self-awareness in her own description of engaged learning:

> I think the most successful way to be an engaged learner is to always take extra steps to making sure you understand the content. It may take longer but it's essential. When given an assigned reading it's important to understand what's really being said. You can outline the reading or even annotate and also asking yourself questions. Being involved in the campus community is also really important.

Engagement and Threshold Learning

When we think of the habits of mind that help students feel connected to their learning community and dedicated to their learning, it's important to consider what entry-level learning looks like on the developmental trajectory. In "Threshold Concepts and Troublesome Knowledge: Linkages to Ways of Thinking and Practising," Jan H. F. Meyer and Ray Land explain how certain disciplinary concepts and skills can seem particularly obscure, disorienting, alien, counterintuitive, and even subversive to new learners. These are the concepts and skills that tend to resist "common sense," such as complex numbers in mathematics or deconstruction in literary criticism (2–3). Although not all academic learning fits this description, much of it does, especially for underprepared students. For instance, in prebaccalaureate writing classes, concepts such as audience, occasion, and ethos can present challenging learning thresholds to many students. When we ask first-year students to identify the audience for a specific text, they often say the text (regardless of whether it was published in the *New York Times*, *Seventeen* magazine, or *The Journal of the American Medical Association*) was written for just "a general reader" or "anyone who's interested in the topic." Discerning distinctions in audience depends on a nuanced, experiential understanding of how real-world texts are written, published, and read.

Prior to crossing a learning threshold, students often experience a great deal of uncomfortable confusion and complexity that may increase their inclination to disengage. They may also substitute superficiality for depth. In describing this pretransformational stage, Meyer and Land note that "difficulty in understanding threshold concepts may leave the learner in a state of liminality (Latin limen— 'threshold'), a suspended state in which understanding approximates to a kind of mimicry or lack of authenticity" (10). We see this in student writing that has the form but not the substance of academic argumentation: the five-paragraph essay, for instance, or a paper full of abstract jargon. Asking students to rely on their own powers of invention instead of a familiar formula can leave them feeling anxious and disoriented.

At this point in their learning, students can have a fairly low tolerance for ambiguity. For instance, they may find our course outcomes and assignments overwhelming and prefer us just to explain exactly what they need to do to earn an A. They may be frustrated when we answer their questions by saying, "It depends." Some may even feel like withdrawing or shutting down. On the other hand, honeymooners who underestimate the effort required to progress beyond this state of liminality may be naively optimistic about the road ahead. Educational scholar Donna Miller describes this developmental stage nicely: "As novices, [beginning students] don't yet know that the path to understanding is cluttered, meandering, and protracted; that understanding requires experience, dialectical practice, and intellectual habituation" (51).

We can foster intellectual habituation by alerting students to the ways an active practice of intentional engagement supports their growth at this stage. We do this by praising students' early progress, focusing on the process before the product, posing intriguing questions, privileging the long view, and encouraging students to embrace change while accepting mistakes and setbacks as a natural part of the learning curve. Our goal is to help students be engaged and intellectually vulnerable risk takers who welcome cognitive dissonance in the pursuit of deep learning.

Among the best defenses against disengagement are the abilities to *postpone judgment* and *tolerate ambiguity* (ICAS 12). Both are aspects of openness and curiosity, which *Framework for Success in Postsecondary Writing* defines respectively as "the willingness to consider new ways of being and thinking in the world" and

> Among the best defenses against disengagement are the abilities to *postpone judgment* and *tolerate ambiguity* (ICAS 12).

as "the desire to know more about the world" (CWPA, NCTE, and NWP 1). Instructors may even want to list these abilities as learning community norms on their syllabi, so that students see this kind of disposition toward "beginner's mind" as a course expectation.

Later in the term—at the point when students feel they've been working hard in our classes for weeks, are dying for spring break or a holiday weekend, have strained all their personal resources and relationships, and are feeling spread too thin in every area of their life— we're going to ask these students to dig deeper and try harder. We're going to make the work more, not less, difficult because we believe that's how we build transferable knowledge and internalized practices.

The only way that increased cognitive demand is going to fly down the road is if our students trust us and themselves. By modeling and coaching the cultivation of habits of mind as learned abilities, we stand in solidarity with our students and affirm our faith in their intellectual growth. We make this commitment knowing that we'll ask our students to give us more just when they feel they've given all they can. Students who aren't emotionally and intellectually engaged early in the academic term—and who don't see habits of mind as something they can change—too often reduce, rather than increase, their efforts once the going gets tough (Dweck 16–17).

Michelle, a first-year student at CSUMB, describes the challenges she faces after the semester kicks into high gear:

> I understand the material that is being taught yet I don't really know how to connect back to my main understanding. Some other thing that I am encountering is the whole situation of not having enough time on my hands and not having enough time to get assignments done and actually do things. It's understandable because it seems like it's crunch time and it's time to get things done.

We want our students to have a substantial cushion of support in place by the time they reach this moment. By foregrounding engagement as a habit of mind, we encourage students to adopt a growth mindset—something that helps honeymooners bounce back from challenges. Carol Dweck, professor of psychology at Stanford University, explains, "Students with

> By foregrounding engagement as a habit of mind, we encourage students to adopt a growth mindset—something that helps honeymooners bounce back from challenges.

a growth mindset are more likely to respond to initial obstacles by remaining involved, trying new strategies, and using all the resources at their disposal for learning" (17). In contrast to a fixed mindset, a growth mindset sees abilities as malleable and subject to improvement through effort and persistence, a perception that encourages a sustained commitment to learning.

Conclusion

Building on the learning communities and communities of learners established early in the term (see chapter 2), instructors have an opportunity to use the embers of trust and collaboration to stoke a burning desire for deeper learning within the students' hearts. Feelings started through community-building activities can stimulate other connections that are both more personal and progressively more academic. Once trust is established within a classroom, the connection is deepened through fun or interesting activities that are related to the curriculum. But engagement does not stop there. As a first-year CSUMB student wrote in a reflection, "Learning is not just sitting in class and listening to lecture, it is more than that. Learning consists of making connections to other concepts." Engagement requires that students utilize critical thinking skills to connect their ideas to a broader intellectual discourse, and, ultimately, engagement helps students to develop intellectual curiosity and fosters risk taking—skills that will be needed to build confidence, which is discussed in the next chapter.

As teachers who work closely with students who are sometimes a little commitment shy, we can attest to the power of engagement. Engaged students accept a level of responsibility that has profound consequences for their future lives and learning. In the lesson exemplars that follow, you'll see numerous ways to help students be connected, committed, and involved. We hope you'll find these activities both meaningful and enjoyable.

Works Cited

Bain, Ken. *What the Best College Students Do*. Cambridge: Belknap Press of Harvard UP, 2012. Print.

Barkley, Elizabeth F. *Student Engagement Techniques: A Handbook for College Faculty*. San Francisco: Jossey-Bass, 2009. Print.

Bean, John C. *Engaging Ideas: The Professor's Guide to Integrating Writing, Critical Thinking, and Active Learning in the Classroom.* San Francisco: Jossey-Bass, 2001. Print.

Bresó, Edgar, Wilmar B. Schaufeli, and Marisa Salanova. "Can a Self-Efficacy-Based Intervention Decrease Burnout, Increase Engagement, and Enhance Performance? A Quasi-experimental Study." *Higher Education* 61.4 (2011): 339–55. Print.

CWPA, NCTE, and NWP (Council of Writing Program Administrators, National Council of Teachers of English, and National Writing Project). *Framework for Success in Postsecondary Writing.* Berkeley: National Writing Project, 2011. Web.

Dweck, Carol S. "Even Geniuses Work Hard." *Educational Leadership* 68.1 (2010): 16–20.

Finding God in All Things: A Marquette Prayer Book. Milwaukee: Marquette UP, 2005. Print.

ICAS (Intersegmental Committee of the Academic Senates of the California Community Colleges, the California State University, and the University of California). *Academic Literacy: A Statement of Competencies Expected of Students Entering California's Public Colleges and Universities.* Sacramento: ICAS, 2002. Print.

Kuh, George D. et al. *Student Success in College: Creating Conditions That Matter.* San Francisco: Jossey-Bass, 2005. Print.

Mery, Pamela M. "Students Leaving before Census." *Survey Series* (Spring 2000). San Francisco: City College of San Francisco, Office of Institutional Development, Research, and Planning. (ERIC document ED455867)

Meyer, Jan H. F., and Ray Land. "Threshold Concepts and Troublesome Knowledge: Linkages to Ways of Thinking and Practising." *Improving Student Learning: Ten Years On.* Ed. C. Rust. Oxford: OCSLD, 2003: 1–16. Print.

Miller, Donna L. "Got It Wrong? Think Again and Again." *Phi Delta Kappan* 94.5 (2013): 50–52. Print.

National Research Council. *Education for Life and Work: Developing Transferable Knowledge and Skills in the 21st Century.* Committee on Defining Deeper Learning and 21st Century Skills. Ed. James W. Pellegrino and Margaret L. Hilton. Board on Testing and Assessment and Board on Science Education, Division of Behavioral and Social Sciences and Education. Washington, DC: The National Academies Press. Print.

Schreiner, Laurie A. "The 'Thriving Quotient': A New Vision for Student Success." *About Campus* 15.2 (2010): 2–10. Web.

Lazy Teacher or Genius? A Case for Vocabulary Enhancement through Playing Scrabble in the Classroom by Hetty Yelland

Activity: building vocabulary while playing Scrabble

Learning Outcomes: increased vocabulary, improved spelling, and enhanced dictionary skills

Habits of Mind: engagement and persistence

If you walked into my English 253 course at 10:10 on a Friday morning, you might be taken aback by the lack of teaching taking place. Students are clustered in small, lively groups. Often there is pizza, chocolate chip cookies, or taquitos with guacamole being shared among the groups. You would hear a couple of phones blaring out fuzzy versions of music on their tiny speakers: hip-hop from one side of the room, Spanish lyrics to a polka beat from the other.

Upon closer scrutiny, you would notice the diversity within these groups. An African American woman affectionately calls a stereotypical computer nerd "B-Rad"—his name actually being Bradly. A working-class young man, a Korean immigrant and mother of three college-age children, and a quiet Hispanic man all huddle around the same focus. What are they doing? They are playing Scrabble and they are learning. As the authors of *Bringing Words to Life: Robust Vocabulary Instruction* emphasize, encouraging students to think about and discuss words—instead of rote memorization—can inspire them to approach meaning in an inquisitive, academic way throughout their lives (Beck, McKeown, and Kucan 1).

In my developmental writing classes that meet one hour a day, five days a week, Friday is always—or almost always—Scrabble day. Although it is designed to be a fun day and a break from the regular project we are working on as a class, it is still a learning day worth participation points that add up to 5% of the final grade for the semester. Students are expected to be on task and engaged.

Doing this activity starting the first week of the semester helps promote the habits of mind persistence as well as engagement. Students bond first with those around them and later are encouraged to branch out to play with other people. They are not just engaged, but engaged with each other. They don't just play Scrabble; they talk about their lives, other classes, this class, and the current assignment. Initially they are interested in the novelty of playing a game, but over time, they learn to persevere together when the classwork engagement gets more challenging and the game itself becomes old hat. They are being entertained and engaged initially, but they are also learning the habit of mind called *engagement*. Maintaining interest and finding new ways to challenge themselves is ultimately up to them. If they

adaptability can apply this to a game, they can apply it to their education.

Method Behind the Madness

By playing Scrabble, students are improving not only their habits of mind but also many so-called basic skills. Students increase and build upon existing vocabulary. They learn to use the dictionary, and by doing so they improve their English language skills by checking spelling, word origins, and parts of speech. I would even argue that students increase their reading success through playing Scrabble. They are having to read a Scrabble game board with words placed horizontally, vertically, and backward. This is good practice for researching and reading college-level articles that progress from one column to the next and that contain sidebars, charts, graphs, pictures, and biographical material. Reading is not just following the words from left to right, line after line. College reading and Scrabble share the need to look at the text with a discerning eye.

Some of these transferable skills happen effortlessly through play, and others require supplementary work in order to achieve the desired outcomes. In "How a Hobby Can Shape Cognition: Visual Word Recognition in Competitive Scrabble Players," the authors state, "The results of a series of cognitive assessments showed that Scrabble . . . expertise was associated with . . . semantic deemphasis" (Hargreaves et al. 1). This means that Scrabble players gain the ability to recognize what is and what is not a real word, but do not usually learn the definitions of words from playing the game. Therefore, playing Scrabble in class gets students thinking about new words, and then I provide opportunities on other class days for vocabulary instruction in context. For example, students collaboratively choose new vocabulary words from assigned readings. The ever growing list of vocabulary is then recorded by each student by annotating the text. I have them circle words and write the definitions in the margins of the reading. The result is that books and articles come out on Scrab-

spirit of ble days for reference and the skills transfer from one assignment to

transfer another. However, you could have them just take notes or require a vocabulary binder of some kind as well. Extra credit and/or prizes can be given for use of vocabulary on the game board.

The Seven Stages of Scrabble

Although a class would not necessarily have to play the game every week in order for this lesson to work, Scrabble should be played no less than every other week. A few games will stimulate a student's thinking about words, but only consistent game play over weeks will lead players through the following seven stages of learning.

The first stage is when the students are learning to play the game. During this process, it is important to keep circling around the classroom answering questions and redirecting those not following the rules properly. At this point students usually can't believe their luck. They can't believe they are getting to have so much fun in English class. They develop friendships with each other, and I even allow them to bring food and play their iPods. I am pleased when I overhear a student saying something like, "Oh no! I missed listening to my favorite song because I was *thinking*." motivation

However, the students soon reach the second stage in which they realize, to their dismay, how little their vocabulary actually is. A great number of the words they know are brand names (which can't be used in Scrabble) and slang (much of which is not found in the dictionary). They find—to their horror—that they are using a great many simple, one-syllable words over and over again, such as *at* and *is*. A few students offer a larger vocabulary, but most are in the same boat.

In the third stage, students either hate the game (they would rather be writing the dreaded in-class essay) or have a difficult time staying on task. At this juncture, it is very important for you, as the instructor, to remain both patient and firm about completing the task. Students will attempt to text on their phones instead of engage. Bathroom breaks will become longer. Students will even begin skipping class. Students may try to stop keeping score or just sit there and talk to each other. Kindly but firmly assure them that this is a natural stage that will pass and redirect them to the game. persistence and self-management

Once students realize that the instructor wants them to succeed and that no one is going to let them just give up or cut corners, vocabulary enhancement begins in earnest. In this fourth stage, students begin to tap into a larger vocabulary they already know. They begin taking the one-syllable words on the board and adding an *s* to make plurals or converting them into longer, more complex words. They start looking at the dictionary and playing Scrabble at home—without being required to do so. They start utilizing the vocabulary words for the class. I start to see significant changes in the words used and the Scrabble scores. Week one may have been dominated with self-efficacy words such as *hat* and *blue* with final scores around 35. Now students are scoring near 100 and using words such as *merit* and *intern*.

The fifth stage is a renaissance. Spontaneous discussions about words start coming up during every class meeting—not just Scrabble day. This stage corresponds with what Susan Ebbers and Carolyn Denton say about learning in "A Root Awakening: Vocabulary Instruction for Older Students with Reading Difficulties":

> Word consciousness—and thus vocabulary development—might be best fostered in a verbal learning environment. . . . Children who are provided with the most verbally supportive atmosphere at home . . . learn far more words than those whose families engage in fewer verbal behaviors. . . . Teachers can emulate such an atmosphere. (91)

Likewise, students experiencing this stage of Scrabble move from focusing on the social interaction of the game day into the inquisitive context of more traditional, academic studies. Students ask me what words from the readings mean on days we are not choosing vocabulary words. They ask each other. They ask to use the dictionary. They discuss words in small groups and we discuss as a class. Smartphones come out of pockets, not to text, but to look up definitions, which are then spontaneously shouted out to the class and compared with other findings from other technological devices. Spelling and meaning are the main topics. Other topics are the use of academic language and the power of words (in both a positive way and the power to offend). "Why are words so powerful?" they begin to ask. They are just letters combined in arbitrary ways, yet saying something one way as opposed to another produces different results. They start to mimic the more academic form of writing from our class readings.

The sixth stage is when the students, realizing the arbitrary nature of language, begin to question all of language. At first they begin asking, "Is this a word? If *cat, hat,* and *rat* are words, is 'gat' a word? It looks like a word." Even words they once thought they knew become strange and hard to recognize. "Is 'net' a word? I'm not sure. It sounds familiar," one student will say. "Of course, it's a word," another student will say. "Net—like using a net to catch a fish!" Now the dictionary starts to come into play. Words are challenged by other players. When the challenged word is a real word and in the dictionary, the meaning is read out loud proudly. "I didn't know that," the students—and the instructor—begin to say.

curiosity

openness and reflection

Just when you feel successful and happy as an instructor, you will hit the final Scrabble stage. It's messy, it's chaotic, and it's creative. You will most likely hate it because it creates more work for you—just when you thought the students were beginning to take on responsibility for teaching themselves vocabulary. Don't panic. This is a natural part of the process and good for the students. At this stage, the students begin to test the boundaries of vocabulary and to experiment with words. They are willing to silently play the word *gat* even though they don't know whether it is a word, and if it is, what it means. Everyone begins making up words. So much so that the instructor must start challenging words, looking them up, and taking the nonwords off the board. However, this comfortableness with being wrong and experimenting with vocabulary is good.

creativity

Have fun!

Challenges

As a final note on Scrabble in the classroom, I would like to discuss the biggest challenge with implementing this lesson plan: getting buy-in from administrators and colleagues. If you are seen rolling your pushcart of Scrabble boards down the hallway and looking too happy, there may be some concern. My advice is to keep dated score sheets and possibly even sometimes take photos of the game boards so that you can show the progress that your students are making if called upon to do so. I have also found it helpful to keep to a schedule. If there is no school on a Friday or we need to finish something else on a Friday, then we simply don't have Scrabble that week in my class; I don't reschedule Scrabble for another day of the week.

Quick Start Guide

1. Plan specific and reoccurring times and dates to play Scrabble in your class. Whether game play is every Friday or every other week, or the last half hour of a three-hour class, students need to be able to look forward to the activity as part of their regular routine.
2. Scrabble allows up to four players per game set, so plan how many boards you will need to buy for your class. It's best to buy new games to make sure all the pieces are there.

3. Give each student a copy of the rules, go over the rules in class (plus any additional rules you require), and have a quiz on the rules of Scrabble. Students can't know everything before they start, but if they haven't bothered to read through the rules once, game play is less engaged.

4. Play! It is best to let the students pick their own partners at first. You can require playing with new partners after the first month.

5. Be sure to have one player per group be the scorekeeper to avoid cheating.

6. Let students talk and interact, but circle around and make sure they are playing correctly, taking score, and staying on task. As the instructor, challenge words anytime you want to, and then have the students alter the score sheet as necessary. Doing so will keep everyone honest and encourage students to start challenging words as well.

7. Give students a full 10 minutes for cleanup. They probably will not need this much time, but I have found that students do a sloppy job putting away games if they feel rushed.

Works Cited

Beck, Isabel, L., Margaret G. McKeown, and Linda Kucan. *Bringing Words to Life: Robust Vocabulary Instruction*. New York: Guilford Press, 2013. Print.

Ebbers, Susan, and Carolyn Denton. "A Root Awakening: Vocabulary Instruction for Older Students with Reading Difficulties." *Learning Disabilities Research and Practice* 23.2 (2008): 90–102. Academic Search Premier. Web. 5 Feb. 2014.

Hargreaves, Ian, et al. "How a Hobby Can Shape Cognition: Visual Word Recognition in Competitive Scrabble Players." *Memory Cognition* 40.1 (2011): 1–6. Academic Search Premier. Web. 5 Feb. 2014.

Recess by Jennifer McGuire

Activity: various games that are adaptable to all disciplines

Learning Outcome: depends on the game

Habit of Mind: engagement

When I tell my students we're going to play a game, they laugh it off. Some give blank stares. This is *college*. I mean, really, a game? Yes. We're going to have recess. Games are familiar. Playing a game provides a feeling of safety and fun, while still allowing students to learn and challenging their intellectual process. It's all about supporting each other and engaging everyone in the classroom. In a game they'll take risks they wouldn't normally take in their writing, and if they mess it up, it's something they'll laugh about and debate with each other. They are not only learning new things from each other, but also utilizing their past knowledge. And it's just fun. It sets the tone for the class. Students realize that the learning process doesn't have to be difficult or exclusively focus on coursework. The learning process can be about engaging in their real lives in a different way. Composition doesn't need to be a drag, or something that they just need to get through to finish their general education requirements. They get comfortable quickly when they know right away that learning and practicing the skills of writing can be a fun and easy process, and they engage quickly and readily with games.

I don't tell them any of this, but they begin to understand with their first questions. Playing a game? Huh? This is not something you can be transparent about. You can tell individuals who are going to have recess that they will be learning social skills and communication, but that's irrelevant and secondary to just letting loose and feeling good about playing with their friends on the playground. They're just doing it and enjoying it. Nothing to explain about that!

The Bell Rings

Early on in the semester, the first game we play can be as easy as Alpha-Omega (discussed later), which is great for introducing new vocabulary and concepts. Depending on what issues I see from the essays, or what strategy for essay writing we're going to practice, I'll choose different games. For example, if I notice that the majority of people are having difficulty with homophones, I'll play a game of Mix and Match. If it's nouns and verbs, I'll play Verbing the Noun (also great to put on Bassnectar's song by the same title). Some games I've made up, and some are altered (not much) from those I learned and used when I taught K–12. They help bring groups together, make students interact, and all with a positive and light learning atmosphere. It's not "edutainment"; it's giving students a safe and familiar format that allows comfort with new things. It turns off those negative associations with difficulties, and makes it fun to learn and teach the others in class.

motivation

With a game in mind, I tell students to get into groups. Sometimes I split the class into halves, sometimes into threes or fours. Group size depends on the game. Once they are in their groups, I tell them to talk with each other to choose a prize (they can ask for the moon, but that doesn't mean they'll get it, so they need to have a reasonable alternative). I give them a minute to come up with one. I write the group on the board and the correlating prize in my notes. Sometimes students ask for a night free of homework, extra-credit points, or a treat, like cookies for everyone. (All prizes must have my approval!)

I explain the game, give them a trial run of the game, and we're off. Once they realize we really are going to play a game, they get a little goofy. Some may be hesitant, some shaking their heads like it's useless, some looking around to see how others are reacting. After we've played a game once in the semester, any following game is met with anticipation of the ensuing group dynamic.

openness

Now, let's take a look at some of the games.

Mix and Match

This simple game helps students to use homophones and correct sentence structure. Students work in groups of three or four, and one person writes the answer. Up on the board, I'll write two homophones. The object of the game is to put the words in a complete sentence using the homophones correctly. Students work in their groups and try to finish first. They raise their hands when the assigned task is completed. It's all about speed and checking in with each other. I'll go to the group that finishes first, read their answer, and if it's not correct say, "So close!" If the answer is correct, I'll read it out loud and write it on the board announcing the winner. The first group that correctly uses the homophones in a complete sentence gets a point.

The game can be played with more than two homophones at a time, or you can incorporate two sets of homophones as you go on. You can do as many rounds as you want and set any point structure you like. It's *fast*! And students sometimes write really funny sentences. It's just as fun when they get one incorrect, and some of the funny ones they come up with just have to be read aloud.

Pieces

For this game, which helps students with sentence structure, conjugation, tenses, and subject/verb agreement, students work in small groups of three or four, and one person in the group writes the answer. Put one noun and one infinitive on the board. You can start out with an already conjugated verb; it just depends on where the class is. If you have it conjugated, students have to use it in that tense. They have to come up with a sentence using both the noun and the verb correctly—no using them as adjectives or adverbs! Oh, tricky! Again, you can add more of either if you want to play with expanding sentences, modifiers, and prepositional phrases. You can always have adaptability them write them on the board.

Alpha-Omega

This game helps students build lexical sets/word banks, details, connections, and examples. It works best in big groups. Split the class into two or three large groups, and tell the students they can get in lines or assign a scribe to their group. Choose a word and write it on the board. Tell the students that they are to write directly under your word a list of words from A to Z that have to do with the word you have written. For example, I'll start off writing the word *hospital* on the board. Then I'll ask the class to come up with words starting with the first letter of the alphabet, then the second letter, and so on that would be associated with the word *hospital*. They might come up with *ambulance*, then *bed*, then *cast*. . . . As the words get written on the board, I encourage and cheer on the students.

The rules include losing a point for skipping a letter. If they do skip a letter and lose a point, then they can't go back if they figure it out later in the game. They can't use proper nouns or adjectives (like *brown* cow for *B* under *animals*). Word of advice: Don't monitor!

When groups have completed their lists, go through them one at a time. Any words that are mentioned by more than one group get crossed out. Any words that don't belong in the set can be debated as a class. You can be the monitor for those. After a few rounds, engagement this game can get very rowdy and energetic. It's practically a guarantee that the answers your students come up with and their creative defense of oddball words will make you laugh.

Collage

This game helps students to provide a description, express a point of view, and think critically. It is a two-part activity with no prizes except bragging rights. The first part is to make a story collage, and the second is to guess the identity of the artist. If you have a stash of magazines, great; if not, your students can bring some in for homework. You can provide glue sticks. Group students so they can share the magazines, and have them rip out images and words that represent them and paste them onto a piece of construction paper. Each collage represents the image that student has of himself or herself, creativity and that student's story. Then have the students write short explanations curiosity of how the collages represent them. No names.

Once done, collect the collages and pass them out randomly. Each student writes a short paragraph on what kind of person he or she thinks the image represents. Then the student is to try to find that person in the classroom. Everybody walks around, talking to each other, finding out who is who. Some get it right away. This game is very interactive. The collage and the other person's description go back to the artist. They ask questions of each other, their thoughts, their explanations. This makes for a huge class discussion while creating the sense that the course is a community of individuals.

Start and Stop

This game helps students write essay introductions or theses, conclusions, and titles. It started out as a regular old lesson plan for introductions, but somehow it morphed into a game. It's really simple. I like to show students the contest results from the San Jose State University Bulwer-Lytton Fiction Contest, in which contestants compete to produce the first sentence of the worst novel, or examples from other short story collections so they can see what a creative beginning to a story can look like.

Students get into groups of five or so. I put a subject on the board, and they have to come up with an introduction or a thesis (depending on what you want to work on) for that subject. The trick is that it has to be the worst one possible. When they come up with their sentence, they write it on the board. Once everyone has written their sentence on the board, the class votes on the ones they like the best—the best of the worst. And, boy, do they come up with some bad ones. Then they have to rewrite the sentence to produce the best thesis sentence for that same subject. It goes up on the board, and then they vote again.

We do the same thing with the conclusion for the same thesis or subject (both worst and best), and again for the title. When the votes are counted from each of the pieces, you have your winner.

Success and Challenges

The wonderful thing about a game is that you immediately have your answers and feedback; there is no waiting to see what will be marked on a paper. The students know, and you know, when they catch on. The game automatically starts picking up; they talk more; they write more and faster; they start shouting out things, debating, asking questions. Students randomly have asked if we can play a game. I'll even challenge them to come up with games. If they want extra credit, they can come up with a game to play with the class that addresses any grammar or mechanics issue or learning outcome that they want. They learn so much more when they get to be the teachers. I don't teach them anything in the games. They have to teach and engage each other.

engagement and responsibility

The main problem that can arise with games has to do with the fact that games are competitive. At times, some students will be disappointed that they didn't win. However, over time it usually evens out in terms of winners. If the class is getting a bit lopsided on which group wins all the time, then bring in a prize for everyone.

When it comes to prizes, I make sure the prize won is something that benefits everyone. In other words, whoever wins the prize wins the prize for everyone in class. No one loses. This is the main thing about what they get to choose for a prize. I will do things that cost me money (usually food), but I'll save those for later, and I will bring it in for the last day. Prizes are things like watching a movie, two extra-credit points, or a homework pass. Usually they are things that I would already incorporate into the class, but the students can come up with whatever they want, and I get to say yea or nay. I do have to admit, I did have to dress up as a ladybug one day for class . . . and it wasn't Halloween. This is when I learned not to write down the prizes on the board; they will slant the game so that the most desired prize wins. No kidding! They work as a whole team that way, which is a whole other dimension to game playing.

Regarding the issue of time, these games can last from 10 minutes to hours. You can split games up, continue the games into the next class, stop them, start them, change them, at any time.

Last, but not least, is your willingness to let this be actual play time. The topics can be addressed in regular lessons, but my experience has been that making them into games engages students right off the bat. When students have a chance to laugh at themselves and the doozies that they can come up with, it makes for a wonderful contrast to how they usually think about the seriousness of institu-

openness tionalized education. They aren't being graded or judged or evaluated in any average sense, but they are definitely learning. It's a lot like recess as a kid: You play with the other kids and you learn social interaction, real-life application of communication. Give them a ball and they'll learn the rules and structure of the game played for that tool; writing skills are like that ball. They'll be learning, sure, but it'll also feel like recess.

Quick Start Guide

1. Try to incorporate one game a week.
2. Start class with a game in order to build community.
3. All these games can be tailored to your specific teaching needs— find the ones that fit you best and then have fun!

The Great Debaters? Well, Close Enough by María Boza

Activity: class debate

Learning Outcome: effectively prepare an argument

Habits of Mind: transfer of learning and engagement

Background

Most students in WRT 95: Integrated Reading and Writing, the developmental writing course at California State University Monterey Bay, write an argumentative essay near the end of the semester. I was a philosophy major as an undergraduate, so to me this sort of writing is second nature. Yet, partly because of lack of prior exposure to the genre, this essay proves to be a difficult assignment for many of our students. Frequently the drafts they submit to me—after peer review—are papers that list information without questioning it and without structuring it as an argument in which a clear claim is made and argued for, taking into account the sides of the controversy.

I tell students to imagine that the audience for their argumentative essay is a panel of objective jurors in an academic setting who are open to persuasion. Furthermore, a skilled opponent, whose points they will have to anticipate and rebut, is attempting to sway these same curious but critical jurors. To enable students to see the back-and-forth of opposing ideas in concrete form while experiencing the rewards of engagement, my classes have a debate the week before their first drafts of the argumentative essay are due.

openness

We employ traditional policy debate format, which I have modified slightly to suit our needs. There are various online sources for the format—and they do not all agree. I have listed two under "Resources for Debate Format" at the end of this activity.

Other Preparation for the Argumentative Essay

The debate is not the only preparation my students get for writing the argumentative essay—far from it. I show them PowerPoint presentations on claims, arguments, critical thinking, and logical fallacies. I follow these with an ungraded quiz to reinforce the material. We look at relevant pages of our textbook, *The Norton Field Guide to Writing with Readings and Handbook*, which has good coverage of argumentation (Bullock, Goggin, and Weinberg 119–49, 726–63).

We read examples of effective argumentative essays and go over them paragraph by paragraph, noticing their structure and evaluating their persuasive tactics. (I draw these examples of good student-written argumentative essays from the Bedford/St. Martin's website for the sixth edition—now superseded—of *Rules for Writers* by Diana Hacker.) I give the students a very long, very specific essay prompt detailing what should be included in the essay. In the prompt I discuss structure, techniques, evidence, and effective strategies, as well as approaches that in the past have proven to be unproductive for

metacognition   students. And, yes, the debates are still necessary. Here's the prompt:

Assignment Directions

Write a three- to four-page essay arguing in support of a definite position about a controversial issue taken from the choices provided. Be sure to do the following:

- In your introduction, state a thesis that clearly, forcefully, and accurately summarizes the principal claim you will argue throughout the essay.
- Persuasively build your argument by following reasonable lines of argument.
- Provide suitable supporting evidence for your position:
    - You must use at least one scholarly source to support your argument. (You may not count unpublished material as scholarly sources.)
    - Other supporting evidence may include facts, statistics, examples, anecdotes, and/or opinions from experts.
- Discuss at least one opposing argument and provide a quotation that represents that position.
- Rebut the opposing argument.
- In a strong concluding paragraph, bring the reader back to the thesis you have just proven.
- Give the essay a title that assists the reader in identifying your focus.
- Properly cite all outside sources in MLA format, providing both in-text parenthetical citations and fuller "Works Cited" end-of-essay citations.

Debate Preparation

To prepare students for the debate, if time permits, I show them the 2007 film *The Great Debaters*, directed by Denzel Washington. Through the film they get an idea of the structure of debate and also become acquainted with serious challenges faced by African American students in the Jim Crow South. My students generally like the movie, but for the class planner it has the disadvantage of running 124 minutes. Last semester I showed only scenes that were directly related to debate.

At least a week before the debate, I give a PowerPoint presentation on preparing for a debate. The first order of business after that is for the class to choose a topic. I like to have the students suggest possibilities, but if they seem stuck, I help out. The topic is never one of the choices I give them for the argumentative essay, for which they will have to engage in independent research and thinking. The debat- responsibilityers will be more engaged if students choose a topic about which the class is divided, so I canvass them about their willingness to argue the particular sides. For example, recently the proposition "The highway speed limit should be raised to 75 mph" drew no opposition, not even from the instructor, so that one was eliminated.

I then ask for three students to volunteer to be judges. Frequently those students who opt to be judges are shy people who recoil from arguments. However, when postdebate analysis time comes, they can be excellent at pointing out the strengths and weaknesses of each side's performance. Thus, students who may be quiet the rest of the semester have the opportunity to show that behind that silence are minds that are taking it all in.

Next, those students who will not be judges choose sides: affirmative or negative. I aim for similar numbers on each side and ask students who are sitting on the fence to go to the side most in need of participants. I explain to them that it is not necessary for them actually to agree with the position they are arguing. The goal is not to find the "right" answer, which may not even be determinable, but to learn to argue well. In fact, frequently in order to maintain evenness of the sides, students whose first choice would have been one position take on the task of arguing the opposite. In academic discourse they will seldom find answers to be reducible to yes or no, so this is in itself tolerance for good preparation. ambiguity

I remind students of the role of the affirmative side and of the negative, which they should have picked up on from the "Preparation for a Debate" presentation and the film. Then I ask each side to choose two speakers. I emphasize that although two students will be presenting the arguments for each side, all members of each side must participate with information and ideas. In fact, I build in opportunities for them to huddle.

As the sides are choosing their speakers, I meet with the judges to explain to them what their job is during the debate. Their duties are to listen carefully; take notes on the arguments; and, at the end, deliver an individual verdict, expressing reasons for the decision. These reasons must be supported by evidence in the notes. This way, although they will be neither speaking with the sides nor lending support to a side, they will be engaged in the entire debate and will see themselves as the active participants that they are.

The sides and the judges gather into their respective groups to examine the color-coded table I have made of the debate format they will follow (see Table 3.1). For example, affirmative speaker #1 is coded blue and #2 green; negative speaker #1 is red, while speaker #2 is orange. I find that color coding helps me, so I assume it also helps my visually inclined students both before and during the debate.

Minutes before the debate I show the students, as a reminder, two PowerPoint presentations they have seen before, one on logical fallacies and another on unfair emotional tactics (i.e., ad hominem appeals, biased language, and ridicule). I emphasize the need for courtesy.

The students follow the official debate format without actually making an effort to figure out if what a student is saying is "constructivist" or "rebuttal." I am glad when they present good points or follow effective strategies of any kind. There is a lot of group consultation during the breaks. This allows students who are not speakers to remain engaged and to see their contributions as valuable to the entire effort—therefore not viewing the debate as something that is being done by others while they remain mere spectators.

engagement

I sit out of the way, only jumping in to clarify questions of procedure. I used to be in charge of a timer that required me to hit multiple buttons frequently, a task that might be easier for a chimpanzee than for me. Then I wised up and asked that a judge be timekeeper. Students use their smartphones instead of my old kitchen timer, and the process goes more smoothly.

TABLE 3.1.
Example of Color-Coded Table for the Debate

Speaker	Time
1 Affirmative constructive	6 min.
Cross-examination	4 min.
1 Negative constructive	6 min.
Cross-examination	4 min.
Break	4 min.
2 Affirmative constructive	6 min.
Cross-examination	4 min.
2 Negative constructive	6 min.
Cross-examination	4 min.
Break	5 min.
1 Negative rebuttal	3 min.
1 Affirmative rebuttal	5 min.
2 Negative rebuttal	5 min.
2 Affirmative rebuttal	5 min.
Break for judges' private deliberation	5 min.
Judge 1's report and verdict	3 min.
Judge 2's report and verdict	3 min.
Judge 3's report and verdict	3 min.

1 Affirmative: Blue; 2 Affirmative: Green   1 Negative: Red; 2 Negative: Orange

Debate Aftermath

When the two sides are finished with their part of the debate, I ask the judges to describe in turn what, in their view, worked and what did not in each side's presentation and to vote on the winner. This activity of analyzing and verbalizing effective and ineffective elements of the arguments is one of the most productive steps of the whole enterprise. The verdict itself is usually unanimous and is less valuable.   reflection

After the judges have had their say, I sit in the midst of the students and draw them to make explicit some of the lessons they might transfer from debating orally as a group to writing an argumentative essay in the loneliness of their rooms. These lessons include the following:

- Evidence strengthens the points of an argument.
- Each building block of a good argument is important.
- It's nice to work with a team.
- Authorities in the field can be brought in as members of one's team through quotation.
- Peer reviewers are also members of one's team.
- Our own arguments become stronger when we rebut opponents' strong arguments.
- Logic is necessary.
- A confident, calm tone boosts the credibility of the speaker or the writer.
- Finding common ground is another way the rhetor can boost his or her credibility; reasonable people are easier to believe.
- It's imperative to keep one's audience in mind.

Student Feedback

In anonymous questionnaires filled out after the debate, students most frequently mention the need to support points with well-researched data as the biggest lesson they have learned from the activity. Some students also mention having learned that in order to debate effectively one has to be well acquainted with both sides of the question.

A common complaint is lack of preparation and information sharing by team members. Several students have expressed discomfort with the activity, one saying that he did not like the confrontational nature of it. However, in a recent semester, out of 46 respondents, only three said they would not recommend repeating the activity in future semesters.

Reflection

Although many students find the debate useful—or at least interesting—this does not mean that the debates are all of high quality. One semester, when there were some particularly strong arguers in the same section, the debate and the judges' analysis were stellar. The previous semester, on the other hand, the class had chosen legalization of marijuana as the debate topic, and some of the members of the affirmative team came to the debate stoned. One of them even threatened an opponent. However, it is rare for debaters to become so passionate about their stance that they behave uncivilly.

I have not conducted an experiment to compare the quality of essays in a "with debate" semester with that of a "without debate" one. I would not want to go a semester without a debate because students are fully engaged during the debate, and that is a habit of mind worth cultivating.

Through the exercise, students develop an awareness of the need to consider multiple points of view and, no matter what the academic task, to provide solid evidence for well-articulated positions. These are skills that will serve them well throughout their academic career and later on as they mature as members of civil society.

Quick Start Guide

Preparation

1. Decide on a debate format. Useful resources on formats are the National Association for Urban Debate League's publication *Learning to Debate: An Introduction for First-Year Debaters* and Wikipedia's "Structure of Policy Debate" entry.
2. Have students elect a debatable topic.
3. Invite volunteers to serve as judges.
4. Have remaining students choose sides.
5. Ask students on each side to choose two speakers.
6. Hand out copies of the format to the speakers and the judges.
7. Emphasize the need for preparation and collaboration.

Debate Day

1. Ask the debaters and the judges to take appropriate positions in the classroom.
2. Ask one of the judges to be the timekeeper.
3. Remind students of the format to be followed.
4. Begin the debate.
5. Ask judges for their feedback at the end of the debate.

6. Ask students how they might transfer skills exercised in the debate into their writing of an argumentative essay.

Resources for Debate Format

Bullock, Richard, Maureen Daly Goggin, and Francine Weinberg. *The Norton Field Guide to Writing with Readings and Handbook*. 3rd ed. New York: W.W. Norton, 2013. Print.

Hacker, Diana. "Model Papers." *Rules for Writers*. 6th ed. Student Site. Bedford/St. Martin's. n.d. Web. 22 Feb. 2014.<http://bcs.bedfordstmartins.com/rules6e/latest/Main_Frame.asp?Id=8&edition=Newed>

National Association for Urban Debate Leagues. *Learning to Debate: An Introduction for First-Year Debaters*. National Association for Urban Debate Leagues. Web. 8 Aug. 2011.

"Structure of Policy Debate." Wikipedia. Wikimedia Foundation, 26 June 2011. Web. 8 Aug. 2011.

The Great Debaters. Dir. Denzel Washington. Perf. Denzel Washington and Nate Parker. The Weinstein Company, 2007. DVD.

Gender and Miscommunication by Sunita Lanka

> Activity: the analysis and evaluation of information while reading college-level texts

> Learning Outcomes: accurate comprehension and evaluation of college-level texts while drawing accurate inferences and devising reasonable conclusions

> Habits of Mind: engagement, transfer of learning, metacognition, creativity, flexibility, and curiosity

It's a Monday morning. For most of my students you could say it's a "black Monday." The attendance is taken and I sense that my talkative students are winding down their exchanges about weekend activities with friends. The quiet ones stop fidgeting, and there is that moment of expectation: "Now what?" Looking around I smile, then force some enthusiasm into my voice as I begin, "Did you have a good weekend?" There are smiles, sighs, comments, hardly audible. I decide to get straight to the point. "Do you ever disagree or fight with your partners/boyfriends/girlfriends/spouses?" Suddenly there's less shifting in the chairs; some bend forward to listen more intently. A couple of them answer in unison, "Oh, God, all the time!" Those who are silent nod agreement, too, and the whole class, without exception, is listening. I tell them that this will be our next assignment: "Miscommunication between couples." I remind them that they were to read the text over the weekend as homework. I soon realize that many have forgotten to read it and they are now quickly turning the pages of the text to browse through it, in case there is a quiz. The assignment is to examine two articles in the course textbook, *Texts and Contexts: A Contemporary Approach to College Writing* (Robinson and Tucker, with Hicks)—"His Talk, Her Talk" by Joyce Maynard and "Man to Man, Woman to Woman" by Sherman and Adelaide Haas (32)—and to recommend one of the articles to a couple who seeks counseling to solve communication problems.

curiosity

I begin a warm-up exercise by asking simple questions such as, "What did you think of the reading?" "Can you relate to the anecdotes described?" and "Do you have similar stories to share?" It's interesting to observe how the silent ones are now giggling and beginning to talk with their classmates. When I call upon them to share their thoughts with the class, they begin hesitantly but soon burst into animated narration. There are peals of laughter when each one is given a chance to speak up about his or her experience.

engagement

This assignment covers the habits of mind of engagement, transfer of learning, metacognition, creativity, flexibility, and curiosity. For instance, the topic triggers inquisitiveness. Even those students who do not report having had communication problems are inquisitive about reading further to find out what happens to the couple. They are interested in participating in the group discussions where their friends share their real-life experiences. I have also seen very shy students share their own stories. This is transfer of learning because they practice transferring real-life experiences into writing. To do this successfully, they process this information and organize it to articulate it in the form of a coherent essay. Habits of mind are evidenced as students move through the activity.

1. Engagement: The assignment is successful in arresting attention to get students to invest effort into the exercise. Engagement is vital to any student activity.
2. Transfer of Learning: Students must transfer their real-life experience into a written product.
3. Metacognition: "Miscommunication between couples" is a topic any student can relate to, and be interested in—a topic that invites a reflection in a variety of contexts.
4. Creativity: The topic encourages the ability to use novel/diverse methods to approach, understand, and investigate an issue, and also to draw upon experiences related to the topic. The process of finding a solution to the problem enables students to not only examine the two articles closely/actively, but also look for the kind of information that will convince a couple of the solution offered by one.
5. Curiosity and Flexibility: The topic is an issue of universal concern, so students develop the awareness/need to adapt to situations, the need to find solutions to problems, manage expectations, and meet obligations of relationships. It also teaches them the abilities to articulate these in a convincing manner.

Analysis and evaluation of information is very important in the writing process. How does one teach students to learn this skill? The process inevitably has to follow a thorough comprehension of the text. It must trigger interest and a strong desire to participate and voice an opinion. Active reading is both essential and vital to doing the assignment.

I begin with a PowerPoint presentation and a handout to guide students on the process. The PowerPoint walks them through the process of preparing to read, or prereading. The handout also provides them with a checklist of activities that I go over with them in class. The students take a couple of minutes to review the checklist handout. The students then take turns reading the text aloud in class. After the reading is done, I divide them into groups of four and ask them to find answers to questions that I present through the document camera:

1. Comment on the titles. Which one of the two articles gives an impression of togetherness, a likely compromise? Some of them dramatically enact the titles, saying "His Talk, Her Talk" is like "you go your way, and I go my way." The other one, "Man to Man, Woman to Woman," they say, is like a man can share conversations easily with a man, and women do so with people of their sex. This second one suggests that the couple communicates readily with people of their own sex.

2. What about the authors? What is the significance of one article being written by a single author, a woman, while the other is written by a man and a woman? The single author, Joyce Maynard, portrays a woman's point of view; it is one-sided and highly opinionated. The second essay, on the other hand, is a collaborative effort. A couple is addressing a common issue; two perspectives, a man's and a woman's, are combined in dealing with the issue. Hence, there is a strong possibility that it might address more comprehensively/justly problems of communication faced by both men and women.

3. Which introductory paragraph has a topic sentence that clearly states what will be addressed in the article? How do the introductions read? Will the couple be able to easily identify the topic—the problem/issue—at hand? Which one of the articles could help the couple to see that it is addressing their problem? Can they identify the thesis statement? The students tell me that the first article has an attention-grabbing introduction but that it is rambling. It is the second one that addresses the problem at hand, communication. It is well organized with transitional words that contribute to effective comprehension.

4. Quality of information/content: Which article creates confidence and credibility in the troubled couple? What is the quality of information? Which is the article that has information to convince the couple that a compromise is possible? Is the information credible, plausible, connected to the topic, relevant; does it prove a point; are there any contradictions? What are the details

that are credible and convince the couple? Have they been able to see that facts are supported by reasonable, convincing data/statistics/research or interviews with couples? How strongly do they feel about such details offering support to prove a point, leading to accurate inferences? Details that explain, substantiate, and illustrate the point help in assessing the quality of information. The credibility of information is established not with opinionated statements, but ample authentic proof (i.e., research, surveys, interviews, and questionnaires).

5. Which one of the articles provides a solution to the problem in a direct and precise manner? Which one of the articles offers a solution to solve communication problems/clear misunderstandings between the couple? The students take turns reading the concluding paragraph of both articles. The two conclusions offer solutions, but the first one is not direct and clear. One has to infer the solution from the situation described by the author. The other article states very clearly that men and women enjoy different topics of conversation, and that by giving each other some space (i.e., freedom) and understanding it is possible to create a lasting relationship without conflict.

The class is able to draw their conclusions with some guidance, questions, discussions, and sharing of information. Monitor students' discussions by asking clarifying questions, moving around from one group to another, and guiding them on how to draw conclusions by examining the text. It's interesting to see the answers that each group comes up with. With gentle coaxing, also have them read sentences from the text that support their answers. Finally, ask students which of the two articles they've chosen to recommend to the couple and the reasons for their choice. They will initially present their preference as an in-class response listing their reasons as brief points.

It is interesting to note that with a little help students on their own are able to discover significant points from the two articles and use them to draw reasonable inferences. They record answers to the questions posed, as part of their preparation for a rough draft. When it's time for them to make the rough draft, I explain the format of the essay as follows:

Learning outcome: By the end of the exercise students understand the process of examining details, making connections, identifying contradictions, and analyzing and evaluating information—the necessary criteria to make inferences and draw conclusions in order to make wise decisions. Most important, they learn to justify the reasons for their choices with evidence and confidence.

Introduction: States the issue and purpose of the assignment.

(Problem of miscommunication between a couple and recommending an article that would help them understand and overcome their problem.)

Body paragraphs:

1. Title: Comparing the titles and inferences from them.
2. Authors: One article is opinionated and solely from a wife's point of view. The other article is authored by a couple and it's reasonable to infer that it holds a comprehensive view of the issue because it has a man's and a woman's point of view.
3. Quality of information in the two articles: Comparing opinions, facts, and evidence that is authentic (i.e., supported by data, research, surveys, statistics, illustrations, and examples).
4. Solution offered: One article offers a realistic solution while the other does not suggest any remedial measures. By now, the students will be able to identify this on their own.

Conclusion: Based on the analysis and evaluation of the two articles a recommendation is made summing up and justifying the reasons for the choice.

Miscommunication Between Couples: Assignment Guidelines Handout

Focus on the following:

- Title
- Authors
- Introduction
- Thesis statement
- Quality of information
- Solution

Checklist for the Recommendation

- Is there an appropriate title?
- Are details of student assignment in MLA format?

- Are there distinct sections?
  - ○ Introduction
  - ○ Points of focus
  - ○ Recommendation
- Does the introduction clearly state the problem at hand?
- Is there clarity and coverage of all the important points of the two essays?
- Is there evidence—points of support that explain why one essay is more suitable than the other to offer as a recommendation to the couple?
- Is there coherence?
- Is there a solution recommended?
- Does the response seem convincing?
- Do you think your response is clear and would help the couple?
- Did you review your writing for proofreading errors?

Quick Start Guide

1. Get students interested in the readings and the topic by discussing miscommunication between couples as a class and in small groups.
2. After the students have read two articles on this subject as homework, use the next class meeting to continue discussion about this interesting topic and also to add a level of learning. Have students begin to analyze the structure of the texts. For instance, point out passages and then ask students to say what they infer, or have the students compare the strength of evidence presented in both articles.
3. Assign an essay in which students evaluate the structure of the assigned articles.

Work Cited

Robinson, William S., Stephanie Tucker, with the assistance of Cynthia G. Hicks. *Texts and Contexts: A Contemporary Approach to College Writing*. 7th ed. New York: Wadsworth Cengage Learning, 2008. Print.

Letter to the Editor by Kathleen Leonard

Activity: writing a letter to the editor

Learning Outcomes: develop a thesis in support of an argument; gain awareness of the audience, tone, and purpose; complete the writing process while discovering the real-world value of their writing (other than for a grade) through engagement with current topics that interest students and have an impact on their local, state, national, or international community

Habits of Mind: engagement, motivation, openness, mindfulness, and confidence

Making Your Voice Heard

All of us get irritated by things in our community, state, country, or the world. We want something changed, and we know just what to do. Who will listen to us? No one, we think, so we just keep quiet. However, there is a forum for speaking out and being heard—the letters to the editor of your local newspaper!

For more than 30 years, I have been writing letters to the editor that have been printed in the *San Jose Mercury News* and the *Monterey Herald*. I write about many topics, such as politics, education, libraries, roads, and mental health policies. Once, in 1982, a newspaper even published my ecstatic letter about the Oscar unexpectedly being awarded to the long-shot, brilliant British film *Chariots of Fire*.

Almost any topic can be covered in a letter to the editor. What is necessary is that you be passionate about the topic because that is what comes through in your writing. Topics that have an argument and a solution are usually best because they give the student the opportunity to define why something is a problem or challenge and how best to correct it.

During the class meeting before this activity starts, I ask students to read the letters to the editor in a newspaper. If they can't afford a newspaper, students can read the letters online. The students are to find letters they think are particularly effective or horrible and bring them to class. They should be prepared to discuss why the letters are effective or not. I then ask students to start thinking about topics they might want to write about.

motivation

At the next class meeting, I distribute a handout called "Tips on How to Write Your Letter to the Editor" (see p. 119) and go over it with students. I put the students into groups, hand out letters to the editor that I have clipped from the newspaper, hand out the Letter to the Editor Critique sheet (see p. 120), and have students review their letters using the sheet. The critique sheet provides the criteria they and I will use to provide feedback on the letters. It facilitates assessing how clear, credible, and compelling the letters are. Then, I have the students pick one student from each group to present the letter and its critique to the class. I encourage the class to comment on the critique and to give reasons why they agree or disagree with the critique. This activity helps the students with their critical thinking skills and gets them thinking about better ways to craft a strong argument.

The assignment for the next class meeting(s) is for each student to bring to class a first draft of a letter to the editor for peer review. Each letter will be reviewed by at least two classmates using the Letter to the Editor Critique sheet. Then, after a class vote, either I will read aloud each letter anonymously, or the students will read aloud their own letters, and we as a class will discuss how each letter might be strength-

engagement   ened to improve the writing and increase the chances of publication.

A revised, edited, and proofread hard copy of the completed letter is due at the next class meeting, but it will not be graded until the student has submitted the letter to the local newspaper and then turned in a printed copy of the letter from the student's sent file so that I can see that the letter was actually submitted. I use the Letter to the Editor Critique sheet to determine the grade for each student's letter.

Successes and Challenges

My experience has been that approximately 50% of the students' letters are published. It is especially thrilling for students when another letter writer from the community outside the class comments on a student's published letter because even when the comments disagree with what the students wrote, the students see that their words have

confidence   made an impression on another reader. They see that their words
and self-   matter and make a difference.
efficacy
I suggest that you teach "Letters to the Editor" only if you believe in the assignment. If you don't write letters to the editor yourself, or at least want to, your students will pick up on your lack of enthusiasm and write poorly argued, uninspiring letters. However, if you believe in the purpose and power of persuasive/argumentative writing and genuinely want your students to see that their writing can make a difference in the world outside the classroom, then this is the assignment for you.

Habits of Mind

Students are always surprised to discover that they care about lots of situations and topics. I've had students write about the Grammys, motorcycle helmets, street names, park closures, gang activity, politics, lack of good childcare options, football, graffiti, immigration, and ways to increase tourism, to name just a few of the topics in student letters that were chosen to be printed in a newspaper.

When students realize they are writing for the real world as opposed to the artificial world of the classroom, they become more engaged and motivated to write a good letter because they are writing about topics important to them, and they are writing for a public forum. Students realize that their letters can be read by anyone who reads the newspaper, so they are especially motivated to write well.

I explain to my students that the criteria for a letter being selected by the editor for print are that it be timely and well written. If the topic of the letter is not timely, then, no matter how well written, it will not be printed. So, the challenge is to make certain that students write timely letters. This promotes openness and mindfulness in the students because they often have to entertain new ideas and consider opposing approaches to solutions if they wish to have a stronger chance of being printed.

openness and responsiveness

When a student's letter is printed, the whole class cheers. This promotes confidence in the students whose work is printed, but it also promotes confidence in the students whose work was not printed because they bask in the reflected glory. Knowing that their peers had letters printed makes every student in the class aware that anyone can have their work printed. You just need the right topic and good timing.

Often, students will write more letters to the editor after the class has ended because they get "bitten by the bug" of civic responsibility. As a teacher, my heart fills with delight when I see these voluntarily written letters in a newspaper because I know that I've given my students a way to have their voices heard, as well as strengthened the habits of mind that will help them lead fulfilling lives.

responsibility

Tips on How to Write Your Letter to the Editor

1. OBSERVE: Read the newspaper every day, paying particular attention to editorials and letters.
2. RESPOND: Letters to the editor typically arise from an emotional response. Look for opinions or events that anger you,

frighten you, amuse you, or strike you as ridiculous. When something riles you, you are onto a possible letter.

3. ANALYZE YOUR RESPONSE: Dig into your reaction by asking that magic question "why?" When you find out why you are angry, frightened, or whatever, you have also found out what you want to say to the readers of the newspaper.

4. SPECULATE AND MAKE CONNECTIONS: Before you establish a thesis, find out how your issue and your opinion fit into the context of contemporary events. Search newspapers (and the TV news) for related material. Know what others think about the issue. Know causes and effects. Timely issues are more likely to be printed.

5. SELECT A MAIN IDEA: By now you are ready to choose a thesis. Make it strong, positive, and specific, and don't apologize by tacking on "in my opinion."

6. SUPPORT YOUR THESIS: Remember that you are trying to convince the readers of the newspaper of your point of view. Select information that best exemplifies or proves your point.

Some General Qualities of a Good Letter to the Editor

1. Letters to the editor are shorter than essays, usually fewer than 200 words.

2. Letters to the editor deal with an issue or event that is timely, important, and of interest to the readers of the newspaper.

3. Letters to the editor express a strong opinion about an issue or give a fresh insight into it. Frequently, they recommend a course of action.

4. Letters to the editor have a strong, direct, brief thesis statement.

5. Letters to the editor often appeal to the human side of the reader.

6. Letters to the editor have catchy openings, dramatic conclusions; make good sense; have a clear, direct style; and are grammatically perfect.

Letter to the Editor Critique

1. Is the letter's thesis or purpose clear? If not, how might it be made clearer?

2. Is the thesis well supported?
3. What is your reaction to the letter? Agreement? Disagreement? Indifference? Why?
4. Is the writer's credibility established?
5. What do you like best about the letter?
6. What do you like least about the letter?
7. Are there any words or phrases you believe should be changed? If so, why and how?
8. Do the opening and closing have punch?
9. Is the letter timely? That is, is it relevant to issues being discussed now?
10. What is the tone of the letter—serious, humorous, sarcastic, other?
11. If a problem is stated, is a course of action also stated?

Example Letter

You may change the example letter each semester to reflect timely issues. This letter is a very good example written in 2007.

Dear Editor,

California moved its presidential primary with the goal of empowering its voters. However, if you, like me, were born between February 5 and June 3 in 1990, you've been effectively disenfranchised.

Dumb luck? Poor planning? Regardless of the cause, it seems to contradict the lip service given to "Rock the vote" and the value of young voters.

If California and the nation are serious about getting the youth involved, then it's time to respect us, not disregard those of us turning 18 next year.

A onetime exemption for the newly disenfranchised would remedy the injustice as well as show the up-and-coming electorate that their opinion and vote do matter.

Sincerely,
Name
Complete address
Phone number

Letters to the editor must have your full name, complete address, and phone number at the *bottom* of the letter. Address the letter to: Dear Editor.

E-mail to your local newspaper, and please put Letter to the Editor in the subject heading.

DATE DUE: _____. Please print your letter from your sent folder and hand in to me so that I can grade your letter and see the date you e-mailed it to the paper.

Quick Start Guide

1. Help students to find a timely issue that speaks strongly to them.
2. Review the purpose and form of letters to the editor with your students.
3. Encourage students to submit their letters for publication.

4

BUILDING CONFIDENCE

Jennifer Fletcher

"To love the plateau is to love the eternal now, to enjoy the inevitable spurts of progress and the fruits of accomplishment, then serenely accept the new plateau that waits just beyond them. To love the plateau is to love what is most essential and enduring in your life."

—George Leonard (48–49)

This chapter describes a special moment in the learning process—that place in the cognitive pool where the instructor has begun to lead the new swimmer out into deep water yet still treads within reach. It's a liminal space between trust and independence. At this stage, teacher and student share responsibility for learning, and both must work hard to promote intellectual growth. We address the promotion of self-efficacy in the next chapter because we believe that an authentic sense of personal responsibility often arises from a transfer of trust. For confidence, after all, is another word for trust. It can also mean courage, comfort, self-assurance, and resolve: that is to say, all the gifts we want our students to have on their educational journeys. Once students have confidence in their own abilities, the burden of instruction largely shifts from teacher to learner. It's that moment of letting go, of crossing the pool alone, that we pursue here.

Learning at this transitional stage is messy, confusing, and often overwhelming. We juggle a load of concepts and skills over which we have yet to achieve mastery. Gone is the blissful ignorance of not comprehending the full difficulty of our task. Progress, too, can seem to stall at this point as we finally realize both how far we still need to go and how unprepared we are to get there. In writing, this moment of total immersion can be particularly discouraging. Trapped between starting and ending, we doubt our ability to find a way out.

As teachers, we know this feeling well. When we look back on our own journeys in higher education, we can see that our most important learning experiences nearly always started with a sense of being in over our heads. Unfortunately, first-year college students don't enjoy the benefits of hindsight. For them, confusion is often an indication that something's wrong. Many haven't yet learned that feeling clueless[1] and unsure isn't a sign you don't belong; it means you're appropriately challenged. We can provide that reassurance.

> Many haven't yet learned that feeling clueless and unsure isn't a sign you don't belong; it means you're appropriately challenged.

Building students' confidence so that they are prepared to learn independently involves several pedagogical moves. One is an increase in the difficulty level of academic tasks. Another is the bridging of in-school and out-of-school identities. A third—and perhaps most important—is the creation of a feedback loop. Taken together, these moves can help students develop both their intellectual identities and habits as they learn more about their own progress and struggles. This often happens sometime around the middle of an instructional cycle, whether that cycle encompasses a whole course or an individual unit. It is at this stage that strategic intervention and effort are critical. Without targeted coaching and feedback from teachers to tell students how well they're performing and what they need to do next, and without greater diligence from students, instruction can languish in the early stages of engagement and community building; everyone's having fun and likes each other, but too many students are just putting in "seat time."

Habits of Mind

Beyond openness and curiosity, then, students need habits of mind such as persistence, flexibility, and metacognition so that they become more than just briefly enthusiastic dabblers in a field. *Framework for Success in Postsecondary Writing* (2011) defines *persistence* as "the ability to sustain interest in and attention to short- and long-term projects" (CWPA, NCTE, and NWP 1). As anyone who has made a

New Year's resolution knows, sustaining interest and attention is far more difficult than engaging them. Malcolm Gladwell's *Outliers: The Story of Success* explores the staggering time commitment needed for interest to turn into expertise: 10,000 practice hours in some cases (47). Like persistence, flexibility and metacognition also require concerted effort. Flexibility, *Framework for Success in Postsecondary Writing* explains, includes the ability to adapt to new demands, and metacognition involves an active assessment of ourselves as learners (CWPA, NCTE, and NWP 5). Students acquire these mental habits when they consistently tackle ever greater challenges, applying what they learn from one endeavor to the next. This isn't a new idea. A few millenia ago Aristotle was telling his students it is "hard work to be excellent" (29). What has changed in recent years, however, is our understanding of how to support students during more challenging phases of instruction through mindful and explicit mentoring.

> Beyond openness and curiosity, then, students need habits of mind such as persistence, flexibility, and metacognition so that they become more than just briefly enthusiastic dabblers in a field.

Research Base

Educational scholarship offers abundant evidence justifying this kind of support. Whether it takes the form of "coaching" (Bean 149), direct or "explicit instruction" (Scarcella 127), or "formative assessment" (Popham 3), the idea that students need an extra boost of awareness and guidance to progress beyond basic proficiency levels has deservedly received much scholarly attention. In *Accelerating Academic English*, for instance, linguist Robin Scarcella argues for the importance of providing direct instruction to English language learners in order to help them overcome an intermediate "plateau" (6). Composition scholar John Bean similarly describes teacher coaching of critical thinking skills as a practice that can "convert students from passive to active learners" (122). And literacy researcher Norman Unrau encourages educators to use "diagnostic teaching" so that they can assess "what is working and what is breaking down" (113)—and then respond appropriately. All of these ideas are predicated on the principle that effective instruction does not march relentlessly forward, indifferent to student needs and learning curves.

The Link Between Learning and Identity

Indeed, honoring who our students are as individuals—their assets, interests, and developmental stages—is essential for moving students from basic proficiency to mastery. This is especially true for our most underrepresented students. Writing on the way first-generation status impacts college students' degree attainment, Jennifer Engle reminds us of the link between learning and identity: "First-generation students need considerable support as they make the complex academic, social, and cultural transitions to college. They need validation that they are not only capable of succeeding in college, but that they belong on campus as well" (39). Academic performance and identity, the research suggests, are two sides of the same coin—and both are critical to college completion. As Elizabeth Birr Moje and Cynthia Lewis observe, "One learns to take on new identities along with new forms of knowledge and participation" (19). In "You Need to Realize It in Yourself: Positioning, Improvisation, and Literacy," Aimee C. Mapes calls academic assignments "opportunities for identity work" (523). Linguist Mary Schleppegrell similarly explores the link between ways of knowing and ways of being in her analysis of how language choices "realize" various social contexts and relationships (114). Perhaps the clearest expression of this idea comes from sociolinguist Paul Gee: "It's not just what you say or even how you say it. It's also who you are and what you are doing while saying it" (2).

As teachers, we make important contributions to our students' identity formation. One colleague, for instance, tells the story of how she excelled in both her high school English and science courses but received praise and mentoring only from her English teacher. Not surprisingly, she believed her best subject was English. Expanding students' repertoire of social roles to include a confident academic identity is as sacred a teaching obligation as developing students' knowledge and skills.

Increasing Confidence Through Rigor

One way to nurture students' academic identities is to encourage them to welcome rigor. This is not only a good practice but also a precondition for developing intellectual habits of mind. Unless students encounter increasingly complex academic tasks and texts,[2] they won't have the opportunity to experience the pitfalls and plateaus that foster persistence, flexibility, and metacognition. By enduring

and surmounting these obstacles, students gain an authentic
sense of confidence as learners.
Thus, while engaging reluctant
or underprepared learners is certainly worthy of celebration, we
also need to consider how we're
going to sustain this engagement beyond the honeymoon
period, particularly when we need to ramp up the difficulty of the
work we ask students to perform.

> Unless students encounter increasingly complex academic tasks and texts, they won't have the opportunity to experience the pitfalls and plateaus that foster persistence, flexibility, and meta-cognition.

The hard truth—the truth we share with our students after they
know and trust us and each other—is that genuine academic confidence results from learning how to manage our struggles, not our
successes. Part of our work as guides and mentors during this challenging phase is to help students see pitfalls and plateaus as necessary
to their growth. Students are often highly optimistic (some might say
too optimistic) before they experience their first big confidence correction. Most students expect to pass a class when they enroll. Most
high school students expect that they will graduate from college. We
wouldn't want it any other way. But we also understand that those
humbling moments of recalibration when a learner recognizes that
the task at hand is much tougher than he or she thought mark a critical threshold on the road to mastery.

The dual notions of "threshold concepts" and "troublesome
knowledge" help explain why this stage of instruction so often leads to
generative confidence crashes. In their preface to *Overcoming Barriers
to Student Understanding: Threshold Concepts and Troublesome Knowledge*, Jan H. F. Meyer and Ray Land describe the liminal, destabiliz-
ing space that divides the known from the unknown in academic
terrain. When students first encounter a "threshold concept" in a
discipline—for example, the idea of "otherness" in cultural studies
(xix)—they often experience an uncomfortable and disruptive sense
of being "stuck in between" as they struggle to reconcile their new
learning with their prior knowledge. At this stage, Meyer and Land
note, learners "oscillate between earlier, less sophisticated understandings, and [a] fuller appreciation of a concept" (xvi). Resolving
this confusion often marks a point of no return:

> A threshold concept can be considered as akin to a portal, opening
> up a new and previously inaccessible way of thinking about some-

thing. It represents a transformed way of understanding, or inter-preting, or viewing something without which the learner cannot progress. As a consequence of comprehending a threshold concept there may thus be a transformed internal view of subject matter, subject landscape, or even world view. (1)

Students who cross this threshold on their way to deeper learning experience a "transformation" that includes "a shift in the learner's identity" (xvi). The knowledge gained is often troublesome, that is to say, "conceptually difficult, counter-intuitive or 'alien' " (1)—and difficult to unlearn. Troublesome knowledge such as the postmodern skepticism of "truth" is indeed both unsettling and (ultimately) tenacious.

In writing, the notions of purpose and audience figure for many students as threshold concepts because they require acts of imagination that reshape how students perceive rhetorical situations. When I worked with younger students, I would often be hard pressed to get them to see books or essays as more than inanimate objects (especially if the authors had been dead a few centuries). Whereas they saw just the printed words on the page, I wanted them to see the living community of idiosyncratic writers, thinkers, and readers of which the text was merely a physical trace. Being able to imagine all the quirky, contentious, and historically situated individuals who are the audience of the text and what the writer wants these complicated human beings to do, think, or feel transforms students' understanding of written communication. Students who pass through this portal have an easier time later on seeing a literature review as a description of an argument among scholars.

Another threshold concept I try to help composition students understand is Charles Bazerman's idea of pseudo-boredom. According to Bazerman, pseudo-boredom is an emotional response to academic tasks that feel too new and difficult, whereas true boredom arises from tasks that are too familiar and easy (23). Because this notion assigns responsibility for academic engagement to the learner and not the text or task, it disarms students of a favorite defense: claiming that whatever they didn't read, write, or complete was just too boring. Pseudo-boredom can be a troublesome idea to understand because it not only makes students accountable for their own learning but also runs contrary to their sensory experiences; although they may feel tired, uninterested, and easily distracted, the high cognitive and linguistic demands of the task or text they're trying to engage actually suggest they are overstimulated, not underchallenged.

Accepting this troublesome knowledge can change how students see themselves as learners.

In my own courses, I've noticed an interesting trend: Students who report that they spend between four and five hours per week on homework say that the class is more difficult than those students who report spending between six and eight hours per week on homework. I suspect that the former group has somehow remained trapped at the threshold; the class still feels really hard to these students because they haven't yet fully contended with and reconciled the troublesome knowledge that presents the greatest barrier to their understanding.

In anticipation of this threshold trap, my coeditor Hetty Yelland has created a smart icebreaker for the first week of class. She distributes long sentence strips to her new students and asks them to write a piece of advice they would give themselves during the middle of the semester when they are most likely to feel stressed, exhausted, and overwhelmed by difficult material. The sentence strips are then displayed on the walls of the classroom or posted on the course website for the duration of the term, reminding students not to be deterred by those obstacles that are an inescapable part of the learning process.

Surviving the Confidence Crash

Admittedly, surviving a confidence crash and crossing the threshold of troublesome knowledge takes courage. Because growth depends on risk taking, helping students to face their fears and not be intimidated by challenging academic work can be an essential first step. Many anxious conversations during my office hours start with students saying, "I'm not sure I can do this." Some are worried about individual classes or assignments; others are worried about the whole college experience. While I eventually want my students to have that kind of confidence that translates into full ownership of their learning process—the "I've got this" confidence—I think there's an intermediary sort that's more the "I can take this" confidence. This is "fake it till you make it" at its best, the daring to embrace rigor before even experiencing success. Making that risk seem like a desirable enterprise is part of our charge as teachers.

Consider Alex, for instance. An 18-year-old, first-generation college student from a local agricultural community, Alex showed up on the first day of our developmental writing class ready to play. He had that "bring it on" expression. Although he had worked hard in high school and been mentored by excellent teachers, he wasn't quite writing at the college level yet. But he was close. And he was hungry. From day one, Alex wanted to know what he needed to do to get to the next level as quickly as possible without taking shortcuts. Driven, but not rushed. Alex would try anything, didn't take criticism personally, challenged my own thinking, and seemed amused when an assignment or text turned out to be harder than he anticipated. After a while, Alex's drive and fearlessness were infectious. I noticed other students became more willing to take risks and endure challenges after watching Alex's example.

While Alex was just one of those gifts teachers accept gratefully, I learned several things from his behavior. One thing that surprised me was that motivation doesn't have to be based on long-term goals. Another was that confidence doesn't have to come from mastery. Alex's confidence manifested itself through the intrinsic love of the plateau that aikido master George Leonard describes in the epigraph that opens this chapter (48–49).

Alex also reminded me of the quirky, almost counterintuitive connection that exists between rigor and persistence. Expressing what has become a standard view, human development scholar Arthur W. Chickering claims that "motivation is the key to persistence" (13). He explains, "The challenge is to help each person clarify his or her important purposes and then to find or create the combination of studies that is pertinent to those desired outcomes" (13). This is very often excellent advice. But there's another way to generate sustained attention that doesn't depend on first-year students knowing important purposes and desired outcomes that may be outside their experience. Many students who attend community colleges or who find themselves in developmental education classes may not be particularly motivated to complete their degrees. Some of our students enroll in college as the default alternative to getting a full-time job; moving out of their parents' home; receiving public assistance; or, in a few cases, returning to prison. In these situations, persistence can be the key to motivation.

Through the present-minded attention Alex gave to intellectual questions, he reminded me that rigor, joy, and persistence are part of the same feedback loop. While clear goals help, we've also noticed that students try harder and work longer when the activity is self-rewarding or generates what Mihaly Csikszentmihalyi calls "flow." In his view, the flow experience trumps outcomes as a motivator:

Concentration is so intense that there is no attention left over to think about anything irrelevant, or to worry about problems. Self-consciousness disappears, and the sense of time becomes distorted. An activity that produces such experiences is so gratifying that people are willing to do it for its own sake, with little concern for what they will get out of it, even when it is difficult, or dangerous. (71)

This absence of self-consciousness is exactly what we're after when we try to build students' confidence through increased rigor. Intellectual curiosity, we find, kills more than cats. It also kills nerves, self-doubt, and indifference. Engagement guru John Bean, for instance, notes how a "response to a significant and interesting problem or question" (197) counters "mechanistic" approaches to research papers that are "disturbingly unlike the motivated inquiry and analysis we value" (197). Thus, authentically rigorous assignments that entice students into taking intellectual risks despite their best defenses can be a surprising corrective for feelings of insecurity— and perfunctory academic performances.

> Through the present-minded attention Alex gave to intellectual questions, he reminded me that rigor, joy, and persistence are part of the same feedback loop. While clear goals help, we've also noticed that students try harder and work longer when the activity is self-rewarding.

The lessons in this chapter offer several ways to combine rigor with emotional support. For example, Lydia Graecyn's "Working the Workshop" tempers a candid approach to peer review with humor and personal anecdotes. Tina Sander similarly lightens a robust lesson on proofreading with self-reflection and a playful poem. Several other lessons also use this two-part approach to intellectual growth, demonstrating that "when students are sufficiently challenged, they give meaning to the work, produce new knowledge, and draw upon the Habits of Mind" (Costa and Kallick 6).

Bridging In-School and Out-of-School Identities

Helping students become comfortable with academic rigor and risk taking not only opens the door to independent learning later on but also encourages students to expand their self-concept to include both in-school and out-of-school identities. This is confidence as self-assurance.

There's a period of apprenticeship in any learning process when we inevitably feel like a bit of an impostor. We try on new personae that are not quite our size or style and worry that the artifice is obvious. First-year college students can find this feeling of not yet being the "real thing" particularly uncomfortable, especially if assuming an academic identity feels like an act of betrayal against their home culture. Some students, for instance, worry that attending college makes them a "schoolboy" or an undutiful daughter. When we honor students' prior experience and social roles, however, we help them see intellectual growth as an extension, not a replacement, of the identities and practices they've developed to meet other needs. "Understanding how meaning is made in school-based texts," Mary Schleppegrell reminds us, "does not require that students change the ways they interact and use language in other contexts" (41).

> When we honor students' prior experience and social roles, however, we help them see intellectual growth as an extension, not a replacement, of the identities and practices they've developed to meet other needs.

Jennifer McGuire, an English instructor from Cabrillo College, demonstrates how to value and extend students' identities in her lesson "A Different You." In this activity, McGuire first asks students to write a description of a special talent they possess. She next directs the students to exchange papers anonymously so they can experience how others perceive this ability. Lastly, she asks the class, "If you were to change something about yourself, how would it change your life?" She invites students to imagine how being "a different you" would impact both their self-perception and their treatment by others, thereby fostering a safe and creative exploration of identity development.

McGuire's approach encourages both openness and flexibility in her students—two habits of mind critical for surmounting the intermediate plateau. Openness includes "a willingness to consider new ways of being and thinking in the world" (CWPA, NCTE, and NWP 4), while flexibility includes a recognition that the moves we make as writers, including our choice of ethos, depend on changing contexts, audiences, and purposes (CWPA, NCTE, and NWP 5). Her approach likewise helps students see, as Jerome Bruner argues, that "the lives and Selves we construct are the outcomes of [a] process of meaning-construction" (138).

Constructing an open and flexible self-concept can ultimately lead to enhanced self-efficacy. Researchers note some important differences between these two terms. Whereas *self-efficacy* is "a context-related judgment of personal ability" (Zimmerman 218), *self-concept* encompasses a much wider range of feelings and ideas about the self, including degree of confidence. Self-efficacy, in other words, is a task-based sense of control whereas self-concept is a more global sense of being. We can think of this as the difference between knowing how to write a research paper (or trusting that we can figure it out) and feeling like a good English student. And although some scholars have given more attention to self-efficacy than to self-concept because of the former's greater predictive abilities (Zimmerman 218–19), we believe that who we are as learners matters greatly. Our identities can not only shape how others perceive our words but also determine which conversations we're willing to join.

From social cognitive theory, we've also learned about the powerful influence of social relationships on learning. This idea is especially important when we think about how we model and mentor academic behaviors. If, as Paul R. Pintrich and Dale H. Schunk assert, "people acquire knowledge, rules, skills, strategies, beliefs, and emotions by observing others" (143), then our work as exemplars and guides is essential for revealing the "hidden curriculum" to students. Disclosing our own (often fretful) processes for reading, writing, studying, and time management can be a form of encouragement. For example, Adela Najarro, English department chair at Cabrillo College, begins her lesson on academic essay structures by telling her students about her own "failures" as a first-generation college student. In this way, she offers her students the support of someone who has "been there" instead of mystifying intellectual labor by concealing its mess. Modeling our own confidence and optimism as learners, research suggests, can have a positive impact on our students' self-efficacy—even when we model how to fail gracefully (Pintrich and Schunk 159).

Having the confidence to engage new social worlds and embody new social roles is a key part of intellectual growth. When students feel respected for who they are and supported in who they might become, they are more open to "learning [that] has the potential to make and remake selves, identities, and relationships" (Moje and Lewis 18).

Creating a Feedback Loop

Confidence can also take the form of resolve. When we say, "I am confident I can get the job done," we mean we are absolutely determined to finish the work, come hell or high water. At the arduous midpoint of an instructional cycle, this type of confidence expresses itself as willingness to accept and apply constructive feedback. It's an openness to troubleshooting, to fixing whatever's not working— and for that attitude to develop, students need formative assessments of their progress. As John Hattie notes in his research on student achievement, "The greater the challenge, the higher the probability that one seeks and needs feedback" (24).

> At the arduous midpoint of an instructional cycle, this type of confidence expresses itself as willingness to accept and apply constructive feedback.

Distinct in purpose from both diagnostic and summative assessment, formative assessment can be thought of as an interactive process that offers teachers and students a "pulse check" on learning; it's a "live" feedback loop, a progress measure, a guide for future actions. Above all, formative assessment is an opportunity for intervention when students encounter bumps in the path of progress. Scholars generally agree on the following purposes of formative assessment (Marzano, Pickering, and Pollock 96–99; Nicol 336–39; Popham 5–7):

- To clarify expectations
- To gather data that can inform instruction
- To increase student motivation, metacognition, and self-regulation
- To provide corrective feedback to students

These goals highlight formative assessment's constructivist approach. Because formative assessment largely occurs during the middle of the instructional cycle, it measures students' developing, procedural knowledge in action while contributing to their learning and agency. In other words, formative assessments help to construct—or form—students' skills, knowledge, and dispositions as they progress toward a summative assessment. When students pause during a reading assignment, for example, to reflect on the strategies they used to make sense of difficult sections of the text, they practice a form of metacognition that gives them greater control over their

own learning. Any time we help
students examine their thinking
and writing processes, reflect on
the texts they read and create,
and transfer their learning from
one task to the next, we encourage their metacognitive abili-

> Formative assessment is hence a
> way to coach students to higher
> levels of achievement as they
> build their capacity to learn
> independently.

ties (CWPA, NCTE, and NWP 5)—and we help them develop the
resolve to keep learning.

Formative assessment is hence a way to coach students to higher
levels of achievement as they build their capacity to learn independently.
The interventions that follow a formative assessment encourage students
to push beyond a superficial understanding of the content or basic proficiency of a skill to increasingly sophisticated levels of mastery. As Leslie
K. Maniotes observes in "Teaching in the Zone: Formative Assessments
for Critical Thinking," "Deep processing fosters higher order thinking
that requires intervention at critical points in the learning process" (37).
This might mean coaching a student through a draft of an essay or a
speech, providing redirection and modeling as needed, as Tina Sander
from Cabrillo College does in her "Proofreading: How Can We Polish
Our Essays When Our Brains and Computers Have Such Limitations?"
activity in this chapter. Or it could mean guiding students through a
deeper reading of a text, as Olga Blomgren from Hartnell College does
in her exemplar ("Group Projects: Turning Students into Teachers") in
chapter 5. The ultimate goal is internalized, automatic, and expressive
learning—and that requires ongoing mentoring.

Specific formative assessments can be intentional (i.e., planned)
or incidental ("on the fly"). Both are useful. Demonstrations, reflective journals, self-evaluations, presentations, observations, interviews,
exit slips, quizzes, and surveys (Shepard 99–101) are among the many
types of formative assessments teachers can use to give customized
feedback to students about their strengths and needs. "Fuzzy/Clear"
cards is one of our favorites: at the end of a lesson, students write
something they now understand on the "Clear" side of an index card
and something that still confuses them on the "Fuzzy" side. Many
other learning activities that might take place during instruction have
formative potential, as well, provided that they are later used to guide
instruction. For instance, if a teacher observes during a class discussion that a majority of students tend to make sweeping generalizations or unsupported claims, she might modify the next day's lesson
to include a review of critical reasoning. The point is that teachers

and students need to do something with the information they gain from the formative assessment—whether that assessment is a formal test or a casual conversation.

In his end-of-semester reflective essay, for instance, Alex wrote, "When I was faced with a barrier in regard to my writing, I knew I could count on my instructor's feedback. From her feedback, it seems my deficiency was in my transitions and a few run-ons and sentence fragments. Therefore, I knew what I had to strengthen." For Alex, being confident as a learner included the fortitude to accept and apply feedback.

Challenges

Our challenge as teachers of students who are transitioning to college is not only to balance rigor with support but also to find creative ways *to use rigor as a means of support*. Building students' confidence during the messy middle of the instructional cycle really means building their pleasure in the endeavor itself. By focusing on habits of mind, we liberate learning from the stick-and-carrot approach that compensates for the difficulty of academic labor with extrinsic rewards and long-term goals. Instead, we embrace the plateau—that place where students engage authentic problems and questions, using "ways of approaching learning that are both intellectual and practical" (CWPA, NCTE, and NWP 1). We embrace exploration, challenge, adaptability, consistency, and self-reflection. We embrace learning in medias res, when all its procedural functions and structures are fully visible. And we understand that persistence, flexibility, and metacognition emerge not from a tolerance but from an eagerness for rigor.

> Persistence, flexibility, and metacognition emerge not from a tolerance but from an eagerness for rigor.

Providing support via rigor requires courage on the part of teachers. We commit to providing access to demanding curricula regardless of our students' preparation levels, we make instructional room for identity work and habits of mind, and we provide strategic and timely feedback to students so that they know where they are and where they're going. We also make ourselves vulnerable as learners, sharing not only our own intellectual passions but also our struggles. Mindful of the delicate balance of agency we seek, we take our soundings carefully. If we increase the cognitive load too soon, students can shut down—too late, and students don't progress toward independence. But when we strike the balance just right, we help students find that confident spirit of adventure that will ultimately help them continue their journeys on their own.

Notes

1. See Gerald Graff's *Clueless in Academe* for a rich discussion of the way higher education disorients those it seeks to initiate.
2. The Common Core State Standards for College and Career Readiness similarly note the importance of creating "a staircase of increasing text complexity, so that students are expected to both develop their skills and apply them to more and more complex texts" (NGA & CCSSO; see Fact Versus Myth).

Works Cited

Aristotle. *Nicomachean Ethics*. Trans. Terence Irwin. Indianapolis: Hackett, 1999. Print.

Bazerman, Charles. *The Informed Writer: Using Sources in the Disciplines.* 5th ed. Boston: Houghton Mifflin, 1995. Print.

Bean, John C. *Engaging Ideas: The Professor's Guide to Integrating Writing, Critical Thinking, and Active Learning in the Classroom.* San Francisco: Jossey-Bass, 2001. Print.

Bruner, Jerome. *Acts of Meaning.* Cambridge, MA: Harvard UP, 1990. Print.

Chickering, Arthur W. "Every Student Can Learn—If." *About Campus* 11.2 (2006): 9–15. Print.

Costa, Arthur L., and Bena Kallick. *Habits of Mind across the Curriculum: Practical and Creative Strategies for Teachers.* Alexandria: Association for Supervision and Curriculum Development (ASCD), 2009. Print.

Csikszentmihalyi, Mihaly. *Flow: The Psychology of Optimal Experience.* New York: HarperCollins, 1990. Print.

CWPA, NCTE, and NWP (Council of Writing Program Administrators, National Council of Teachers of English, and National Writing Project). *Framework for Success in Postsecondary Writing.* Berkeley: National Writing Project, 2011. Print.

Engell, Jennifer. "Postsecondary Access and Success for First-Generation College Students." *American Academic* 3.1 (2007): 25–48. American Federation of Teachers.

Gee, James Paul. *Social Linguistics and Literacies: Ideology in Discourses.* London: Taylor & Francis, 1996. Print.

Gladwell, Malcolm. *Outliers: The Story of Success.* New York: Little, Brown, and Co., 2008. Print.

Graff, Gerald. *Clueless in Academe: How Schooling Obscures the Life of the Mind.* New Haven: Yale UP, 2003. Print.

Hattie, John. *Visible Learning: A Synthesis of Over 800 Meta-analyses Relating to Achievement.* London: Taylor & Francis, 2009. Print.

Leonard, George. *Mastery: The Keys to Success and Long-Term Fulfillment.* New York: Penguin Books, 1992. Print.

Maniotes, Leslie K. "Teaching in the Zone: Formative Assessments for Critical Thinking." *Library Media Connection* 29.1 (2010): 36–39. Print.

Mapes, Aimee C. "You Need to Realize It in Yourself: Positioning, Improvisation, and Literacy." *Journal of Adolescent & Adult Literacy* 54.7 (2011): 515–24. Print.

Marzano, Robert J., Debra Pickering, and Jane E. Pollock. *Classroom Instruction That Works: Research-Based Strategies for Increasing Student Achievement.* Alexandria: Association for Supervision and Curriculum Development, 2001. Print.

Meyer, Jan H. F., and Ray Land. *Overcoming Barriers to Student Understanding: Threshold Concepts and Troublesome Knowledge.* New York: Routledge, 2012. Print.

Moje, Elizabeth Birr, and Cynthia Lewis. "Examining Opportunities to Learn Literacy: The Role of Critical Sociocultural Literacy Research." *Reframing Sociocultural Research on Literacy: Identity, Agency, and Power.* Ed. Cynthia Lewis, Patricia Enciso, and Elizabeth Birr Moje. Mahwah: Lawrence Erlbaum Associates, 2007. 15–48. Print.

NGA & CCSSO (National Governors Association Center for Best Practices and the Council of Chief State School Officers). Common Core State Standards for English Language Arts & Literacy in History/Social Studies, Science, and Technical Subjects. Washington, DC: NGA & CCSSO, 2010. Web. <www.corestandards.org/read-the-standards>

Nicol, David. "Assessment for Learner Self-Regulation: Enhancing Achievement in the First Year Using Learning Technologies." *Assessment & Evaluation in Higher Education* 34.3 (2009): 335–52. Print.

Pintrich, Paul R., and Dale H. Schunk. *Motivation in Education: Theory, Research, and Applications.* 2nd ed. Upper Saddle River: Merrill Prentice Hall, 2002. Print.

Popham, W. James. *Transformative Assessment.* Alexandria: ASCD, 2008. Print.

Scarcella, Robin C. *Accelerating Academic English: A Focus on the English Learner.* Oakland: Regents of the University of California, 2003. Print.

Schleppegrell, Mary J. *The Language of Schooling: A Functional Language Perspective.* Mahwah: Lawrence Erlbaum Associates, 2004. Print.

Shepard, Lorrie A. "The Role of Assessment in a Learning Culture." *Educational Researcher* 29.7 (2000): 4–14. Print.

Unrau, Norman. *Content Area Reading and Writing: Fostering Literacies in Middle and High School Cultures.* 2nd ed. Upper Saddle River: Pearson, 2008. Print.

Zimmerman, Barry J. "Self-Efficacy and Educational Development." *Self-Efficacy in Changing Societies.* Ed. Albert Bandura. Cambridge, UK: Cambridge, 1997. 202–231. Print.

Boredom Busters by Jennifer Fletcher

Activity: analysis of the concept of "boring"

Learning Outcomes: understand the special demands of academic reading, develop metacognitive or "self-awareness" strategies for monitoring comprehension, and explore "fix-up" strategies to help with boredom or confusion

Habits of Mind: persistence and metacognition

"The essence of boredom is to be found in the obsessive search for novelty. Satisfaction lies in mindful repetition, the discovery of endless richness in subtle variations on familiar themes."

—George Leonard (83)

I have great faith in writers. And so I tend to trust that what they have to say is important—that even if I'm at first bored or resistant as a reader, there is still valuable meaning to be had. Knowing firsthand the struggle of finding just the right word or phrase to express a thought, I also tend to believe that the writers I read have already labored extensively over their craft before their texts ever fall into my hands—and that their effort obligates me to work hard at making meaning, too.

However, for many students in my classes, the struggle to comprehend a challenging text often results in disengagement, not increased effort. Academic reading can trigger an understandable defense mechanism in students; they can avoid the discomfort of some difficult tasks by calling the work "boring." This is a special kind of boredom. Unlike the boredom we associate with repetitive or simplistic tasks—think assembly line work here—academic boredom results from cognitive overload rather than lack of stimulation. The brain has too much to deal with, rather than too little, and so it shuts down, says, "Thank you, but I've already had my fill today," and defends the student against further stress by allowing him or her to "tune out" for the class. Academic boredom, or what composition scholar Charles Bazerman calls pseudo-boredom, is thus a type of guard dog against feelings of confusion and insecurity.

I've seen this happen in my own classes more times than I like to admit. I distribute a reading to a class that I consider absolutely fascinating—say, an excerpt from Edward Said's *Orientalism* or some passages from Thoreau's *Walden*—and the students make a good-faith effort to dutifully read what I've assigned for about five minutes.

Then it starts: the shifting, the sighs, the slumping, the cell phones. *I* know that what I've distributed is life-changing, electrifying material that should rivet my students' attention to the page. *They* look like they've been in line at the DMV for days—exhausted, resigned . . . broken. This is not the face of engagement.

Yet I also know that this is boredom with a difference. Reading *Walden* is not the same as standing in line at the DMV, reading *Orientalism* is nothing like capping bottles in a factory (although students may at first experience similar reactions). As Bazerman explains, "Genuine boredom occurs when you are reading material you already know only too well. . . . Pseudo-boredom comes when you feel you just cannot be bothered to figure out what all the new information and ideas mean" (22–23). Scholars from The Boredom Research Group (real name) offer a more technical distinction: Whereas the academic boredom associated with overchallenging situations can produce complex feelings of anger, anxiety, hopelessness, and shame in some students, the boredom induced by underchallenging tasks simply results in low levels of enjoyment (Acee et al. 25). Students can thus mean many different things when they say, "I'm bored" (Acee et al. 26).

My job as an instructor is to alert my students to these situational differences in meaning. One of the ways I've tried to help my students distinguish between real boredom and "fake" (i.e., academic) boredom is through a metacognitive approach to academic reading that asks students to notice when they're feeling tired, disengaged, confused, frustrated, and disinterested, and then to apply a "fix-up" strategy to deal with the source of boredom. In other words, I try to train students to develop their "radar" for situations that might trigger defensive boredom. The goal of this approach is improved self-awareness, persistence, and personal responsibility.

metacognition and self-management

We begin by completing an anticipation guide, or survey, that asks students to agree or disagree with various statements related to academic reading and boredom (see the appendix at the end of this lesson exemplar). For example, "It's not fun to do something until you're good at it" or "The best way to handle confusion is to just keep reading." I usually follow this with a whole-class discussion and freewrite on the most divisive statements. Statements on how to handle distractions tend to draw the biggest reactions ("Ignore them!"; "Be disciplined!"; "Take a break!"). Because I'm asking my students to consider an attitude change—somewhat of a risky and presumptuous venture—I ensure that they have sufficient time and support to explore their feelings. Next, we discuss the special features of academic reading that can induce pseudo-boredom—such as assumed background knowledge, dense information, and academic English (Schleppegrell 16–17)—and compare academic texts to materials they might read for pleasure. The important point for students to understand is that academic boredom is a response to tasks that feel too hard, not too easy.

I then share with them the following "Top 10 List of Things Students Really Mean When They Say, 'I'm Bored'":

10. I don't want to work this hard.
9. I'm confused.
8. I don't have a purpose for reading.
7. I've never done this before.
6. I don't have any questions I want answered.
5. I'm tired or hungry.
4. I'm preoccupied with something else.
3. I don't feel like I'm very good at this.
2. I don't see the connections between this activity and future learning or work.
1. I have another agenda.

Although this list is mostly a conversation starter based on what I think students mean by "boring," the general idea of multiple meanings of boredom is research based (Acee et al. 2011; Pekrun et al., 2010). To introduce the idea that students have some control over their responses to texts, I ask them to talk with a partner about one counterstrategy they could use for one of these causes of "boredom." For example, pairs might brainstorm ways to generate questions or make predictions for number six or might discuss sources of support and clarification for number two. After participating in this activity, one student wrote, "It's almost as if my mind wants to distract me." Some of her "boredom busters" included stretching for 10 minutes, drinking a full glass of water, or even swimming laps when stressed or preoccupied.

self-efficacy

We then discuss strategies for making difficult reading assignments active and engaging. In particular, we focus on self-monitoring and "fix-up" strategies to improve students' comprehension while also reflecting on how, where, and when they read can affect what they understand. I ask students to generate their own list of "What Good Readers Do." We then match their responses to the research findings using the following behaviors of effective readers as identified by Nell K. Duke and P. David Pearson:

- Good readers are active readers.
- Good readers have clear goals in mind for their reading.
- Good readers typically look over the text before they read.
- Good readers read selectively, deciding what to read carefully, what to read quickly, what not to read, what to reread, and so on.
- Good readers monitor their understanding of the text, making adjustments in their reading as necessary.
- Good readers read different kinds of text differently. (107)

Although the first three items on this list are familiar to many students (and often match the students' responses), the last three tend to elicit some surprise. "What do you mean we can read selectively?" students will ask. "Don't we have to complete the assignment?" This gives us a great chance to talk about how having clear goals—one of the best boredom busters—allows readers to make adjustments and read different kinds of texts differently because they know what they're supposed to be getting out of the experience and when the job is done.

Finally, we try the strategies in practice. Now is a good time for me to trot out *Walden* or *Orientalism* again to see if the strategies and increased awareness of defensive boredom make a difference. First, I distribute water and trail mix to combat pseudo-boredom attributable to fatigue or hunger. Second, I ask students to do the following while they read: (a) identify passages in the text that cause confusion; (b) keep your place with a pencil or note card; and (c) stop reading when you become confused and use one of the following fix-up strategies:[1]

flexibility and reflection

intellectual stamina

- Survey the text again.
- Reread.
- Write about your confusion/questions.
- Talk to a friend and/or your teacher.
- Take a walk or eat a snack.
- Check your predictions.
- Read the introduction or preface to find a purpose for reading.

A word of caution: I've learned that increased awareness of effective reading strategies sometimes does not lead to improved practice. Knowing, in other words, is not the same as doing. And to be fair, I am often not the best teacher I know how to be. I do believe, however, that this kind of awareness can put a voice in a reader's head that speaks against complacency.

reflection

We conclude the lesson by reflecting on the difference that active reading can make in our experience of difficult texts. When Thoreau describes reading as "a noble intellectual exercise" that requires us to "stand on tip-toe" and "devote our most alert and wakeful hours to" (94), I want my students to know exactly what he means. These activities help students see that meaning-making is not shouldered by writers alone; readers, too, have to work hard to create tip-toe standing literacy experiences, especially with academic texts. As Bazerman says, "The cure for real boredom is to find a more advanced book on the subject; the only cure for pseudo-boredom is to become fully and personally involved in the book already in front of you" (23).

Quick Start Guide

1. Explain to your students the differences between pseudo-boredom (a response to tasks that feel too hard) and genuine boredom (a response to tasks that are too easy).
2. Ask students to complete the "Boredom Busters" Anticipation/ Reaction Guide.
3. Facilitate a class discussion on the "Top 10 List of Things Students Really Mean When They Say, 'I'm Bored.'"
4. Identify "fix-up" strategies for each cause of pseudo-boredom.
5. Instruct students to read a challenging academic text independently. Ask students to note how their use of active reading strategies and increased awareness of defensive boredom make a difference in their reading experience.

Note

1. See Chris Tovani's *I Read It, but I Don't Get It: Comprehension Strategies for Adolescent Readers* for excellent suggestions for fix-up strategies.

Works Cited

Acee, Taylor W., et al. "Academic Boredom in Under- and Over-Challenging Situations." *Contemporary Educational Psychology*. 35.1 (2010):17–27. Print.

Bazerman, Charles. *The Informed Writer: Using Sources in the Disciplines*. 5th ed. Boston: Houghton Mifflin, 1995. Print.

Duke, Nell K., and P. David Pearson. "Effective Practices for Developing Reading Comprehension." *Journal of Education* 189.1–2 (2008): 107–213. Print.

Leonard, George. *Mastery: The Keys to Success and Long-Term Fulfillment*. New York: Penguin Books, 1992. Print.

Pekrun, Reinhard, et al. "Boredom in Achievement Settings: Exploring Control-Value Antecedents and Performance Outcomes of a Neglected Emotion." *Journal of Educational Psychology* 102.3 (2010): 531–549. Print

Said, Edward W. *Orientalism*. New York: Vintage, 1979. Print.

Schleppegrell, Mary J. *The Language of Schooling: A Functional Linguistics Perspective*. Mahwah: Lawrence Erlbaum Associates, 2004. Print.

Thoreau, Henry David. *Walden*. 1854. New York: The Modern Library, 1937. Print.

Tovani, Chris. *I Read It, but I Don't Get It: Comprehension Strategies for Adolescent Readers*. Portland: Stenhouse, 2000. Print.

Appendix 4.A: "Boredom Busters" Anticipation/ Reaction Guide

Directions: Read each statement. Then, in the first space, write a plus sign if you agree with the statement, a minus sign if you disagree, or a question mark if you are unsure about your opinion. For many statements there are no right answers. At the end of the term, you can indicate your reactions in the second space.

Agree = +   Disagree = −   Don't know = ?

1. _____ _____ The best way to handle confusion is to just keep reading.
2. _____ _____ It's best to completely ignore personal problems when studying.
3. _____ _____ Having surgery is less stressful than essay tests.
4. _____ _____ Students who are strong in math are usually poor writers.
5. _____ _____ Great writers are born, not made.
6. _____ _____ It's easier to write academic essays if you warm up by reading.
7. _____ _____ I do my best work late at night.
8. _____ _____ I do my best work early in the morning.

9. _____ _____ I often feel sleepy when I try to read academic texts.

10. _____ _____ Reading textbooks is boring.

11. _____ _____ I enjoy writing short stories or autobiographical incidents.

12. _____ _____ Reading literature is boring.

13. _____ _____ It is difficult for me to find time for pleasure reading.

14. _____ _____ Most careers require critical reading and writing skills.

15. _____ _____ Daily writing produces better results than "binge" writing.

16. _____ _____ I consider myself a skilled and competent writer.

17. _____ _____ I find it hard to concentrate when I write essays at home.

18. _____ _____ It's not fun to do something until you're good at it.

19. _____ _____ I enjoy writing poetry or song lyrics.

20. _____ _____ Writing essays takes too much time.

A Different You by Jennifer McGuire

Activity: writing an identity essay that expands students' capacity for empathy

Learning Outcomes: write an essay that expands self-awareness and compassion while demonstrating sustained clarity of intention, awareness of audience, and various writing techniques

Habits of Mind: metacognition, openness, and mindfulness

It's amazing to me how students gain perspective of themselves and the world around them by examining their connections and prejudices toward words. Through a close examination of words, I have students write an identity essay that expands their compassion toward themselves and others. One of the best parts of doing this exercise with students is being able to see them see themselves. It gives them a kind of ownership and responsibility with their communication. It doesn't just make them mindful about words; it makes them mindful and open to what words actually mean.

Having grown up with a grandpa who was paraplegic, I never thought twice about someone needing a wheelchair to get around. My sister and I "rock-paper-scissored" over who got to wheel him around and who got to sit on his lap. He taught bowling to mentally challenged adults, was an English tutor to ESL students, participated in the Paralyzed Veterans of America games (discus and shot put), and loved to travel. Members of the American Wheelchair Bowling Association came from all over for his funeral—at the bowling alley. Yeah, he was that kind of guy. Anything he wanted to do, anywhere he wanted to go, I just assumed he would.

It wasn't until years later, when a friend of mine said, "If I lost a limb, I wouldn't want to live," that I had a glimpse into how others might see a physical disability. To me, wheeling around in the wheelchair was the height of fun. My goal was to be able to pop a standing wheelie like Grandpa and so many of his friends were able to do; I got blisters on my hands and bumps on my head from the ground, but that was all I earned for my efforts. I knew I had use of my legs, and playing wasn't the same thing as permanent change, but I never thought of living without limbs as traumatic. The only things I saw as traumatic were the accidents that led so many people into wheelchairs. I never once thought of a person who had lost a limb or who was paraplegic living a life that was less than anyone else's. I never associated not having the use of a limb as anything that really made a person, or his or her abilities, different.

The term *disability* is a bit of a misnomer. The term *handicapped* came and went and has various negative connotations. When it comes down to it, ability varies from one person to the next. I have friends who have all sorts of different abilities. Some abilities are beneficial, and some make it difficult to get around. My sister can swim like a fish, Grandpa could swim like a madman, and I sink like a stone. Does that mean I'm disabled? Certainly differently abled. *Physically challenged* is another confusing term, as is *mentally challenged*. Again, this is subjective. Aren't we all challenged with certain things? Sure, there are medical definitions, but the terms we use—such as *disabled, handicapped, challenged*—take on their own connotations past medical terminology. What do you call your abilities? Considering that everyone is not able to do everything, we are all in some way disabled. Each of us has extraordinary abilities as well. I let students know that openness this assignment is our chance to change our perspectives.

I tell students that we're going to look at ourselves. First, we will look at what we can do, maybe even something we are proud of. Then, we will look at what we cannot do. Finally, we will look at what we could and could not do if our bodies or our minds were other than what they are. I tell students to let themselves take in the world around them with new eyes.

Assignment

Students are to describe an ability that they are proud of, something that they are able to do mentally, emotionally, or physically. Maybe a student has won the high jump in track or can put both legs behind his head. Maybe he can remember all the states and their capitals in reverse alphabetical order. Maybe a student is the kindest person she knows or loves her family to the point where she feels she is going to bust. I ask students to write at least a few solid paragraphs about their ability.

After the students have written their descriptions, their papers are collected and then passed around anonymously. Each student writes a response to the person whose paper he or she has received. You can give them prompts like the following: What kind of person do you imagine him or her to be? What does the person look like? What is the person's personality like? How would you define or describe the person? Can you tell any limits of abilities? Once students are done imagination writing their responses, they seek out the writer. Look around the and empathy room. Whom do you think those abilities belong to?

The next step is for the students to do this assignment describing what they cannot do. Again, after students have written their descriptions and the papers have been collected, they are randomly passed out to the class. Each student writes a response and tries to guess whom those limitations belong to. I ask, "Is how we see ourselves the same as how others see us?"

The final step is for the students to consider how making a change in themselves would affect them and those around them. I ask the students, "If you were to change something about yourself, how would it change your life? Imagine if your sight changed, your hearing, or your mobility. How would you see yourself, and how might others treat you?" The responses to each of these questions can generate a good two or three solid paragraphs of description and reflection.   reflection

These parts and paragraphs make up one assignment/lesson but can be broken down into several days. At the end of this assignment, we link the paragraphs into a cohesive and full essay.

Student Response

I haven't yet run into a student who isn't interested in at least one of the sections of this assignment. Some like to talk about what they do well, some can see their limitations more than anything, while others wish they could be other than what they are. It creates a great dynamic in the class by fostering a safe place to explore and share each other's perspectives.

One of my favorite tangent essays resulting from this assignment was a student's request to be a bird. Although it didn't conform with the type of change I was asking students to envision in the last part of the assignment, the student took a leap I hadn't anticipated, making the difference a spiritual one, rather than a physical, emotional, or mental one. He wanted to get out of the human mind-set, which he found restrictive.

Successes and Challenges

This lesson can be done with all levels of English classes. It also allows students to be mindful of others around them as well as themselves. However, some students may find it challenging to find positive abilities or aspects of themselves or their lives. The flip side of this is that difficulty allows the teacher to recognize how those challenges present themselves in the students' writings, and how they see their ability as a writer or communicator.

Quick Start Guide

1. Begin with a group exploration of what people do well.
2. Have students write what they do well.
3. Collect the writings and then randomly pass them out. Have students respond to the writer's strength.
4. Follow the same pattern for exploring and writing about what people do not do well and the types of changes for which people hope.

Working the Workshop by Lydia Graecyn

Activity: peer review

Learning Outcomes: develop personal responsibility, self-management skills, and self-awareness through the examination of peer essays for clear analysis and sound logic

Habits of Mind: persistence, openness, and metacognition

Most of us have been taught that we must choose between politeness and honesty. Teaching English at Cabrillo College, I find that during peer workshop students often feel hesitant to give useful, real feedback because they do not want to hurt anyone's feelings or, worse, have other students think of them as mean and rude.

I find peer workshops an invaluable teaching resource, once I can convince students to participate fully and honestly. Before our first workshop, I tell them a story. After I greet the class and hear a bit about their weekend, I tell them how happy I felt to get to see my good friend Lucy for lunch. I begin this minilecture just as a conversation:

"Lucy and I are both very busy people: working single moms with classes or big art projects always in the works. I treasure the rare opportunities we have to get together and share the adventures of our full lives. We ate at a local vegetarian spot called The Saturn Café. She had a veggie burger. I had a spinach salad. After the meal we hugged good-bye, and I felt so happy that I was all smiles while running my next errands. I went to the bank and even flirted with the teller. I bought groceries while beaming at everyone.

"I put my groceries in my car, and while looking in the rearview mirror to back up, I noticed a giant piece of ugly, slimy, green spinach stuck to my front tooth! I was horrified. None of the people I had smiled and joked with had said a word about it. The server at the restaurant didn't say anything when I paid the check. The handsome bank teller, the sweet grocery clerk, the old lady I helped pick out tomatoes, none of them wanted to tell me the truth that obviously stood out to them. Most disappointing, my dear friend Lucy didn't even clue me in. I would have appreciated the opportunity to remove that spinach and save myself some embarrassment. Class, raise your hand if you would want someone to tell you if you had something stuck in your teeth."

Usually every student will raise his or her hand. Then we discuss gentle ways to inform others about something in their teeth, hair, or nose; on their clothes; or even in their essay.

Now that we agree that we would all like to know, I expand the comparison between spinach in our teeth and places in our essays where we need improvement. I explain that we are all going to behave as good friends and classmates and *gently* raise each other's awareness. Our shared understanding that we indeed do want honest feedback and that we intend to give feedback kindly helps students to open up to the workshop process, encouraging another habit of mind.

I give students a workshop worksheet that helps to direct them and encourages them to stay on task. At the end of this lesson exemplar, you can find a sample to use as a starting point in creating a worksheet that will work for you and your students. I usually customize worksheets with relevant specifics for each essay prompt (depending on the learning objectives of the assignment) that complement the grading rubric. In class students exchange papers, and I ask them to first read their peer's essay all the way through once. On a second reading, they begin to respond to questions and tasks on the worksheet. The reader completes the worksheet and gives it to the author. The author reviews it, thanks the reader, and tells the reader which part of the feedback the author finds most useful. Through this process, the students develop metacognition as they increase their understanding of their own learning process, their strengths, and the areas

metacognition that need improvement. (I also often follow up the in-class workshop with a self-evaluation worksheet that reinforces the metacognition aspect. A sample is provided at the end of this exemplar.)

I know this lesson works for students when I hear them say things to each other such as "Thanks for pointing out that piece of lettuce!" or "I'm glad this essay didn't smile at the teacher yet."

Sometimes, however, a student will tell me that she feels disappointed with the workshop. "I put a lot of effort into providing thoughtful, useful feedback, but I didn't get any helpful comments." To this student I explain that she is doing good work developing her critical eye. When we read our own work, we often see what we intended to create rather than what is actually there on the page. Sometimes we find it easier to see errors, typos, faulty organization, paragraphs that need more development, and awkward sentence structure in the work of others. She will be able to apply to her own work what she learns from evaluating others' essays. I ask her to begin

spirit of transfer now. Looking at the workshop worksheet questions, does she see any area in particular where she would like feedback? I then work with both her and her reader to help direct the reader where to focus.

In addition to improving student papers, workshops develop the habit of mind of persistence. Successful students are able to keep working on a project and not give up when challenges arise. "Working the Workshop" supports students as it reinforces that, as writers, we all share the same struggles. Students gain a greater understanding and appreciation that writing is a process. They practice giving and receiving criticism, learning that politeness and honesty are not mutually exclusive. In fact, politeness and honesty can enhance each other's effectiveness as well as the effectiveness of writing workshops and the resulting essays.

persistence

Quick Start Guide

1. Before class, develop a workshop worksheet for students (see the sample on page 154).
2. Think of an anecdote, or use the one I provided, and share with students to illustrate how we all value and appreciate honesty when it can spare us from mistakes and embarrassment.
3. Explain that workshops serve two important purposes: receiving feedback and developing a critical eye.
4. Instruct the students to exchange papers and complete the worksheet.

Essay #1 Workshop Worksheet

MLA Format: Check format and circle any errors and questions for the author. Does it meet the length requirement?

MLA Works Cited: Double spaced throughout? Alphabetical order? Complete entries? Use your MLA book for help!

MLA In-Text: Does the author need more documentation? Does the in-text citation correctly correspond to the Works Cited entry?

Introduction: Which one of the six introductions does the author use? Suggestions?

Strong Thesis: Write the thesis here. How can the author make it more specific, clear, and/or arguable?

Paragraphs: Put an *S* next to the central statement of each paragraph.

Specific Examples and Evidence: Do they support the paragraph's central statement? Mark in the text where more description would help the reader.

Sentence Construction: Do not make corrections. You can circle or underline areas that lack clarity.

Refutation: Does the refutation address your objections or objections you thought of while reading? If not, what other reader concerns should the writer consider? Does the writer's response seem reasonable, logical, and in support of the reader? Write the objection and the reply here.

Word: Mark any words that distract the reader, wrong words, or imprecise words. Write suggestions here.

Conclusion: Does it sum up everything? Which one of the five conclusions does the author use? Suggestions.

Careful Proofreading: A second pair of eyes helps. Gently mark any errors or questions.

Essay #1 Self-Evaluation (Option A)

1. I chose my essay #1 title because . . .

2. On a scale of 1 to 10 with 1 representing least arguable and 10 most arguable, I give my thesis a _____ because . . .

3. I feel happy/proud/disappointed/concerned/confused/excited about my introduction because . . .

4. Someone would want to read my essay because . . . (How can your reader benefit? What will he or she find valuable?)

5. I found _____ the most interesting thing I learned. I did not know it before and . . .

6. Out of the body paragraphs, #_____ supports my thesis best because . . .

7. I did or did not include a refutation because . . .

8. Out of the five conclusions on The Meal of an Essay handout, I chose _____ because . . .

9. In essay #1, I feel most proud of . . .

10. For the next essay I want to . . .

11. Optional:
    I would appreciate your comments on this particular, specific area of my essay:

I would like help with . . .
I want you to notice . . .

Essay #1 Self-Evaluation (Option B)

Please use complete sentences and careful consideration to create insightful answers to each of the following questions. You may hand write on this sheet, type, or create a new document. Keep your work clearly readable.

1. What part of your finished essay do you like best? Explain why.

2. What part of the essay writing process did you enjoy most? Describe.

3. What part of the writing process did you find most challenging? Why?

4. Where do you think your essay needs work? *or* Where would you like to improve?

5. How could you improve your *experience* of writing? How can you better support yourself in creating strong work that inspires in you a sense of pride?

6. Specifically, how can your instructor better support your learning and development as a writer, reader, and critical thinker?

Proofreading: How Can We Polish Our Essays When Our Brains and Computers Have Such Limitations? by Tina Sander

Activity: proofreading

Learning Outcomes: understand the need for using proofreading strategies and incorporate proofreading into the writing process

Habits of Mind: persistence and openness

As a teacher, I am tired of seeing typos and simple mistakes in the polished work of my students. Students are tired of seeing red marks all over their essays after they have spent hours researching, drafting, and writing. What do we do about proofreading and polishing?

I have found that many students either do not take the time to proofread or waste their valuable time by simply rereading their essay many times with glazed-over eyes. My solution is to focus specifically on proofreading early on in the semester.

I introduce this lesson, which takes about 50 minutes, on the day the students turn in their first essay. The objective is to make students aware of the limitations of their brains and computers while seeing the importance of using specific strategies to proofread in order to polish their essays and eliminate many of the extraneous red marks. Persistence, in the form of students finding and applying strategies to work on perfecting their work, and openness, in the form of students accepting the limitations of their tools and trying out new strategies, are habits of mind that this activity develops.

persistence and openness

Journal Writing: How Did You Do on Your First Essay? What Are Your Experiences with Proofreading? (10 minutes)

We start with a few minutes for self-reflection. Students are asked to write about their experiences with the essay that they are turning in. In a freewriting kind of format, they should analyze their feelings delving into what they liked and didn't like, what was easy or difficult, and what they learned from this essay. I suggest these topics, but I let them go where they want because this is only for their eyes.

reflection

The next part of the journal involves students writing about their experiences with proofreading. Again, it is a freewrite in which students can focus on what they have done and learned in terms of proofreading with other classes as well as how they proofread the essay that they are about to turn in. I ask them to think about what specific strategies they used and which strategies have worked or not metacognition   worked in the past and why.

Partners and Proofreading (10 minutes)

For this part of the lesson, students line up along the sides of the room in order of how much time they spent proofreading. Students who spent a short time proofreading are at one end, and at the other end are students who spent more time proofreading. Students then partner up (starting with the two people from either end being one team and moving toward the middle of the line). They sit together and share a bit about what they wrote in their journals.

Proofreading: Your Brain Does Not Work! (10 minutes)

I elicit a few responses from the students' journals and guide the discussion toward proofreading. I ask how many times the students reread their essays and if they used specific strategies. Usually students will just say they reread their essays or they used spell-check.

I then inform them that without using specific strategies their brain will not be very effective at proofreading simply because of the way it is wired. To illustrate this I have them read "The Proofreading Brain" (see part 1 the proofreading handout of in the appendix at the end of this lesson exemplar). Students are asked to count the letter *F* in a simple sentence: "Finished files are the result of years of scientific study combined with the experience of years." Many find only three or four *F*s because their brain skips the *F* in the word *of*. When given more time and prompted to look for more, they usually find the *F*s in the word *of* and see that there actually are six *F*s in that one sentence.

I next help them apply this to their writing by seeing how if they skip one letter in this simple sentence they are very likely to skip quite a few words and letters in the essays that they have been working on for many hours. Thus, our brains are not always reliable when it comes to proofreading and finding mistakes! This leads me to introduce the importance of proofreading strategies rather than simply rereading the same essay many times over.

Proofreading—Your Spell-Checker Does Not Work! (5 minutes)

Before we get into specific strategies, I like to show the students how another popular tool, the spell-checker, also has limitations. I direct them to the poem "Candidate for a Pullet Surprise" by Jerrold H. Zar (see part 2 of the proofreading handout), which beautifully illustrates this concept. The poem is about a spell-checker that has checked the words as correctly spelled but then cannot determine whether they are correctly used (example: "My checker tolled me sew."). Because the spell-checker does not identify any of the words as wrong, the poem is cumbersome to read. This shows the students in a fun way that even though their computers can be helpful they are not perfect. Students usually love this activity.

Proofreading Strategies (5 minutes)

I now ask students to come up with effective proofreading strategies. I list the strategies that students suggest on the board as they describe them. Then I direct the students to the list of strategies on the proofreading handout. Either they read over the handout by themselves or we do this as a class, and I ask them to circle at least three new ones or ones that they would like to try. We briefly review the strategies by clarifying ones that students don't quite understand and by having students share the ones they want to try.

Use a Strategy! (10 minutes)

Students are given time to use a specific strategy to work on their essay and proofread it one more time in a different manner before turning it in. I accept and highly encourage changes in pencil to their final drafts.

Teaching Note

"The Proofreading Brain" and the "Candidate for a Pullet Surprise" poem were both found on multiple sites on the Internet. This lesson can be done with all levels of English classes, and the journal part of this lesson can also be done orally with students talking in pairs.

Student Responses from the Actual Lesson

- "I felt insufficient because I thought I had done enough by just going over my essays but there's so much more I could have done. I'll try harder next time by using various strategies."
- "The lesson about proofreading and talking about different ways and things to do was very helpful. I was interested in the lesson because there were some ways I've never tried before."
- "I learned a lot of new proofreading skills. The lesson made me feel more confident about my writing and editing. I was definitely interested. Editing is always something I get stuck on. I enjoyed when we did the 'How Your Brain Plays Tricks' thing on the board. Lessons where you are participating in a fun way always get me much more motivated about the lesson and make me want to learn."
- "I am glad I got to view this because now I know what doesn't work for proofreading."

Quick Start Guide

1. Incorporate this lesson at the beginning of the semester. Students need to have their first essay with them, ready to be turned in.
2. Allow students to make revisions to their essay before they turn it in if they find mistakes as a result of this activity.
3. Have students turn in answers to specific self-reflective questions for you to read before you read and respond to their essay. These questions cover similar topics ("What was easy/hard?") as well as direct ones to guide you in your responses ("What do you want me to focus on? Do you want me to mark every mistake or only the important and recurring ones?").

Appendix 4.B: Proofreading Handout

Think or write about these questions before you read the handout:

> How much time do you spend proofreading?
> After you finish typing your essay, do you go back to it? What do you do? Is it effective?

Many students spend hours and hours writing and rewriting their essays and then turn them in without any real proofreading. Some quickly reread their essay and count that as proofreading. Some rely on their computers to fix mistakes for them. Neither method catches everything, as is shown by the next two exercises.

Part 1: The Proofreading Brain

Count the *F*s in the following text but do not count them more than once: "Finished files are the result of years of scientific study combined with the experience of years."

How many did you find?

If you only found three or four, then it is proof that your brain does not work like you would want it to.

(See part 4 of this handout for the answer and an explanation.)

Part 2: Poetry—What Do You Think about Your Computer? Read and Enjoy!

Candidate for a Pullet Surprise
  By Jerrold H. Zar

> I have a spelling checker,
> It came with my PC.
> It plane lee marks four my revue
> Miss steaks aye can knot sea.
>
> Eye ran this poem threw it,
> Your sure reel glad two no.
> Its vary polished in it's weigh.
> My checker tolled me sew.

A checker is a bless sing,
It freeze yew lodes of thyme.
It helps me right awl stiles two reed,
And aides me when eye rime.

Each frays come posed up on my screen
Eye trussed too bee a joule.
The checker pours o'er every word
Too cheque sum spelling rule.

Bee fore a veiling checker's
Hour spelling mite decline,
And if we're lacks oar have a laps,
We wood bee maid too wine.

Butt now bee cause my spelling
Is checked with such grate flare,
Their are know fault's with in my cite,
Of nun eye am a wear.

Now spelling does knot phase me,
It does knot bring a tier.
My pay purrs awl due glad den
With wrapped word's fare as hear.

Too rite with care is quite a feet
Of witch won should bee proud,
And wee mussed dew the best wee can,
Sew flaw's are knot aloud.

Sow ewe can sea why aye dew prays
Such soft wear four pea seas,
And why eye brake in two averse
Buy righting want too pleas.
(Published in the *Journal of Irreproducible Results*, January/
February 1994, page 13)

Strategies

As you can see, your brain is not perfect and neither is your computer.
Is that a good excuse for why you can have errors and mistakes? NO!

Mistakes will take away from the careful research, thorough
thinking, and clear presentation that you have devoted your time and
energy to. Avoid them by tricking your brain by using various strategies. What strategies have you used?

Part 3: Strategies for Proofreading

Circle three new ones to try.

1. **Give yourself plenty of time:** Proofreading takes a lot of time, but it works! You will find and correct a lot of errors if you give yourself a chance to do it.

2. **Proofread more than once:** Wait several hours after you've printed out your essay to proofread it for the final time. The more you can detach yourself from your work, the easier it is to proofread. Always proofread at least once with the hard copy instead of just looking at it on the computer screen. Don't wait until just before class to do this final step.

3. **Trust your instinct:** If you read a sentence carefully and get confused or feel something doesn't sound right, there is probably something wrong with your sentence. You need to find the error and fix it.

4. **Know your typical mistakes:** Before you proofread, look over any papers you've already gotten back corrected. Recall the errors you need to watch for. As you're writing this paper, take 10 minutes to learn from the last one.

5. **Proofread actively:** Read your essay very slowly, sentence by sentence. Stop at each verb and underline it. Look for a time expression, put a wiggly line under it, and check the tense you are using. Then look for the subject, circle it, and check the agreement and the form of the verb.

6. **Proofread for one or two errors at a time:** Read your essay again in the same way to catch other errors.

7. **Use reference books:** When you are unsure, check a grammar book and/or your dictionary. Your dictionary gives you a lot of useful information about a word such as the part of speech and which preposition you can use with it. If you are looking up a verb, you can find out whether it can have an object or not. Moreover, the dictionary often gives sample sentences for you to see how a word is used in context.

8. **Read your essay out loud:** In a room where you can hear yourself, read exactly what is on the page. You'll find that you can hear errors, particularly missing or misused "–s" or "–ed" endings.

9. **Read backward:** If you have difficulty seeing your errors, you may be focusing too much on the meaning, what you meant to write, instead of what is actually there. To distance yourself from what you meant to write, try going through your paper backward. Begin with the last sentence, read it out loud, then proceed to the second to last sentence, and continue until you reach the beginning.

10. **Use help sparingly:** If you have a friend proofread your essay, you are relying on someone else to do something you should learn to do for yourself. Proofread your paper yourself several times first, and then if you have a friend help you proofread, have that person circle any sentence with an error in it and see if that helps you find the error. This will teach you more than just allowing someone to fix it for you.

11. **Use the resources your computer offers:** Always run the spell-check after you have entered changes and before you print a final copy. If your computer has a grammar check, you can also try it but beware of its limitations as well.

Part 4: Proofreading Brain Explanation and Answers

Your brain will count the *F*s in the big-content words that add meaning to the sentence: *finished, files, scientific*. Did you find those three?

Your brain, however, will skip over the little function words such as *of* that make sentences grammatically correct but that add little meaning to them. To confuse your brain further, the *f* in *of* sounds more like a *v* than an *f*, making it harder to find. Did you count the three *F*s in the *of*s? If you did find all six *F*s, then give yourself a pat on the back but still use proofreading strategies.

DEVELOPING STUDENTS'
SELF-EFFICACY

Adela Najarro

> *"To perform its democratic function, basic writing sits not at the point of exit from high school, but at the entry point to higher education."*
>
> —Sugie Goen-Salter (98)

After investing our time and energy developing a semester course, we all hope that students will do more than just pass the class. We hope that they will move forward with knowledge and new strategies that will serve them well as they progress through college and then on to their futures. We want students to internalize what we teach so that eventually our influence contributes to a fully rounded and thorough education, hopefully culminating in a college degree and successful career. Teaching is an art that my coeditors and I view as best beginning with an assets-based approach, moving on to community building, the development of self-confidence, and now self-efficacy—the ability to complete college-level work independently and effectively. How do we know that when students pass our classes they have also internalized knowledge and become independent learners who navigate their own success?

Developing Students' Self-Efficacy

Two thirds of the way through every semester, I'm hoping that students are finally getting it, the "it" being the habits of mind that lead to success at the college level. I've asked them to trust me, that it will all make sense, that eventually each student will experience the "aha" moment when he or she gains the skills and confidence to succeed, not only in my class but also permanently as part of who the student becomes. As instructors, this is the point of nervousness and worry about our teaching effectiveness, and that worry rests in the project that we are undertaking: preparing underprepared students to attain their goals and potential. Can we actually do this? And how do we know if we have done so?

As educators, we enable students to reach the heights of their own possibility. At the same time we have to admit that serving underprepared students presents unique challenges that are seen across disciplines in open-admission four-year campuses and throughout the community college system. The idea resting behind open admissions and community colleges is that higher education should be available to all who have the inspiration. This is an egalitarian notion in regard to whom society should educate: We've chosen everybody. Both the individual and society as a whole benefit when our systems of higher education create generation after generation of college graduates who can think, read, and write critically—and the more the better. As Goen-Salter (Goen-Salter and Gillotte-Tropp) states, this is part of a democratic function, it's part of American culture, and it's part of the American dream. Ultimately, we are teaching more than content; we are fostering habits of mind that develop students' self-efficacy in and out of our classrooms. It's at two thirds of the way through the semester that we can begin to see students enact self-efficacy.

What Do We Mean by Self-Efficacy?

Self-efficacy entails the individual student's ability to enact her own success. It is an essential ingredient of a self-regulated learner: one who knows what she wants, what she needs to learn, and how to learn it. Besides course content, there is so much students need to know. First-generation college students as well as those who may be underrepresented and underserved through our educational system are required to learn the content matter of the general education curriculum along with the content of their chosen major, but they also have to learn the unspoken standards and expectations of academia. I routinely tell students that grades are not mysteriously granted by instructors, but that there is actually a set of criteria that most instructors have internalized and by which they grade and judge achievement. Some of us have begun to place these criteria on rubrics as part of our standard practices, but, unfortunately, not all instructors make these internalized realities obvious to students—too many of us simply expect students to know. Self-efficacy arises when students begin to internalize these systems that are the "norm" within university culture. They begin to know what is expected and how to reach those expectations.

As students gain a greater sense of self-efficacy, or trust in their own ability to meet learning outcomes, the responsibility for scaffolding instruction and providing support shifts from the instructor to the student—an essential requirement for success in higher education. Two thirds of the way through every semester, students should have had enough positive learning experiences to foster a growing sense of self-efficacy. The growth of self-efficacy is part of a process in which students develop the belief and knowledge to enact personal and educational goals. Barry J. Zimmerman proposes that there is a cycle of behavior that leads to student success, which includes setting specific goals, monitoring one's progress, making necessary changes, using time efficiently, accurately attributing causes for outcomes, and being able to adapt (205). Students who can self-regulate their learning through this cycle gain confidence in themselves and grow in their self-efficacy or belief that they can accomplish their goals, which hopefully means passing our classes and earning college degrees.

When considering the topic of student success and study skills, Russ Hodges, in *Teaching Study Strategies in Developmental Education: Readings on Theory, Research, and Best Practice*, proposes that a student's belief system affects his educational performance because beliefs become self-fulfilling realities. Hodges notes that "educational psychologists have coined the term *self-efficacy*—one's beliefs about one's capabilities to produce designated levels of performance" (189). Hodges contemplates why students react differently to similar grades. If two students each receive a B, their reactions may completely differ, with one viewing this grade as a defeat and the other viewing it as a confidence builder. Future performance builds on past accomplishments filtered through the student's belief system about her own abilities and her understanding of the world around her. As instructors, we must realize that a student's sense of self-efficacy is fluid and malleable through the result of new experiences. In other words, we can set up our courses so that students experience success, which then builds self-efficacy and thus leads to further academic accomplishments.

Myron H. Dembo and Helena Praks Seli, in "Students' Resistance to Change in Learning Strategies Courses," suggest that there are "four reasons why individuals have difficulty changing their behaviors: (a) they believe they can't change, (b) they don't want to change, (c) they don't know what to change, or (d) they don't know how to change" (194). Some students may have a low sense of self-efficacy reinforced by low performance, or their sense of self-efficacy may be artificially high, leading them to blame poor performance on outside factors such as the instructor or the course itself. Other students may see that they have a problem learning the material but don't know what to change, and others simply may be completely unaware of what went wrong. Along with teaching course content, we can structure instruction so that students have positive academic experiences, and when change is needed we can set up procedures by which to teach students how to change, when to change, and what new methods and approaches to take.

Nick Tingle, in *Self-Development and College Writing,* views the first two years of college composition as opportunities for students to learn how to write effective college-level essays, as well as to adopt the behaviors for lifelong learning. The writing classroom can be the entryway into the university culture: "A teacher may assist students in finding and developing their particular relationship to the larger academic terrain" (4). Tingle concurs with Dembo and Praks Seli on the idea that change is key to academic success; students need to be comfortable with the changing landscape of themselves. At the college level, we are not simply asking students to master empirical data sets; the college experience, especially for first-generation students and those who are underserved and underrepresented, entails making an inner change to accept and use what may be a different worldview. Self-efficacy grows as students enact academic performance to levels they desire, which is in itself a sign of accepting change and integrating change into one's self-concept.

In *The Community College Writer: Exceeding Expectations,* Howard Tinberg and Jean-Paul Nadeau conduct a study of composition at the community college in a variety of academic disciplines. Their study includes analyzing the expectations and performance of both faculty and students as they engage in writing across the curriculum. One major factor that coincides with Dembo and Praks Seli's ideas of why students don't change their behaviors is that Tinberg and Nadeau conclude that the problem lies in a student's ability to understand faculty expectations in writing assignments; students can't change what they don't understand: "The source of this frustration was often a lack of clarity, particularly in terms of a disjuncture between the guidelines offered, the task itself, and what the instructor seems to be emphasizing when responding to a draft" (119). Student frustration feeds into the idea that they can't write, don't know how, and writing is just not for them. If we are to change these attitudes, which is necessary because behavior arises from students' beliefs about their ability to perform, then we too have to realize that learning how to learn and learning how to compose an essay, or any other discipline-specific task, is not a mystery demanding a magical solution. We have to communicate with students the process involved for academic success, and in regard to composition, students need to internalize the process of writing, revising, and trying again as the norm. We can teach students to self-regulate their learning in our classes, improve academic performance, and in this manner continually add to their belief of their own self-efficacy, which leads to future academic accomplishments.

Habits of Mind: Self-Efficacy and the Learning Cycle

After surveying instructors and professors in all three California systems of higher education, the Intersegmental Committee of the Academic Senates (ICAS) published and widely distributed *Academic Literacy*. ICAS set upon the task of discovering the expectations that college teachers have for entering students. *Academic Literacy* does not contain surprises but instead articulates what we all know: "Competencies for entering students cannot be reduced to a mere listing of skills. True academic competence depends upon a set of perception and behaviors acquired while preparing for more advanced academic work" (ICAS 12). The report shows that throughout the educational system in California, from K–12 and on to the California Community College, California State University, and University of California systems, we all need to work on the development of critical reading, writing, and thinking skills along with the use of effective listening and speaking skills as well as technology (ICAS 35). But teaching all of these skills depends on the "dispositions and habits of mind that enable students to enter the ongoing conversations appropriate to college" (ICAS 13). And at the heart of these "dispositions and habits of mind" is self-efficacy, students' internalization of knowledge and skills combined with the belief that they can accomplish their goals.

Academic Literacy articulates a variety of student attitudes and behaviors that comprise self-efficacy as a complex dynamic. We need to not only teach the content of our courses, but also do so in a way that cultivates critical thinking, writing, and communication skills while building each student's belief that he or she understands and can fulfill academic norms and expectations. The idea is to structure our teaching so that we are not only teaching content but also fostering habits of mind. *Academic Literacy: A Statement of Competencies Expected of Students Entering California's Public Colleges and Universities* notes that college faculty expect students to analyze, interpret, question, synthesize, hypothesize, challenge their own beliefs and those of others, and "develop a capacity to work hard and to expect high standards; and show initiative and develop ownership of their education" (ICAS 13–14). We help promote these capacities when we plan instructional activities that give students a sense of greater control over their own learning.

In 2011, *Framework for Success in Postsecondary Writing* (CWPA, NCTE, and NWP) reaffirmed the claims in *Academic Literacy* about the need not only to teach content but also to move to teaching critical thinking, communication, and technology while wrapping it all up in the development of habits of mind. *Framework* places habits of mind in the forefront of the learning process, so teaching habits of mind should be a priority when implementing our teaching methods and activities: "Habits of mind refers to ways of approaching learning that are both intellectual and practical and that will support students' success in a variety of fields and disciplines" (1). Regarding self-efficacy, several of the eight habits of mind listed in *Framework* apply: persistence, responsibility, flexibility, and metacognition. If self-efficacy is the belief in one's ability to accomplish one's goals, then persistence or the ability to keep going when the going gets tough is paramount. At the two-thirds point in the semester, students know their instructor's personal style and taste, they have read the syllabus and completed assignments, and now it is their responsibility to make it to the end.

Framework also posits that flexibility and metacognition are necessary habits of mind to foster in our students. At the threshold to the final third of the class, students should be aware of the nuances that arise with each new task, that a college-level course will never request the simple answer, that a true college education is filled with change, challenges, and new twists on previously learned materials and ideas. Metacognition is the process of being aware of how one is changing. Because college is about change, students need to understand that this is the norm. They need to be metacognitive about the nature of success and self-efficacy. When students use persistence, responsibility, flexibility, and metacognition, they come to believe in themselves and their abilities. Now all we have to do is teach course content along with the habits of mind!

Both *Academic Literacy* and *Framework* contain a variety of course techniques and activities that activate critical thinking and habits of mind. *Academic Literacy* proposes that we teach students the behaviors we wish to see and points to teaching and reviewing academic reading strategies: "Reading is repeatedly identified as a most significant factor in the success of students in their college classes. Three fundamental reading competencies prove essential: reading for literal comprehension and retention; reading for depth of understanding; and reading for analysis, and interaction with the text" (ICAS 17). If we are to teach course content and the listed reading strategies while developing each student's self-efficacy, we must break down our assignments and offer multiple opportunities to practice. *Scaffolding* is a term routinely used in English departments to discuss what we mean by breaking down our expectations and teaching students how to succeed. Basically, every assignment we teach can be broken down into parts that build one onto the other, creating a "scaffold" from which each student can complete college-level assignments.

Take, for example, *Academic Literacy*'s suggestion to teach academic norms for reading. Instead of assigning 37 pages to read and telling students to "come prepared" for class discussion, we can break this process into steps and create a "scaffold" of activities that create in-depth analytic reading comprehension on the part of each student. When there are five minutes left of class, the process can begin by reminding students of the reading assignment they are to undertake prior to the next class session. The reading selection can be previewed by asking students to hypothesize what the reading might entail based on the title and what has been covered in class that day. Along with reminding students of the assignment and previewing the main concept, we can also assign students to write a summary paragraph, free-write in a journal, analyze the central conflict, or make a presentation about their own personal connection to the text. Reminding students of the assignment, previewing the main ideas, then assigning some sort of "note-taking" task all "scaffold" the reading assignment so that students read, understand, and interact with the assigned reading selection prior to class. If this is done for every reading selection assigned throughout the semester, then at the two-thirds point students will have internalized this process and will be going deeper into the material on their own; in this way scaffolding nurtures self-efficacy. Here's a little secret about making a career in teaching: It's got to be fun, and the fun starts when we begin to develop the habits of mind students may not have at the beginning of the semester.

Framework echoes that teaching habits of mind doesn't have to be a monumental shift or a burden; teaching habits of mind should be part of our teaching tool kit, the grease by which we guide students toward an in-depth and rich college education. *Framework* lists several activities or teaching methods that cultivate habits of mind. For example, in regard to responsibility, students should "recognize their own role in learning" (CWPA, NCTE, and NWP 5). Again, if scaffolding types of activities have been used through the semester, after the midterm students should know what is coming next and how close they are to the end. As instructors, we plan the entire semester and incorporating habits of mind into our classrooms may take as little as a five-minute review of the syllabus after each major assignment. We can set up small group sessions in which students are asked to identify the remaining major assignments, due dates, and possible points. The idea of incorporating habits of mind into our teaching is that we can do so one small step at a time, and then by the two-thirds mark of the semester students will have a full-blown sense of self-efficacy, the knowledge to successfully complete the remaining course content, and the belief that they can do so.

Teaching habits of mind, including nurturing and developing a sense of self-efficacy, is work that we already do, but perhaps work that we should do more of. The task is not to completely redesign instruction, but instead to realize that meeting student needs requires continual attention. Every time we are about to draw up a syllabus, an assignment guideline, a PowerPoint for tomorrow's class session, here rests an opportunity to push our own methods of instruction so that we are cultivating critical academic discourse while empowering students with the internalization of academic success.

> Teaching habits of mind, including nurturing and developing a sense of self-efficacy, is work that we already do, but perhaps work that we should do more of. The task is not to completely redesign instruction, but instead to realize that meeting student needs requires continual attention.

The chapter's exemplars begin with my "Academic Essay Structure," on how I teach the outline for the basic college essay from the beginning to the end of the semester. It is through repetition and consistency that students begin to internalize college expectations concerning essay writing. The goal of this exemplar is to help you gain valuable insights into how to scaffold essay writing. Olga Blomgren's "Group Projects: Turning Students into Teachers" presents an assignment where students develop skills in critical reading, advanced comprehension, analysis, and interpretation of texts while independently conducting basic research from a variety of media; Blomgren's project builds self-efficacy in the group setting where students learn most by teaching others. In "Students Respond to Instructor's Comments on Essays," Rhea Mendoza-Lewis presents her class project that ensures students realize that self-efficacy means change, and that change involves accurately interpreting instructor comments for revision. Finally, in "Cheating? Everyone Cheats," Daphne Young provides a lesson for delving into the age-old problem of plagiarism. Young suggests that we tackle the beast head-on and make cheating the subject matter for one of our essays.

All the exemplars in this chapter focus on that part of the semester that is a bit past midway when we are preparing students to make it on through and finish. We all want students to pass our classes, but a college education is more than a passing grade. We hope that the ideas in this chapter inspire in you new ways to build self-efficacy in your students.

Works Cited

CWPA, NCTE, and NWP (Council of Writing Program Administrators, National Council of Teachers of English, and National Writing Project). *Framework for Success in Postsecondary Writing*. Berkeley: National Writing Project, 2011. Web.

Dembo, Myron H., and Helena Praks Seli. "Students' Resistance to Change in Learning Strategies Courses." *Teaching Study Strategies in Developmental Education: Readings on Theory, Research, and Best Practice*. Ed. Russ Hodges, Michele L. Simpson, and Norman A. Stahl. Boston: Bedford/ St. Martin's, 2012. 191–208. Print.

Goen-Salter, and Helen Gillotte-Tropp. "Integrating Reading and Writing: A Response to the Basic Writing 'Crisis.'" *Journal of Basic Writing* 22.2 (2003): 90–113. Print.

Goen-Salter, Sugie. "Critiquing the Need to Eliminate Remediation: Lessons from San Francisco State." *Journal of Basic Writing* 27.2 (2008): 81–105. Print.

Hodges, Russ, Michele L. Simpson, and Norman A. Stahl. *Teaching Study Strategies in Developmental Education: Readings on Theory, Research, and Best Practice*. Boston: Bedford/St. Martin's, 2012. Print.

ICAS (Intersegmental Committee of the Academic Senates of the California Community Colleges, the California State University, and the University of California). *Academic Literacy: A Statement of Competencies Expected of Students Entering California's Public Colleges and Universities*. Sacramento: ICAS, 2002. Print.

Tinberg, Howard, and Jean-Paul Nadeau. *The Community College Writer: Exceeding Expectations*. Carbondale: Southern Illinois UP, 2010. Print.

Tingle, Nick. *Self-Development and College Writing*. Carbondale: Southern Illinois UP, 2004. Print.

Zimmerman, Barry J. "Self-Efficacy and Educational Development." *Self-Efficacy in Changing Societies*. Ed. Albert Bandura. New York: Cambridge University Press, 1997. 202–31. Print.

Academic Essay Structure by Adela Najarro

Activity: making outlines for college-level essays

Learning Outcome: organize essays to meet college-level expectations with an emphasis on generating text and critical thinking

Habits of Mind: engagement and self-efficacy

The Face-Off: Meeting the Class at the Beginning of the Semester

The classroom is usually dark. The room is usually crowded. Students are already chatting with one another. Three rows down, best friends from high school sit next to each other in the middle of the class, while the girl who has stopped partying and is ready to get on with school sits by herself toward the end of the row. The room is set up in rows, old school—10 × 8, for a total of 80 possible students; luckily this is a college composition class and the enrollment cap is set at 29. Each of those 29 students needs to pass the class to reach sensible goals: graduation, transfer, a good-paying job. Each of those 29 students also fears failure and desires a future different from working as agricultural laborers in the strawberry fields or salesclerks at Macy's or some other retailer. What does success mean to these students?

For many it is a dream that has not been articulated. It is just a sense—a sense that to get ahead in our culture, one earns a college degree. And so the classroom is full. The faces are expectant. Everyone is ready to give it a try. So now it turns to me, the instructor of record. There I am, standing at the front of the room. There they are, sitting in rows. Based on my own experience as a first-generation Latina who sat in a similar classroom with similar dreams, I begin with a story of failure.

As a freshman in college I had no clue what an "essay" entailed or what was expected. I simply did my best. I wrote the pages. I typed them up. I turned them in on time on the due date. They came back with Ds or maybe a C+. I was sure the professor thought I was a slacker, or that I didn't care. I did care. I just didn't know the parameters of the expectations—that I should think a certain way and then be able to articulate those thoughts by writing in a certain way. I have always wondered how anyone can expect a person to know what the person does not know. Developing an open framework by which to structure college-level essays allows students to grasp expectations about academic writing; it is only when students know what is expected that success can happen.

Writing the Essay: One Step at a Time

Simplicity. At times, we forget that what is obvious to us may be mysterious to others. The basic essay format is obvious. It is simple. It is what we have written so many times that we can't count the quantity of essays completed. But we are teachers, instructors, professors of English composition—we'd better know how to write an academic essay! But our students may not. To convey the basic essay structure to students, it is necessary to create learning opportunities where students practice once, and then once more, how to structure an essay; it is also paramount that students write the essay in sections in order to generate a more thorough and connected understanding of what

metacognition constitutes college-level writing and critical thinking.

When those 29 students walk into the room, I pass out manila folders and have them label their folder "Assignments." On the left, we staple the syllabus, and on the right we staple the assignment guidelines for the first essay. We use these folders throughout the semester, and for each paper a new assignment guideline is stapled on top of the old one. A common thread to all the guidelines is that each one contains a section outlining the basic academic essay structure. To the experienced academic writer these categories will seem obvious: introduction with a thesis statement, body sections, and a conclusion. However, to first-generation college students or those for whom academic writing is a new and perplexing task, presenting the facility of these three sections over and over throughout the semester

self-efficacy creates a sense of empowerment within the student that they "know
and self- what college writing is about."
confidence

The trick is to get students to internalize the simplicity of the basic college essay structure combined with the rhetorical power, fluidity,

flexibility and grace of language. To do that I provide numerous approaches and techniques for writing the various sections of the college-level essay while allowing each student's voice and perspective to appear. With any student, at whichever level, we must encourage that their own knowledge, experience, and thoughts enter their writing. It is by validating the students' ability to communicate and think through written language that we build their self-esteem and value as capable college students, which in turn enables them to engage with the assignment, the course, and their own education and future. Along the way we can explain and require academic writing norms.

In the introduction section, I encourage students to begin with a creative introduction but require that they conclude with a one- to two-sentence thesis statement (see Appendix 5.A: Essay Outline Handout). I do not simply say, "Write a creative introduction." Instead, I present a list of possible creative approaches for writing an introduction. In the assignment guidelines under the introduction section, I note that they may begin their essays by relating background information, telling a story, defining a key term, presenting examples, devising an analogy, or asking a question. For the creative introduction or hook to work, students must in the middle of the introduction explicitly state the essay topic, and name titles and authors under consideration. The final section of the introduction is to end with a thesis statement. So that students gain a sense of what a creative introduction sounds like and what an effective thesis may entail, we review professional and student samples. I also ask students to begin their introduction and thesis during class time. A benefit of having students think creatively while composing the introduction is that at the essay's start students turn to their own life experiences and push their thinking into a realm beyond summary and recitation. They have to come up with something new and interesting to engage the reader within the essay's first page, which sets the tone and approach for the entire paper.

In the body sections both the student's own perspective and academic norms come alive. As with the introduction, in the assignment guidelines I present a list of possible approaches for writing subsections that can make up the body of the essay (see Appendix 5.A: Essay Outline Handout). The body may include article summaries; article analyses; freewrite responses to classroom prompts; personal narratives; interviews; philosophical reflections; arguments; or analyses of fiction, poetry, drama, song lyrics, or other art forms such as sculptures, posters, or photographs. This list can be tailored to the particular needs of an assignment or proclivity of an instructor. To ensure that students generate text, I usually begin each body section in the classroom as a 15-minute freewrite. Students then finish and polish the section at home; in this manner students generate text, address a rhetorical task, and practice academic norms. For each assignment, *responsibility* I vary the choices depending on the level of the course and where we are in the semester, though article summaries and analyses are required for every essay I assign, along with a personal narrative or philosophical reflection. This combination stimulates students to write about concepts and ideas attained through textual analysis while tying in the outside source to their own personal knowledge, opinions, and points of view. A side benefit of this approach is that I never get the two-page paper! Actually, the top third of the class routinely exceeds the minimum page requirement.

For the conclusion, I suggest echoing their introduction or choosing a different approach, the main point being that these are the final words the reader will encounter. They had better be interesting and more than a recitation of the thesis! As with the introduction and body, in the assignment guidelines I present a list of possible creative approaches for writing a conclusion, and these categories are those listed for the introduction: present background information, tell a story, define a key term, present examples, devise an analogy, or ask a question (see the appendix at the end of this lesson exemplar). The conclusion is the final piece students write, and throughout my years of teaching, for the majority of students it flows. The reason these students are successful at writing their conclusion is that they are engaged with the assignment and have found something worthwhile to communicate through the process of breaking down, internalizing, and writing within the structure of the basic college essay, a standard that they now understand and can manipulate to express their knowledge.

How It Really Works in the Classroom: Points and Pitfalls

The essay-writing method takes a long time and requires patience. To write a five-page essay with an introduction, body sections, and a conclusion requires multiple class sessions. Each body section needs to be introduced with its corresponding freewrite, along with the introduction and conclusion. The assignment also needs to go through peer review and include one or two more class sessions where students unify the essay with transitions and by proofreading. However, the benefit of slowing down the writing process and providing scaffolding is that almost the entire class turns in work of passing quality, with the majority turning in work that is authentic, articulate, and accurate.

The most common detractor is that the essays may feel disjointed or choppy, depending on the students' ability to grasp and manage the finesse required of transitions and their ability to weave the thesis throughout the entire essay. Beginning writers often struggle to unify the entire essay, but these would be the same students turning in a shallow two- to three-page summary. To have an authentic personal voice and accurate textual analysis appear in the writing is worth stylistic clunkiness, the point being to have students progress. It is only by completing assignments that students will move forward.

A benefit of this method is that peer review is done per section so that an entire class session is not required. When peer reviewing one section of the body, for example, 20–30 minutes will suffice, which then allows time for discussing readings, beginning another body section freewrite, or other activities. Having a variety of classroom activities during one session also leads to higher engagement simply because change alleviates tedium.

Finally, the most important benefit to this method is that it alleviates students' fear of writing. They do not stare at a blank screen intimidated by the 5, 7, or 10 pages they have to write by dawn. Instead they write the one, two, or three pages required per section, and before they know it the essay has written itself. Also by using this method students go through the entire writing process, and I have yet to receive a paper written the night before the due date.

If we truly desire to increase the number of students graduating college, then as composition instructors what we do really matters. Students need to know what we know. They are there waiting for us to show the way. Sometimes what is most obvious to us is the very thing that is the most elusive to them. Let's teach the basic structure of the college-level essay, scaffold, bridge, and get those students writing.

Quick Start Guide

1. Adapt the essay outline handout to meet the needs of your own teaching style.
2. Include the outline handout with the guidelines for each essay assignment.
3. Schedule one class session for making an outline as part of the assignment writing cycle.
4. Be prepared to read longer papers!

Appendix 5.A: Essay Outline Handout

Putting It All Together

Your essay must include the following parts: introduction with a thesis statement, body sections, and conclusion. Use the following outline to specify the various parts of your essay:

Outline

Section 1: Introduction

    a. Begin with a general overview:

        i. Tell a story, propose a question, present an example, relate background information, define a key term, draw an analogy.

        ii. State the subject of the essay.

    b. *The final sentence must be the thesis statement.*

Section 2: Body sections. The body of your essay may include article summaries and analyses, interviews, philosophical reflections, arguments, personal narratives, analyses of fiction, poetry, drama, song lyrics, or other art forms.

    a. These sections make up the body of your paper.

    b. They may go in any order.

    c. Each section should be **at least two paragraphs** in length.

    d. At the end of each section, you will need to add transitions that link to the next section.

    e. *Transitions should also mention and reflect the thesis.*

Section 3: Conclusion

    a. These are your final words on the topic. What do you want the reader to remember?

        i. Echo the strategy used in the introduction or choose a new one: Tell a story, define a key term, propose a question, present an example, draw an analogy, or relate background information.

    b. Do not, I repeat, do not state, "In conclusion, . . ."

    c. Do not summarize your paper with phrases such as, "In this paper, I've shown . . ." or "My paper has been about . . . ."

Using the previous sections as a guide, write an outline for your essay.

Group Projects: Turning Students into Teachers by Olga Blomgren

Activity: group project and presentation

Learning Outcomes: develop skills in critical reading, advanced comprehension, analysis, and interpretation of texts while independently conducting basic research from a variety of media

Habits of Mind: engagement, motivation, persistence, creativity, and responsibility

Introduction and Goals

A few semesters ago, a colleague shared a conversation she had with a student. The student was planning her schedule for the next semester and asked my colleague to identify the most "entertaining" instructor teaching the next-level class. Alone in an office, we laughed at the idea that entertainment relates to learning! Sometime later, I had to admit that entertainment, or as instructors think of it in the classroom, engagement, goes a long way in the learning process. This student was simply expressing her desire to be engaged and motivated in class. As I was developing a group presentation project for a college-level composition class, this memory came back to me. My initial idea was to make the student groups into teachers of their content, but after the first semester, I learned many more advantages come with group project activities.

I know that there are immediate objections to group work: How do you grade the students? What if only one person does all the work? Who has the time, there's so much content to cover? (Insert your favorite objection here.) In response to the objections, I wish to share two key ideas (my "aha!" moments) learned from this group assignment:

1. In structured environments, students can often engage and teach one another just as effectively as an instructor, if not more so.
2. Group projects can use student energy and creativity to complete tasks and outcomes already established by the instructor or course.

Lesson Sequence

The following example for this assignment takes place in a college-level reading and writing course, but this activity can be adapted to meet course objectives across levels and disciplines. The coursework asks students to read multiple articles and essays on a topic, analyze the information, and then write their own persuasive essay on the topic. The focus is on explaining their own ideas; as such, the objective is to move beyond comprehension to student analysis and application. Finding a visual or other media source that reflects the main ideas of a reading is a concrete demonstration of these skills. The more comfortable group dynamic, as opposed to an individual one, allows each student to practice and develop these skills. Each student will share and discuss his or her ideas with peers in order to agree on one group example to complete this assignment. The version of this project I conduct extends over seven consecutive class days in a four-week period. However, it can be adapted to as few as three or four days depending on the needs and dynamic of the class.

Slips of paper with the name of an author from the next unit we will study are dropped into a bag. Students draw a slip of paper out of the bag to divide themselves into groups of four. There are enough slips to make groups as random and even as possible. Everyone is instructed to join the three other members of their group and introduce themselves. I then pass out the directions for the project and review the assignment with the class (see the appendix at the end of this lesson exemplar).

The author's articles are found in one unit of the class textbook and the groups are instructed to skim their article and make predictions about the content. For homework they are asked to read their article and identify the thesis and main points of the argument (this and all other assigned reading and work is detailed in the class syllabus). The points they identify will be discussed with their team.

I know that group work can result in one or a few people completing most of the work. Because this outcome defeats the purpose of this assignment, I have developed a few strategies to foster responsibility in each member. One of the requirements of this activity is that all students participate by completing the group work as homework. For example, all four members will bring in a visual they believe relates to their article. When the group meets, they and I can easily see who is contributing and the team benefits from having a variety of visuals from which to select. I explain that the benefit of a

responsibility

group is having many views and minds focused on the same goal and then ask the students to tap into that resource.

At the next class meeting the groups are given 20–30 minutes to discuss their reading of the essay. They are instructed to come to a team consensus on the thesis and main points of the essay. Each day the group meets, students are asked to bring their ideas to contribute to the group. This work is assigned as homework and clarified in class. In class, I spend time with each group, listening in on the discussion and monitoring their progress. For homework I ask that each student bring a visual argument (this concept is explained in the homework reading) he or she feels represents a main idea in his or her group's essay. These visuals will be shared with the group in class.

At the third class meeting the groups are given 20–30 minutes to discuss their visuals. As a team, they select the visual they think best represents their assigned essay. Once they have chosen, the group is instructed to analyze the visual as explained in the text and practiced in class. For homework each student is asked to come up with some other form of media that represents the ideas of his or her group's article. Finally, they need an activity that will involve the entire class. The only direction is that the activity must be relevant, instructive, and grounded in their article's main ideas. These will be shared with their team in class.

In the directions for this assignment, creativity is mentioned explicitly a few times. I follow up by encouraging the students to be creative in their presentation, methods, and class activity. Some groups dream up fun games and activities for their peers; others work hard developing insightful questions to pose to the class. Groups often create PowerPoints or use Prezi (free, web-based presentation software), posters, and original artwork to summarize and illustrate the ideas they wish to share with the class.

On the fourth and final day that the groups meet in class they are instructed to decide on their other media source. They also finalize the class activity. (Although not required, at this point groups often decide to meet outside of class to complete the work before they teach their article and visual to the class.)

On the following class day the two teams are given 30 minutes each to present their work. They are asked to first explain the key ideas of the essay and then analyze the visual. In whichever order they prefer, they then lead the class activity and share their media selection, explaining the reasons why they chose it and how it relates to their article and visual argument. This process is repeated over the next few days until all the groups have presented.

After all the groups have presented, I ask each student to write a memo detailing the work he or she contributed to the team project. The students explain what they liked or disliked about the project, the specific work they contributed to the team, and also evaluate the contribution of each of their group mates. I ask them to be as specific as possible in order to help me understand the tasks for which *self-efficacy* they took responsibility. The memos help me recall what I saw of the *and* group's work in class and the presentation itself. These memos, along *responsibility* with daily group observations and the presentations, are the basis for evaluation. Much of the feedback I receive on this assignment comes from these memos.

Student Response

Perhaps surprisingly, it is the group dynamic that encourages participation and interest. In essence, this is a jigsaw activity. The entire class reads six relatively short essays from the textbook on one topic, in this example the topic is gender. Each group become "experts" on their article and then teach that essay to the class after this article has been read by all students for homework. Groups feel responsible to themselves and their peers to do a good job, and each team tries to *motivation* improve on the previous presentation. Students overwhelmingly say that watching their peers' presentations not only engages them but also clarifies the concepts of each article.

Students are often extremely comfortable both working in groups and making presentations. Although not required, they often make impressive PowerPoint and video presentations of their work. They also have very strong insight into how to motivate their peers. As students, they know what their peers will and will not respond to in class. Students who have taken classes in psychology, child development, human sexuality, sociology, and other social sciences have often studied various issues related to gender and bring that knowledge, along with their life experience, into their discussions.

Asking students to bring in visuals and other forms of media that relate to their assigned article allows them to bring their nonacademic interests into the classroom. Because this activity is about gender, students also have opportunities to share what they have learned about gender performance from their families and friends.

Successes and Challenges

In addition to motivating and engaging students, a goal of this activity is to foster critical reading of the textbook and argument essays. The assigned essays are discussed with the instructor in a very limited manner so as not to guide student interpretations. We discuss specific homework questions, as opposed to general responses to the articles. I am careful not to introduce or cite any evidence that the group may wish to analyze in their presentation. A new objective for this project is to identify and analyze visual arguments. Practicing this analysis, and any other new concepts, in class via assigned homework and then in the groups allows the students multiple opportunities to achieve comprehension and comfort with the activity before explaining the group's visual to the class. Additionally, students often respond that visuals engage various learning styles.

One challenge is time. Groups requested more time to sufficiently prepare. In subsequent versions of this activity, I added a few minutes to each in-class meeting and added one more day for groups to prepare.

Students are usually familiar with and enjoy working with their peers. Some even prefer small groups and feel greater freedom to express their ideas. I have found that a group project where each member is held responsible for his or her own work is an effective way to engage students, particularly those who often hesitate to participate regularly in class. Working for and with a team also motivates students to persist in the class activities. Everyone looks forward to presentation days. After all groups have presented, almost all students say how much they enjoyed watching their peers explain their work.

Although group work is not entirely new, perhaps the greatest challenge for students is figuring out how to cooperate effectively within a group. The culmination of their efforts, the presentation, demands that they produce work they feel will be valuable to the rest of the class. A polished and complete effort requires coordination and agreement—in a word, flexibility. Impressively, groups often meet outside of class and try to work on their presentation together as much as possible.

Overall, this activity increases student engagement and comprehension. The discussion that each group creates with their presentation is genuinely thoughtful and rich. This activity feeds into an essay each student will write on the topic of gender. If they have understood the articles and how to analyze visuals they will successfully demonstrate those skills in the essay. On average, the quality of the essays students write after this project is an improvement on the previous assignment. I learn from my students each time I conduct this project. As a result of this particular activity, there are too many other successes to count!

Quick Start Guide

1. Select enough course texts or readings for the amount of groups you will make. Texts may be loosely or closely grouped around a theme or concept.
2. Divide students into groups by title or author of the assigned reading.
3. Distribute and review the directions for the group project so that students understand the tasks and timeline for completing the assignment. Although this project requires that groups complete four tasks, in other courses I have conducted the project with only three: Teach an assigned reading, share and explain a related media source, and create and lead a class activity.
4. Allow students sufficient time and days to meet in class to work on the project. The length and number of in-class group meetings are determined by the scope and demand of the project. Deliverables in the form of homework may be collected from students to mark their contribution and progress. Float between the groups to answer questions and ensure time is used wisely.
5. Sit back and enjoy the presentations! Encourage presenters to manage their own discussions.
6. Collect student memos on the project.

Appendix 5.B: Group Project and Presentation Guidelines

Directions: In this assignment you will work in a group to help yourself and your peers evaluate the way media promotes images of, and ideas about, gender. You will use your critical reading skills to analyze *Dialogues* chapter 8, "Using Visual Arguments" (219–263), and the articles assigned in chapter 11, "Gender Matters: Fitting In" (424–468). The rest of this assignment is left up to your creativity, group collaborations, and critical thinking skills.

As a team, you will complete the following tasks:

- Discuss the key points of the chapter 11 essay, including those you may disagree with.
- Select a visual that best represents a main idea from your assigned chapter 11 essay.
- Incorporate another form of media (novel, music video, TV show/commercial, film, magazine, newspaper, etc.) <u>relevant</u> to your group's discussion of gender.
- Create and lead a class activity based on your group's ideas about gender in the media. Use your creativity and imagination to assign <u>relevant and instructive tasks or classwork</u> for your peers.

A note on the grading: <u>All group members must participate equally.</u> I highly suggest you discuss all of your ideas as a group and then agree on the best way to explain your collective analysis to the class. It is also wise to divide the responsibilities on the day you lead your class activity. Although you will be working as a team, you will be graded as an individual. I will ask everyone to explain their contributions to the team in writing. There is no need to cover or compensate for an absent or noncontributing group mate; this behavior will only impact their grade.

Students Respond to Instructors' Comments on Essays by Rhea Mendoza-Lewis

Activity: responding to instructor's comments on essays

Learning Outcomes: identify the instructor's concerns and employ proper responses

Habits of Mind: engagement and confidence building

On the day essays are returned, how many times have instructors witnessed students flipping to the last page to see their grades and then tossing the essay into the abyss of a backpack never to be seen again? How many countless hours do instructors spend writing these comments and searching for the right words to convey the necessary feedback? The activity in this exemplar was created to assist students in understanding the instructor's comments and, partly, to help redeem instructors, so our work is not in vain.

This activity calls for students to spend some time reviewing what their instructor wrote on their essays in order to ultimately take this feedback to build stronger writing skills necessary for success in college classrooms. Simply put, the activity requires students to respond to *every single mark* placed on the essay by the instructor.

Introducing the Activity to Students

I use class time early in the semester to review graded assignments; later on, students review graded assignments at home. This enables students to be successful at understanding instructor comments.

On the day I return essays to students, I tell them to pull out a colored pen, preferably pink, green, or purple because I use blue to write my comments during the grading process. They are not to use a pencil or black ink. I make sure to have colored pens on hand in case anyone doesn't have one.

I tell them I am going to pass back their essays, and they are to respond to *every single mark* I have placed on their essay. This includes smiley faces and "Good job!" notations. Throughout the activity, I reiterate how they are to respond. I also warn them that this will get messy. Between my comments and the students' responses there may be little space left when all is said and done.

Discussing the Grading Key

I distribute to students a grading key. (The first grading key is always in paper form. The ones to follow for later essays are in electronic format.) We review it, and I tell them that a lot of the comments I have placed on their essays are things they learned about during the writing process. The grading key reflects the essay prompt and aspects of curriculum that we have covered in class.

The grading key also changes depending on the English level and essay topic. In addition, each grading key handout is different for each essay and each class because I create it as I grade essays. While grading, I make a note of the types of issues students are having and place these on the key. I also have examples handy to help explain the various comments on the key.

Returning Essays

Once students are clear on the expectations, I model the activity asking one student to volunteer an essay. We work through a portion of the essay continuously switching from the essay to the grading key. I have the owner of the essay step forward and write the comments while I guide from the sidelines.

When students get their essays back, the actual grade is not on it; the grade sheet is in my office, so once they respond to *every single mark* I have placed on the essay I will attach their grade and give that back to them during the next class. When I tell them this there are usually a few groans, so I make sure to reinforce the idea that this activity is important for helping them to understand the grades they earned.

metacognition and self-efficacy

Responding to the Comments

As students respond to the comments on their essays I offer lots of guidance and encouragement. There are times when there is too much to say on an essay, so I write in the margin, "Ask me." When a student sees this, he or she raises a hand, and I go over to explain and perhaps show examples. If the comment requires more time, I will tell the student to stop by during office hours.

Resubmitting Essays

When students have responded to all comments, they resubmit their essays. I verify that there is a colored-pen comment or correction for every blue one. If something is missing, I hand the essay back and tell the student to go back over it until all comments have responses.

Reviewing Students' Responses

I review the students' comments checking to see if any issues or questions arise. Sometimes this activity leads to an in-the-margin dialogue between instructor and student.

Attaching the Grade and Returning the Essays

Once I feel that all comments are responded to properly, I return the essays with the grade sheet/rubric attached. Students are warned not to lose the essay because they will revisit comments and responses for the next writing assignment.

Successes and Challenges

I have found that students sometimes are frightened by the task of reviewing their essay because when they get their essay back and see a lot of blue comments they worry about how this will be reflected on their grade. But one thing they realize as they begin the task is that it isn't as bad as it seems, and they begin to understand learning as a self-efficacy process. They also build more of a connection to their writing. I have had students tell me that they enjoyed this activity after dreading it at first.

During this activity, students actively are looking at their written work and the instructor's comments. They are engaged in this task because the focus is on their own ideas and writing. The more comfort students have in utilizing instructor feedback the better off they are because, as we all know, instructor feedback is beneficial. This activity is extremely important for imparting comments to students on their strengths as writers as well as where improvement is needed. Additionally, students generally are not used to writing in the margins of and fixing errors in their own essays. Usually they are told to work on various aspects of composition ranging from grammar issues to overall organization for the next essay, but they are rarely held responsible for responding in the present. Therefore, they feel good about themselves when this task is completed. This confidence is essential for them to be successfully prepared for college-level coursework.

One thing instructors need to keep in mind is that the comments they place on an essay need to be limited to higher-level concerns of the rubric. Also, comments are guided by the essay's objectives as well as the course objectives. Knowing what to comment on is a challenge at times, but as we all know, the more we respond to essays, the easier it is to discern the comments we need to be making to our students.

Quick Start Guide

1. Prepare the assignment guidelines, grading key, and rubric.
    a. The assignment guidelines contain everything: explanation of the assignment, minimum requirements, examples, grading key, and rubric.
    b. The grading key contains three to five major concepts students need to master for that particular assignment. Items can range from rhetorical concepts, such as argumentation for mat, to grammar, such as writing complex sentences.
    c. The rubric is a grid stating standards of performance and where the instructor evaluates the essay. The rubric can also state the final grade and overall comments from the teacher to the student.
2. Introduce the assignment and review the guidelines. Try to have fun. Bring in a YouTube video clip, music, a poem, or read an excerpt from a story or an article. Make sure to let students know that they will review your comments as the final session for this assignment.
3. Schedule the date when you will return essays; otherwise, you might skip this step due to the midsemester hustle and bustle. This activity takes one class period, but the final section of this class period can be used to introduce the next assignment.

Cheating? Everyone Cheats by Daphne Young

Activity: annotation, crafting a thesis statement, developing supporting details, and learning proper citation of sources

Learning Outcomes: close reading, writing a reflective response, synthesis, and critical thinking

Habits of Mind: responsibility and transfer of learning

Laughter erupts. I repeat, "Cheating? Everyone cheats." Each by turn, students share with the class the everyday plagiarism they witness, and some of the ingenious methods used to get away with cheating. Then the conversation shifts to why. Voices change from laughter to more candid discussions of pressures to perform, of GPAs, college entrance exams, and the need to prepare for the future by any means necessary. The honest disclosures of why students cheat and plagiarize, even when couched in humor, reveal their fears about being left behind in a competitive world, and the rush-to-the-top pressure students feel in almost all their endeavors.

The initial in-class conversations about cheating and plagiarism are the setup for a sequence of class activities to explore "the cheating culture." More than teaching the practical side of avoiding plagiarism (cite sources) and what not to do (copy and paste) when preparing work for classes, the sequence of lessons provides opportunity for honest self-reflection and discussion of personal integrity and ethics. Ultimately, the lesson plan deals with how cheating and plagiarizing in academic settings is symptomatic of a larger, more serious cultural attitude about success, one that impacts all of our lives, and how we all can promote change.

The lesson sequence focuses on the overall impact of cheating—the ripple effect of academic plagiarism: from fudging on taxes, padding résumés, and forging business documents, to engaging in unethical practices in professional sports, the business world, and

integrative thinking — even personal relationships. The students begin by reading selected articles and essays on academic dishonesty and cheating, then move to the bigger picture, weighing in and connecting intellectually regarding the impact of a "cheating culture." The purpose of the lesson sequence is to go beyond the types of cheating that students are already acquainted with, such as downloading papers or copying and sharing test answers, to dishonesty at work, in corporations and government, and interpersonal betrayals. The activities for the cheating lesson include viewing films and TEDTalk clips, as well as reading journal, magazine, and newspaper articles. The cumulative effect is to help move students toward the larger social consequences of cheating—the impact dishonesty has on self and identity, on society, on the world, and how their future might look if cheating becomes a cultural standard. This allows students to examine themselves not only in terms of their own wants and needs, but also with fresh insights as citizens of a community, a society, the world.

In this exemplar I present the lesson plan I follow leading up to the paper on cheating. Discussions, films, and readings before the essay is written serve as groundwork materials as students learn to write papers that require research and outside sources. They learn how to distinguish between using sources properly and plagiarizing. More important, they become aware of what constitutes plagiarism and understand the importance of academic integrity. It is not an external force anymore; the integrity is now personal.

Day One: Introduction to Cheating and Plagiarism

- Discuss cheating and plagiarism in school (personal experiences and observations).
- Write journal responses to the discussions.
- Homework reading assignment: Read several articles from online databases. Students can choose from a bank of readings. (One article I always assign is David Callahan's "On Campus: Author Discusses the 'Cheating Culture' with College Students.")

To achieve the goals of the lesson, I open up a general discussion on cheating by asking students to offer examples from personal experience or observation. The conversations are surprisingly candid, even humorous. One student related this example: "The guy in my history class who wrote the entire geological timeline inside his tie, then flipped his tie over when he needed an answer!" Once students begin sharing experiences, the class relaxes. They say things such as, "The worst cheaters were in AP!" or "We never had to do anything in class—we just copied all the answers, and our teachers didn't care." The most common statement was: "Everybody cheats in school. You have to just to pass." Students then write journal responses to the discussion and to a prompt such as, "What is the main reason students cheat?"

metacognition

The activity allows students to engage and respond to the ideas exchanged. Reflections set up the reading assignments and the next day's work. Readings from the library's online academic databases and professional websites are assigned as homework for discussion the next class meeting. I use at least one current event to ground the lesson—there is always a cheating scandal in news headlines that can be used as class reading material. Students are asked to download, print out, read, and annotate the assignments.

Day Two: Journal Reflections/Group Discussions on the Reading Assignments

I assign four to five questions for quick in-class responses (one or two sentences each) and then divide the class into four or five groups. Each group focuses on a single question, and then we all report back and discuss the answers as a group.

Day Three: Viewing of the Film, Journal Writing, and Group Work

- View the film *Caught Cheating: The Cheating Crisis in America's Schools* (from *Dateline* with Charles Gibson).
- Write journal responses to the film.
- Class groups: Have each group discuss a segment of the film and its relationship to the readings, and then share their group discussion with the class.
- From the group discussions, pull out possible paper topics.
- Homework writing assignment: Formulate a working thesis statement for a paper.

engagement

The class views the broadcast *Caught Cheating*. Before the class breaks into discussion groups, students respond to the film in their journals to a prompt such as, "What part of the film stood out the most? Why?" Then the class breaks into groups of three or four to discuss the film and its relationship to the assigned readings. Students write down their responses as a group, and then each group shares their discussion with the whole class. From the group work, the class brainstorms topics for papers on academic cheating and plagiarism. Homework for the next class is to find a topic and prepare a working thesis statement for a paper.

Day Four: The Writing Assignment

- Brainstorm paper topics and craft a suitable thesis. Work on how to develop and organize supporting points.
- Discover solutions and creative ways to promote integrity in academic settings.
- Go over examples of MLA source documentation and produce a works-cited page.
- Writing Assignment: Write a paper based on the findings from the class discussions, along with information from the film and the articles.

During class, students exchange and peer critique several thesis statements by their classmates. Then they discuss supporting points that can be used from the film and the articles for their papers. We go over basic citation of sources in text and how to compile a works-cited page using MLA style. This first attempt at citation is done as a class participation exercise, supplemented by reference to an MLA handbook. Sometimes I use a PowerPoint or online source to illustrate citations. Students can then refer to their notes and review the citation format on their own once they are home writing their own papers.

Key Points

The film and readings on plagiarism and cheating provide diverse viewpoints—practical, political, social, and cultural sources—all concerned with ethics and potential outcomes of a "cheating culture" mindset. Students more actively participate in the cheating segment, through reading and discussing the material, than almost any other issue I cover in class. There are many creative possibilities to develop and add to this lesson sequence because new material is, unfortunately, constantly available. The lesson sequence works for pretransfer levels to upper-division college courses. Students learn about themselves when they critically examine the effects of cheating and what it means to be an ethical person.

Older, returning students can be key, because they are student peers (advocates) with more life experiences in employment, family, and education, where lapses in integrity and character may have been evident or even personal. Students of all ages and academic levels who have held jobs have anecdotal stories of cash disappearing, lies found on résumés and applications, accounting irregularities, and bosses who cheat on taxes. Students who are parents relate discussions they have with their own children about lying and cheating, and how they observe the pressure their children experience in the quest for good grades. These exchanges provide rich, shared perspectives.

My role is to act as a mediator, coach, and devil's advocate during discussions. Students then feel free to struggle with their own beliefs and attitudes about cheating through fact gathering, discussion, argument, and contemplation. They are often surprised to discover that, ultimately, cheating and plagiarism are choices. Even under pressure, a student chooses to cheat rather than employ other honest, ethical options. The bottom line is, no matter what, cheating is always a choice.

Every teacher knows how pervasive the cheating problem is—how difficult it is to police—and how pointless. Classroom conversations may not eradicate the problem, but presenting the topic openly is a powerful way to acknowledge the impact of cheating and plagiarism, and to give students a safe forum to examine their own motives, openness actions, and, ultimately, personal integrity and ethics. And when students become leaders of the conversation, and the discussions expand beyond simply reciting mantras such as, "Cheating hurts everyone" or "If you cheat, you only cheat yourself," students begin to acknowl-responsibility edge their own responsibility on a deeper level. David Callahan, author of *The Cheating Culture*, and of the source article I use in class, leaves his audience with this call to action:

> I do think we all have a say in how our society ought to be, even if just in our own little corner. And I believe we all have a responsibility to make personal choices that line up with our views of how things ought to be. Mahatma Gandhi said "Be the Change you want to see in the world." A very powerful piece of advice. (4)

I agree, and I believe that teachers can be a force for change. We can foster integrity, one student at a time.

Quick Start Guide

1. Go to YouTube and gather film clips, especially TEDTalks, that discuss plagiarism, cheating, honesty, and our moral culture. Dan Ariely's "Our Buggy Moral Code" is one example of an outstanding TEDTalk on the subject.

2. Copy David Callahan's "On Campus: Author Discusses the 'Cheating Culture' with College Students," which is readily available free online.
3. Make up essay assignment guidelines where students must include both of the previous sources cited correctly.
4. Devise an online reading bank from which students must draw their sources. This way, as a class, you can discuss correct citation using articles with which everyone is familiar.
5. Be sure to allow enough time for discussion; students love sharing their knowledge of cheats, cheaters, and plagiarizers.

Works Cited

Callahan, David. "On Campus: Author Discusses the 'Cheating Culture' with College Students." *Plagiary: Cross-Disciplinary Studies in Plagiarism, Fabrication, and Falsification* 1.4 (2006): 1–8. Web. 18 Sept. 2009.

Caught Cheating: The Cheating Crisis in America's Schools. ABCNews, 2004. DVD ROM.

6

PROMOTING TRANSFER OF LEARNING

Jennifer Fletcher

"The greatest thing by far is to be a master of metaphor. It is the one thing that cannot be learnt from others; and it is also a sign of genius, since a good metaphor implies an intuitive perception of the similarity in dissimilars."

—Aristotle (*Rhetoric* 255)

One of the great gifts of having spent 10 years as a high school English teacher before becoming a college professor is the connected understanding I now have of both worlds. Having not too long ago made the transition from high school to college myself (albeit as faculty), I found myself following in the footsteps of the students I tried to prepare for higher education. I, too, stood in line for my campus ID card and parking permit, secured university housing, learned the best places for lunch and coffee, and juggled a new lifestyle that often left me struggling to find the continuity between my former and present work.

As I adjusted to life on the tenure track, I was fascinated by the vantage point I now enjoyed of the postsecondary lives of students. Being a high school teacher can feel like only ever getting to read the second book in a trilogy; we don't know the backstory and never get to the conclusion. But as a college professor, I was finally able to see what happened to those scared and hopeful high school graduates after we said our teary farewells in June. The students in my first-year writing courses gave me a critical understanding of how students transfer learning from one context to the next and how educators can help facilitate this process by keeping the full trajectory of a student's intellectual growth in mind.

What Is Transfer of Learning?

For both teachers and students, transfer is a simultaneous act of hindsight and foresight. It's that ability to mine the past for relevant, analogous experiences while imagining their future, recontextualized applications. Without this expanded vision, learning is seldom meaningful or retained.

> For both teachers and students, transfer is a simultaneous act of hindsight and foresight.

Educational psychologist Robert E. Haskell defines *transfer of learning* as "our use of past learning when learning something new and the application of that learning to both similar and new situations" (xiii)—abilities Haskell sees as the basis of human compassion and reasoning (xiv and 64). Rhetorician Rebecca S. Nowacek gets at the contingencies of transfer by calling it an "act of recontextualization" (8). Other scholars have described transfer of learning as a way to help students improve their work beyond a single class or content area (Graff 376) or to understand the limits of universality (Downs and Wardle 552–53). These definitions share the common idea that in order for students to successfully transfer their learning from one assignment, class, discipline, or even institution to another they must recognize—at some level—the similarities and differences between their past and present situations. They then must be able to translate this recognition into principle-based generalizations they can apply to new contexts.

For instance, a college freshman who successfully wrote a research paper in her twelfth-grade English class will likely be able to transfer her knowledge of how to support claims with evidence to a similar assignment in her first-year composition course. A more challenging kind of transfer happens when this same student can then modify what she knows about evaluating evidence to suit the demands of a history paper. In these examples, the student's deep procedural knowledge of research methods and writing conventions is the key to transfer of learning.

Transfer also happens when students have a deep conceptual or theoretical knowledge of a subject. A mathematics student who understands that a function is a way to describe a relationship between two things can metaphorically apply the principles of exponential and linear functions to nonmathematical relationships—like the way a bond between father and son increases in intensity over time or the way the steady loyalty of an old friend provides constant support. An apt ability to extract generalizations of this kind is the alchemy that turns science into poetry.

As a practitioner, I understand the concept of transfer more fully in relation to two of its etymological kinfolk: transformation and transparency. When Pulitzer Prize–winning novelist Junot Diaz spoke at my university a few years ago, he told us that you haven't been educated until you've been transformed. I think this is where deep learning parts ways with rote memorization, and where narrow, school-to-career-based definitions of *transfer* part ways with the transformative experience we embrace in this chapter. Achieving proficiency on a task for a onetime goal—such as passing a test or class—doesn't change you as a human being. Diaz noted that there are lots of people out there who graduate from college without being educated. When learning is passionate, procedural, and internalized, however, you can't help but do things differently in the future. That's the whole point. Transfer happens as a result of transformation.

Transfer also happens more easily when the once and future applications of learning are clear. That's why transparency is important. Many teachers I know tell frustrating stories about having former students again in new classes only to find that they've seemingly retained little of what they previously learned. When I taught high school seniors, I would often encounter students I'd had in earlier grades who would no longer be using the skills and knowledge I had personally seen them master a few years before. I knew they had the content knowledge (e.g., literary terms, rhetorical appeals) and the procedural knowledge (e.g., invention and revision strategies) because I'd seen this firsthand. Yet when I asked, for example, why they didn't continue to use a prewriting activity that had once been a routine part of their composition process, the students explained that they thought this was a different class. Many of my students saw each new class they took—even with a familiar instructor—as an idiosyncratic game with its own arbitrary rules. The connections were not transparent.

> Transfer happens as a result of transformation. Transfer also happens more easily when the once and future applications of learning are clear.

And, to be fair, these students had a point. To use Nowacek's understanding of transfer as a rhetorical act, my students did need to figure out the moves needed for each new situation, to observe "in any given case the available means of persuasion" (Aristotle, *Rhetoric*, Book I, Chapter 2, 26–27), and to write a variety of genres for a variety of purposes and audiences—even if those audiences included the same teacher in a new role. I could do a better job, however, facilitating all this intellectual agility by telling students that they will be expected to use and adapt skills from our course in their other classes and by helping them to see the similarities. Sometimes a brief reminder is all that's needed: "You know that thing we used to do? Keep doing it."

Transfer and the Learning Cycle

Transfer is, quite literally, what students often do after completing a diploma or degree, and this prosaic meaning can help clarify the term's figurative use as a theoretical model. Preparing students to transfer from a two-year college to a four-year university, for instance, is all about aligning what students need to know and be able to do to satisfy their general education requirements with what they need to know and be able to do in their major. It's about vertical articulation. Educators have had lots of practice correlating outcomes across different systems, and initiatives such as the Common Core State Standards Initiative, Liberal Education and America's Promise, and the Degree Qualifications Profile ensure that we will continue attending to transferable learning at the institutional level.

Although the latter is far more complex, the literal and metaphorical meanings of transfer share an emphasis on portable competencies and a longitudinal view of learning. The two meanings also help us situate the idea of transfer in the instructional cycle. Throughout this book, we've offered strategies for promoting a gradual release of responsibility from instructor to student, and transfer represents those moments of release. It's the pivot point between novice and expert, our cue to let go. Although transfer certainly happens throughout a recursive learning cycle, we've placed this chapter last in our book because we believe that transferable learning is the best measure of mastery and independence.

Key Principles of Transfer

Haskell asks the centuries-old question at the heart of teaching for transfer: "What is it that enables a person with specific knowledge, learning, understanding, or skills learned in one area and/or social context to adapt, modify, or extend it in such a way as to be able to apply it to other areas?" (54). The answers to this question have important implications for classroom practice. Scholars generally agree on four key elements that contribute to transfer of learning: (1) expert content knowledge, (2) conscious procedural knowledge, (3) a disposition toward making connections, and (4) internalized practices. While each of these is itself a pathway to deeper learning, taken all together, they describe a fully independent learner.

1. *Expert content knowledge.* Because transfer depends on an informed ability to see the "similarities in dissimilars," students must have a strong command of the content knowledge to discern when it's appropriate to apply in new situations (Haskell 45–46). Transfer also depends on the ability to make generalizations based on underlying principles; thus, a close study of key concepts in a field is an essential part of teaching for transfer. For example, a student who has been studying 19th-century American transcendentalism would need a thorough understanding of transcendentalist principles and characteristics before being able to determine to what extent 20th-century writers such as Wallace Stegner or Michael Pollan could be described as following in this intellectual tradition. Without this subject matter expertise, generalizations are likely to be sweeping, not principled.

2. *Conscious procedural knowledge.* In addition to content knowledge, students need to be aware of the processes they use for different academic tasks in order to strategically adapt those procedures to new contexts or classes. This could be as simple as modifying the reading strategies one uses for a textbook to suit the needs of a journal article. Or it could be as complicated as drawing on the research methods learned in a social science class to design a community service project. Procedural knowledge is "the ability to apply conceptual knowledge to new problems by using the discipline's characteristic methods of thinking" (Bean, Chappell, and Gillam 4)—it is, as George Hillocks says, knowing "how, when, and for what purpose to use procedures that are

the province of that art" (124). In his review of experimental studies on writing pedagogy, Hillocks notes that "the treatments with the largest gains all focus on teaching procedural knowledge,

> In addition to content knowledge, students need to be aware of the processes they use for different academic tasks in order to strategically adapt those procedures to new contexts or classes.

knowledge of how to do things" (223).

3. *A disposition toward making connections.* Researchers have also identified a transfer habit of mind. Haskell calls this a "spirit of transfer" (116) and relates this special trait to an "animating principle" or "vital essence" (117) that can drive students to seek connections among diverse learning experiences. This striving, searching sense of interconnectedness becomes a type of moral and intellectual courage for Haskell (126–29); he calls it "a motivated, affective personality matrix" (117). We see this spirit of transfer in deeply passionate and curious students. These are the students who stop us after class to request recommendations for further reading or to ask, "Is what we discussed like . . . ?" or "Is this similar to the film on . . . ?" or to say, "This reminds me of . . ." Such students not only actively make connections for themselves but also help others do so as well.

4. *Internalized practices.* Transfer often happens after learning has become internalized or automatic. Students need loads of practice with the abilities we target for transfer. The aim is to create a kind of "muscle memory" of transferable skills and knowledge, so that students reflexively apply these competencies in new situations. This is not to say that we need to spend more time on drill-and-kill activities, but rather that we need to make space for intentional repetition that increases in difficulty. As one colleague says, "We need students to keep doing things until they're good at them." Such go-to content and procedural learning eventually become part of how students do business in academic settings. Internalized behaviors of this kind might include an ability to postpone judgment while gathering data—a skill that must be rehearsed repeatedly before it becomes automatic.

> Transfer often happens after learning has become internalized or automatic.

The lesson exemplars in this chapter offer concrete ways to address these key principles in our work with students. For instance, Ken Rand, a math instructor at Hartnell College, helps students find ways to reduce math anxiety while learning from their mistakes. Students who face these difficulties need more than just help with content knowledge on their journey toward independence; they also need help developing the procedural knowledge, dispositions, and internalized practices that will ultimately produce transferable learning.

Why Does Transfer Matter?

In his 2005 commencement address at Stanford University, Steve Jobs told the story of how a calligraphy course he dropped in on at Reed College later influenced the elegant typography of the first Macintosh computers. In addition to the art and history of hand-drawn calligraphy, the class taught Jobs about various typefaces and letter spacing—subjects he found fascinating but believed at the time would have no practical application in his life. However, a decade later when Jobs was creating the first Apple products, he said those calligraphy lessons came back to him:

> And we designed it all into the Mac. It was the first computer with beautiful typography. If I had never dropped in on that single course in college, the Mac would have never had multiple typefaces or proportionally spaced fonts. Of course it was impossible to connect the dots looking forward when I was in college. But it was very, very clear looking backwards ten years later.

Transfer of learning is always about connecting the dots. Sometimes we have a clear enough view ahead of us to predict where the connections will occur. Other times we have to trust that the content and procedural knowledge we've internalized will ultimately serve us well if we keep watching for the right moments.

Habits of Mind

As the story of the link between computers and calligraphy illustrates, transfer of learning is especially powerful when it arises from intellectual courage and passion. A disposition toward making connections—or "spirit of transfer"—is thus one of many key habits of mind that contribute to students' success. In *Education for Life and Work: Developing Transferable Knowledge and Skills in the 21st Century*, the National

> A disposition toward making connections—or "spirit of transfer"—is thus one of many key habits of mind that contribute to students' success.

Research Council argues that "productive beliefs about learning are an essential component of transferable knowledge" (4–17). These beliefs include motivation, creativity, metacognition, and self-regulation.

The Association of American Colleges and Universities (AAC&U) also views transfer of learning in terms of intellectual habits. In its "Integrative Learning VALUE Rubric," the AAC&U describes integrative learning as a dispositional capacity: "Integrative learning is an understanding and a disposition that a student builds across the curriculum and cocurriculum, from making simple connections among ideas and experiences to *synthesizing and transferring learning to new, complex situations within and beyond campus*" (emphasis added). The rubric identifies "transfer" as an outcome of "integrative learning" and states that a student who has mastered this competency "adapts and applies, independently, skills, abilities, theories, or methodologies gained in one situation to new situations to solve difficult problems or explore complex issues in original ways."

So important is the idea of transfer to the AAC&U that it also appears as a competency in the "Foundations and Skills for Lifelong Learning VALUE Rubric"—another indication that AAC&U sees a disposition toward making connections as an enduring personality trait, not a course-specific learning outcome. Here, mastery of transfer is expressed by student work that "makes explicit references to previous learning and applies in an innovative (new and creative) way that knowledge and those skills to demonstrate comprehension and performance in novel situations." Creativity is clearly also a habit of mind that facilitates transfer.

Integrative and lifelong learning have other habits of mind in common: *metacognition* and *self-regulation*, for instance. Literacy researcher Cynthia Shanahan defines the second of these in terms of the first, calling self-regulation "students' metacognitive awareness of their own understanding (or lack of it)" (77). As its name suggests, however, self-regulation is about more than just self-awareness; it's also what learners do to control or regulate their own learning. It's about the actions students take as a result of monitoring and reflecting on their own comprehension (Hattie and Timperley 93–94).

This one-two punch of metacognition cum self-regulation is a potent recipe for transfer of learning. We know our students have reached this point of independence when they start to generate their own feedback on their work, can accurately assess the correctness of the feedback they receive from others, and know if and when they need help and where to get it. These students—and I meet a handful of them every semester—are reflective self-managers who parlay the enhanced confidence and self-efficacy they've developed into a spirit of transfer. They are, in Nowacek's words, "agents of integration" (35). Writing on students at this stage, Costa and Kallick note, "Through reflection and self-evaluation, [these students] begin to see how the application of the habits transfers to all subject areas" (6).

The Trouble with Transfer

Transfer undoubtedly matters, but it's also tricky. Like its close etymological cousin the metaphor, transfer relies on the right kind of connections being formed. Both the word *transfer* and the word *metaphor* have morphemes meaning "to bear or carry"; each term represents a bridging of differences. *The Oxford English Dictionary*, in fact, defines *metaphor* as "a figure of speech in which a name or descriptive word or phrase is *transferred* to an object or action different from, but analogous to, that to which it is literally applicable" (emphasis added). Not for nothing does Aristotle say that mastery of metaphor is a sign of genius. Connecting the wrong kinds of images or ideas results in comic disasters or logical fallacies. Best-selling author Richard Lederer has made a career out of collecting mixed metaphors, such as "the light at the end of the tunnel is just the tip of the iceberg" and "let's bite the bull by the horns" (149–52).

> Like its close etymological cousin the metaphor, transfer relies on the right kind of connections being formed.

Consider the deft use William Shakespeare makes of metaphor in *King Lear*. In the following example, Shakespeare transfers the image of a weapon to his title character's emotional state. When the loyal Kent attempts to intercede on the wrongfully disinherited

Cordelia's behalf, an outraged Lear warns him that the "bow is bent and drawn; make from the shaft" (Act I, scene i, line 141), meaning that Kent had better get clear of Lear's rage. This martial metaphor both expresses the intense aggression Lear feels toward those who oppose his will and foreshadows the imminent destruction of his kingdom by civil war. The mental discipline required to create a metaphor that can do this much heavy lifting for a text is indeed a mark of genius.

With transfer of learning, too, the aptness is all. The dangers of false analogies, ahistorical conclusions, inappropriate writing styles, or sweeping generalizations understandably must give us pause. I think of those student essays I've read that claimed that Romeo and Juliet's relationship is exactly like the writer's own doomed 21st-century teenaged romance—Elizabethan gender norms, power dynamics, and family structures aside, of course.

However, I resist viewing these strained connections as acts of what some scholars call "negative transfer," or a misapplication of prior learning or experience in new settings. The five-paragraph essay, for instance, often features in conversations on "negative transfer" as an example of students inappropriately applying an essay structure they learned in high school to their college writing classes—a place where this artificial formula is typically no longer valued. Yet rather than seeing these infelicitous connections as mistakes to be avoided, we can see them as opportunities to draw on students' assets while sharpening their critical reasoning abilities. Our most vulnerable students need to know that what they bring to our classes is valuable, that knowing, for instance, how to write a five-paragraph essay can be part of the transfer process. Effective transfer is about extending and adapting, not replacing, what students already know and can do.

> Our most vulnerable students need to know that what they bring to our classes is valuable, that knowing, for instance, how to write a five-paragraph essay can be part of the transfer process. Effective transfer is about extending and adapting, not replacing, what students already know and can do.

At the same time, practice in discerning appropriate transfer opportunities—and pitfalls—is a powerful way to develop students' critical reasoning skills. As students view the varying conditions of their academic lives with an eye to useful similarities, they learn to avoid false analogies and hasty or sweeping generalizations. They learn to distinguish the coincidental from the comparable. Composition scholar Nelson Graff notes the power of discernment behind acts of transfer: "Our recognition of similarities matters because we must know that the knowledge and strategies we have learned apply in the new situation" (2). Students need to be able to tell if the new situation is just a little different from what they've already experienced or significantly different, yet still relevant . . . or not relevant at all.

Connective Thinking in the Classroom

In our classrooms, we explicitly teach for transfer when we choose learning experiences that prioritize synthesis and reflection. For example, we can ask students to describe how the writing skills they learned in their high school classes relate to their college courses or we can encourage students to metacognitively reflect on their learning process. Forget subtlety. If we want our students to make connections, we need to tell them to make connections. As part of our work with colleagues in other disciplines, we use the following questions with our students to promote this kind of connective, reflective thinking:

- How is this assignment similar to work you've done in other classes? How is it different?
- To what extent did your prior knowledge contribute to your success on this assignment?
- Where do you see yourself using this knowledge and these skills again?
- How might you need to adapt what you've learned for another genre or discipline?
- Which habits of mind most contributed to your success on this assignment? Why?
- What are the key principles, or "big ideas," behind this text/task/lesson?
- What generalizations can you make about what you learned?
- What did you most enjoy about this work? What would you like to do again?

Nowacek offers a useful analogy of her own to illustrate the different ways students can demonstrate connective thinking in the classroom: the brick versus the blueprint (26). In my developmental writing class, one student asked if she could add references to Andrew Lam's *Perfume Dreams: Reflections on the Vietnamese Diaspora* (2005)—a text she'd read in another course—to a paper she was writing for me on Maxine Hong Kingston's *The Woman Warrior: Memoirs of a Girlhood among Ghosts* (1975). I enthusiastically told her, "Yes, use it! It's a perfect fit." The text-to-text connection this student made between two courses is a good example of transfer as brick laying (or application); she added knowledge she already had to something new she was building. Transfer as blueprint (or reconstruction), on the other hand, is about using an entirely new framework as a result of a previously transformative experience. For instance, one student I had taught in both a British literature course and a grammar course successfully combined linguistic and literary frameworks in her analysis of Ursula Le Guin's novel *The Left Hand of Darkness* (1969). This student used what she'd learned from M. A. K. Halliday's work on the social contexts realized by different language registers to produce a novel interpretation of the characters' personal and political relationships.

Another outstanding student at my university, Liliana Castrellon, helped me to see why integrative learning is especially important for 21st-century learners. Liliana, who served as the student assistant for this project while an undergraduate at California State University at Monterey Bay (CSUMB), shared her view of why connective thinking is essential for her generation: "Millenials have grown up in a very interdisciplinary world; new fields have emerged and fields have merged together. Yet the education system has maintained its traditional teaching methods in separating each subject. Thus, we need to learn how to connect our thinking and learning across disciplines." And that's something that students will largely have to do on their own.

The Long View

If our ultimate goal for our students is independence, then we're going to have to be prepared to do some serious letting go. One of the greatest challenges of teaching for transfer is that we rarely get to see evidence of success. By definition, *transferable skills* and *knowledge* manifest themselves in places other than where they were first learned. We're suspended in that second book of the trilogy, wondering what becomes of the characters we've so grown to love.

This is the story I come back to on those days when I question whether I'm making a difference. Let me introduce you to Alma. She's now so astoundingly accomplished that she's generously granted me permission to share her story as inspiration to other students who are waiting for their moment to shine. I first met Alma when she was a tenth grader in my Advancement Via Individual Determination (AVID) class at Buena Park High School in southern California. Quiet, thoughtful, and composed, Alma had a way about her that suggested she was biding her time. Although she was clearly very bright and had a strong sense of intellectual curiosity as well as a good deal of personal fortitude, she wasn't a grade grubber. I had a sense that Alma was still figuring out to what extent she wanted to play the academic game—that is, earn those As and lock down those stellar SAT scores. And, indeed, Alma's academic record in high school was pretty mixed although her GPA was still probably higher than my own; I failed algebra twice in high school and blew off my health class to read novels in the back of the room.

During the years I had Alma in my AVID classes, I'd push her to excel in her studies, encourage her to take advanced coursework, and question her when her grades weren't what they could be. When she graduated, she enrolled in a community college.

A few years later, after I'd left Buena Park High School and joined the faculty at CSUMB, I heard from Alma. She'd completed her general education and was preparing to transfer to a four-year university. Then, a couple of years later, I reconnected again with Alma, who is now thriving as a senior at CSU Los Angeles, where she majors in sociology with an emphasis in inequalities and diversity. Alma has become a powerful and eloquent advocate for immigrant youth. These days, as a member of the Orange County Dream Team, Alma can be found working tirelessly to secure access to higher education for undocumented students. She has both found her passion and fulfilled her promise.

Not that I take credit for Alma. I'm just glad I recognized her potential. Alma's story is important because it can help us imagine where our students might be going before their path is clear. I also like the selfish kick of reassurance I get from Alma's success. I knew she was going to be fabulous down the road, and her process of intellectual maturation keeps me hopeful that all my students will eventually find their way. Alma didn't quite get it together during those years she was in my class, but she sure did later on.

Understanding transfer as transformation means accepting that we may never know the influence we have. When our students are ready, they'll use what they learned. Sometimes we even get to see this happen. And that's the best gift of all.

Works Cited

AAC&U (Association of American Colleges and Universities). "Integrative Learning VALUE Rubric" and "Foundations and Skills for Lifelong Learning VALUE Rubric." Web. <https://www.aacu.org/value-rubrics>

Aristotle. *Rhetoric*. Trans. W. Rhys Roberts. New York: McGraw-Hill, 1984. Print.

Bean, John C., Virginia A. Chappell, and Alice M. Gillam. *Reading Rhetorically*. Brief ed. New York: Pearson, 2004. Print.

Costa, A. L., and B. Kallick, eds. *Habits of Mind across the Curriculum: Practical and Creative Strategies for Teachers.* Alexandria: ASCD, 2009. Print.

Downs, Douglas, and Elizabeth Wardle. "Teaching about Writing, Righting Misconceptions: (Re)envisioning 'First-Year Composition' as 'Introduction to Writing Studies'." *College Composition and Communication* 58.4 (2007): 552–84. Print.

Graff, Nelson. "Teaching Rhetorical Analysis to Promote Transfer of Learning: This Strategy Has the Potential to Help Students Develop the Rhetorical Awareness and Meta-knowledge about Writing That Can Help Them Transfer Their Learning about Writing to New Contexts and Tasks." *Journal of Adolescent & Adult Literacy* 53.5 (2010): 376–85. Print.

Haskell, Robert E. *Transfer of Learning: Cognition, Instruction, and Reasoning*. San Diego: Academic Press, 2001. Print.

Hattie, John, and Helen Timperley. "The Power of Feedback." *Review of Educational Research* 77.1 (Mar. 2007): 81–112. Print.

Hillocks, George, Jr. *Teaching Writing as Reflective Practice*. New York: Teachers College Press, 1995. Print.

Jobs, Steve. Commencement Address. Stanford University Commencement Weekend. Stanford, CA. 12 June 2005. Web. <http://news.stanford.edu/news/2005/june15/jobs-061505.html>

Kingston, Maxine Hong. *The Woman Warrior: Memoirs of a Girlhood Among Ghosts*. New York: Knopf, 1975. Print.

Lam, Andrew. *Perfume Dreams: Reflections on the Vietnamese Diaspora*. Berkeley, CA: Heyday, 2005. Print.

Lederer, Richard. *Fractured English*. New York: Pocket Books, 1996. Print.

"Metaphor." Entry 1. *The Oxford English Dictionary*. 2014. Web.

Le Guin, Ursula K. *The Left Hand of Darkness*. New York: Ace. 1969. Print.

National Research Council. *Education for Life and Work: Developing Transferable Knowledge and Skills in the 21st Century*. Committee on Defining Deeper Learning and 21st Century Skills. Ed. James W. Pellegrino and Margaret L. Hilton. Board on Testing and Assessment and Board on Science Education, Division of Behavioral and Social Sciences and Education. Washington, DC: The National Academies Press, 2012. Print.

Nowacek, Rebecca S. *Agents of Integration: Understanding Transfer as a Rhetorical Act*. Carbondale: Southern Illinois UP, 2011. Print.

Shakespeare, William. *King Lear. The Norton Shakespeare*. Ed. Stephen Greenblatt, Walter Cohen, Jean E. Howard, and Katherine Eisman Maus. 2nd ed. New York: Oxford UP, 2008. 2325–567. Print.

Shanahan, Cynthia. "Teaching Science through Literacy." *Adolescent Literacy Research and Practice*. Ed. Tamara L. Jetton and Janice A. Dole. New York: Guilford Press, 2004. 75–93. Print.

Using the Habits of Mind as a Reflective Tool by Natasha Oehlman

Activity: a three-part reflective writing assignment over the semester

Learning Outcomes: identify habits of mind and connect them to students' development as learners through major writing projects completed over the semester

Habits of Mind: metacognition and reflection

Introduction to Habits of Mind

I first was introduced to the habits of mind within the context of a "college readiness" conference aimed primarily for educators teaching in secondary classrooms. As I learned more about these habits, or dispositions, and the work of secondary educators to use the habits of mind to support deeper learning, I began to think about the postsecondary university students I teach—a lively bunch—and how they too could possibly benefit from learning about the habits of mind. Maybe these dispositions and ways of thinking would help them discover and unearth patterns and habits about themselves that they might not know exist. And maybe these habits of mind would help them respond to tasks in meaningful, reflective ways as well as develop successful approaches to learning. I thought about the junior-level students in an upper-division professional writing course I teach and how often they struggle with the execution or completion of complex writing tasks. Even at the upper division level, students question their self-efficacy as writers—their "personal belief about one's capabilities to learn or perform skills at designated levels" (Bandura 391). I wondered if use of the habits of mind could be used as an instrument to help students reflect on their behaviors and monitor their growth as learners and writers and challenge their self-efficacy. If I could stress these habits of mind at the beginning of the semester, maybe I could help students identify their strengths and challenges with these habits of mind and encourage them to critically think and reflect on their own thinking processes when faced with complex challenges and tasks in the classroom. But, then I revised my thinking to infuse the habits of mind at key times during the semester to help them systematically reflect and evaluate their own thinking throughout the semester. So, I designed a three-part reflective writer's memo assignment that supported the deep thinking I wanted students to do.

The Beginning of the Semester

At the beginning of the semester, I introduce my students to the habits of mind (see Appendix 6.A at the end of this lesson exemplar) and then ask my students to complete a short reflective assignment called the Writer's Inventory[1] (see Appendix 6.B at the end of this lesson exemplar) detailing their relationship to writing, reading, and research. Included in this assignment is one question that invites students to think of themselves as learners in this course and to reflect: Taking into consideration the eight habits of mind discussed in class, reflection   describe your plan for success this semester.

In addition to helping students self-regulate their behaviors, I am interested in helping students develop their metacognitive abilities— thinking about thinking. On the surface, I want students to devise a plan for success thinking about using the eight habits of mind in terms of the course and their success. But, on a deeper level, I want to stress that success in the course is not wholly dependent on me, their instructor, but on their willingness to embrace these habits of mind as learners and active participants preparing to participate in the learn-

self-regulation   ing community. I want these habits of mind to facilitate self-directed
and   learning and growth, at a metacognitive level.
metacognition

At the Midterm

The midterm reflection is the next stage of the three-part written assignment. After the students have completed a large midsemester writing project, I ask them to reflect on the use of the eight habits of mind when composing, drafting, and finally publishing their midsemester writing project. My question to them is as follows:

> How did the eight habits of mind discussed at the beginning of the semester play a role as this writing project evolved? Select several to discuss. Describe your experiences.

At the End of the Semester

By now, as a class we have reflected on the habits of mind in two formal written memo assignments, including other small in-class writing assignments. They have been visible in class discussions and the work we do.

For the last assignment, I ask students to produce a final reflection on their overall semester.

> Writer's Task: Write a 2- to 3-page memo, single-spaced, highlighting (1) the key concepts you have learned in response to the goals set at the beginning of the semester in your writer's inventory; (2) the specific methods, techniques, and/or strategies you have learned and plan to transfer from this class to future professional writing situations (course based or otherwise); and (3) the key habits of mind that played a role in your success this semester and why. The memo should draw on your major writing project, along with minor assignments as examples to support your writing and learning.

spirit of transfer

Student Reactions to Lesson

Overall, I find that students learn a lot about themselves as learners and writers through the lens of the habits of mind, including what it takes to persist in an upper-division intensive professional writing course. One student mentioned his motivation to learn about the habits of mind "would make me a successful student." However, this same student admitted, "Applying such habits takes time and patience." I agree with this last statement and feel that the more frequently the habits of mind can be revisited in class discussions, the better.

patience

Of the student reflections on the lesson itself, the majority of comments reflected on personal growth in the course, as well as the individual as a learner. One student mentioned that the habits of mind "helped me in my growth to become a better student writer." The same student admitted to "never thinking much about my learning process. I self-managed by allowing myself the freedom to reflect to dig deeper into my own personal learning process." Another student mentioned learning about metacognition and that she "never really thought about 'why' she does what she does [in terms of learning]." Yet another student commented, "I liked best that this lesson taught me about myself. It's helpful to know what is behind what I am doing and that my thinking is going through many phases." This student's comment, examining the metacognitive aspect of the lesson, is exactly why I bring the habits of mind into the course. Students have an opportunity to really examine their thinking as they complete complex written tasks, which helps further develop their written communication skills.

Successes and Challenges

This three-part assignment has evolved from asking students to reflect once during the semester to reflecting at several strategic times over the course of the semester. I revised this lesson to include multiple reflection points because I found that I needed to continually revisit and repeat the habits of mind in order to support the deeper transformative learning I wanted to see take place. In some cases, a three-part reflection is still not enough and repeated reminders are necessary almost on a weekly basis to help keep the habits of mind "fresh" in the students' thinking and "alive" in the classroom environment. So, to that end, I find myself trying to remember to mention the habits of mind as I am introducing other class material or during general classroom discussions. This can be a challenge; the ability to constantly weave in and integrate the habits of mind needs to be habitual for the instructor as well as the students. One possible solution might be to write the habits of mind into the course goals or outcomes.

In reading all the reflections, though, I witness that students think critically about the ways they are learning as they begin to recognize how certain habits of mind help them solve problems that arise over the semester. Students are assuming responsibility for their own behavior and use these habits as resources to understand and solve their own problems. Students are thinking cognitively about their thinking.

I also witness a change in their attitudes as writers. At the beginning of the semester, most students admit to feeling helpless as writers. Usually, they are not familiar with their own processes as writers and feel they have "little control" over the writing process and the work they produce. Their confidence levels are shaky upon entering this professional writing class. But, when they use the habits of mind as a vehicle to understand their own processes as writers, they begin to recognize that these habits, or dispositions, feed into their psyche. For example, once they know *persistence* as a disposition exists, and we make this term explicit as a part of the learning process, they self-efficacy then have the ability to "control" the outcome. Learners can begin to understand how they can modify their own behaviors and writing practices to achieve completion of long-term writing projects and complex tasks set before them. They can sustain long writing projects without losing focus and arrive confidently at the other end of a challenging writing project having used "persistence" to carry them through.

While students work on developing coherent paragraphs, sentences, style, voice, and tone, essential elements for professional writing, they are also working to achieve a deeper understanding of themselves as writers and complex problem solvers by using the habits of mind—and especially one habit of mind: metacognition, thinking about thinking. When students are able to think and ask themselves why they think a certain way and what is influencing this thinking, and then to reflect and evaluate their thinking patterns to make conscious decisions to change certain patterns of thinking, that can be really powerful in the writing classroom—maybe equally as powerful as exercises on paragraphs and sentence structure.

metacognition

Supporting Activities

The following activities support discussion of the habits of mind at the beginning of the semester:

- During the first or second class, I introduce and engage the students in a discussion about the eight habits of mind. Using a KWL+ chart (i.e., finding out what they know, what they want to know, and what they learned) is a great activity that accompanies this discussion.
- I follow up the KWL+ activity with a presentation called "Habits of Mind: Toolbox for Success." This presentation explains how the habits of mind will give students the tools to be reflective, creative thinkers in college while developing transferable skills for the workplace.
- The first question I ask in the presentation is: What have been your prior experiences with writing? I ask the students to meet a person in the class and discuss for three minutes their experiences. Then I ask them to share and we talk as a large group. Next I ask them to participate in a small activity: to write their name using their nondominant hand. They quickly begin to see that something as simple as writing down their name can be cognitively challenging at first when it requires the use of a different part of the brain. I then ask students to discuss the following in small groups:
  - Is it harder to be precise and accurate writing this way?
  - Do you feel like you did when you first started writing?
  - Does it feel awkward and uncomfortable?

We next discuss their experiences, which mostly reflect their frustration with trying to write the letters of their name straight or trying to write their name quickly on the page, things they easily do with their dominant hand. I tell them that this task should be difficult because the brain is learning a new skill. I also tell them that they might feel this way during parts of the course when they experience new ideas, new perspectives, and engage in more rhetorically complex written communication tasks. Then I invite them to focus on the habits of mind as a strategy to help move through or overcome difficulties, noting Arthur L. Costa's point that these dispositions help students "behave intelligently when confronted with problems" (80). Finally, we move to discussion of the eight habits of mind (see Appendix 6.A).

Quick Start Guide

1. Schedule at least 30–45 minutes of class time for initial discussion on the habits of mind—and then plan accordingly throughout the semester to introduce the other scaffolded assignments.

2. Plan to have the students review the list and definitions of habits of mind in Appendix 6.A before the initial class discussion to front-load these terms. Students often know the terms independently, but framed together as "habits" may be a new concept. Asking the students to think about these terms before the initial instructor introduction encourages schema building as well as active engagement with these terms.

3. Think about how to utilize collaborative strategies (i.e., pair share, small-group discussion) to engage students in the discussion of habits of mind when first introduced. Students have a lot to say about how these habits play a role in their everyday, and academic, lives. Sharing with peers allows for a richer and livelier discussion, as well as thoughtful discussion as to the application of these habits in different contexts.

Note

1. The Writer's Inventory assignment was adapted from *Critical Situations: A Rhetoric for Writing in Communities* by Sharon Crowley and Michael Stancliff (New York: Longman, 2008).

Works Cited

Bandura, Albert. *Social Foundations of Thought and Action: A Social Cognitive Theory.* Englewood Cliffs: Prentice Hall, 1986. Print.

Costa, Arthur L. "Habits of Mind." *Developing Minds: A Resource Book for Teaching Thinking.* 3rd ed. Ed. Arthur L. Costa. Alexandria: Association for Supervision and Curriculum Development, 2001. 80–86. Print.

CWPA, NCTE, and NWP (Council of Writing Program Administrators, National Council of Teachers of English, and National Writing Project). *Framework for Success in Postsecondary Writing.* Berkeley: National Writing Project, 2011. Print.

Appendix 6.A: Habits of Mind

For the purpose of this exemplar, I use the following eight habits of mind[1] from *Framework for Success in Postsecondary Writing*:

- Curiosity—the desire to know more about the world.
- Openness—the willingness to consider new ways of being and thinking in the world.
- Engagement—a sense of investment and involvement in learning.
- Creativity—the ability to use novel approaches for generating, investigating, and representing ideas.
- Persistence—the ability to sustain interest in and attention to short- and long-term projects.
- Responsibility—the ability to take ownership of one's actions and understand the consequences of those actions for oneself and others.
- Flexibility—the ability to adapt to situations, expectations, or demands.
- Metacognition—the ability to reflect on one's own thinking as well as on the individual and cultural processes used to structure knowledge. (CWPA, NCTE, and NWP 1)

Appendix 6.B: The Writer's Inventory

Part I: Answer the following 13 questions in short paragraphs. Make sure to develop and support your ideas with examples. Include the question.

---

1. Costa posits 16 habits of mind but also notes this list is not exhaustive.

1. Describe your relationship to writing.

2. What do you currently understand to be "good writing"?

3. Discuss some specific piece of writing for which you have respect. Give as much detail as possible about what made the writing worthy of that respect.

4. Where do you need experience and practice as a reader?

5. Consider the writing process. Where do you need experience and practice as a writer?

6. Consider the research process. Where do you need experience and practice as a researcher?

7. What aspects of writing are most interesting and enjoyable for you? Most challenging?

8. What role does writing play in your life right now?

9. What do you project for your future as a writer? What kinds of writing will your profession or future course of study demand?

10. What situations and questions do you need to address as a writer?

11. How comfortable are you navigating new technologies and finding online resources to help you navigate new technologies?

12. Taking into consideration the eight habits of mind discussed in class, describe your plan for success this semester.

13. Review the course outcomes—see syllabus. What areas are you most interested in learning or finding out about?

Part II: Once you have completed the 13 questions in the inventory, look for common themes and pull out what you think are "most strongly indicative of your strengths, weaknesses, and interests as a writer." Then, make a list of three goals to set for yourself as a writer. For each goal, explain briefly why you consider this goal to be important.

Reading, Writing, and Habits of Mind Reflection Essay by Olga Blomgren

Activity: college-level essay on reading, writing, and habits of mind

Learning Outcomes: write an essay reflecting on reading and writing strategies and processes; discover the relationship between habits of mind and literacy and learning skills

Habits of Mind: metacognition, openness, engagement, persistence, flexibility, creativity, responsibility, and curiosity

When my colleagues and I first began to discuss how we ask students to reflect on their habits of mind in writing, we realized that we have different iterations of this prompt for the varied levels of writers whom we teach. We agreed that this exercise may benefit students differently at different points in their college careers. Although we all work with developmental writers in some form, we also teach college-level and upper-division writers. These different courses have preestablished outcomes and objectives and we have had to find a way to make habits of mind meaningful and useful to students within these existing contexts. Courses such as a first-year reading and writing class may feel like an isolated learning experience, more difficult to relate to other courses. However, this essay provides students an opportunity to note the skills they can transfer to other assignments and courses that call on these abilities. Incorporating instruction and reflection on habits of mind helps students understand that their learning is in their power if they persist, take responsibility, remain open, and so on. Utilizing different versions of this assignment in both general education and upper division courses can provide a moment of self-comprehension for those new to this exercise, or a timely reminder for students who have prior knowledge of the relationship between habits of mind and learning.

spirit of transfer

self-efficacy

This assignment demonstrates how I integrate the habits of mind into my classroom dialogue and reflective writing assignments. Early in the semester, I introduce habits of mind as integral to learning. In this course, we use the eight habits identified in the *Framework for Success in Postsecondary Writing* (CWPA, NCTE, and NWP), although instructors may select any of the 16 habits they want students to work with in a course. In this first discussion, students are asked to reflect and briefly write on their own habits and those they believe will aid them throughout the course. This writing is not collected. As we close the discussion, I share with them that they will be asked to write more about their habits later in the semester and that they can utilize this exercise as prewriting and information on how they viewed their habits at the start of the course. Throughout the semester, we briefly discuss habits of mind and sometimes students will bring them up on their own. Later in the term, I pass out and review the reading, writing, and habits of mind reflection prompt. At reflection this point, the language is familiar to students.

This particular prompt was created for a developmental, first-year integrated reading and writing course. The outcomes for the course include learning and applying reading and writing strategies to help students develop confidence in their own reading and writing processes. Coursework includes creating multiple drafts of essays that are read by peers, revised, and collected in a portfolio. These essays become the work that students will reflect on in this assignment. This prompt asks students to reflect on their reading and writing processes alongside the habits of mind. All three areas are grouped together in the same assignment to encourage students to develop the habits they feel will help them meet their academic goals. However, the nature of the prompt is flexible. For an idea of how this assignment can be adapted for upper-division writers, see Natasha Oehlman's "Using the Habits of Mind as a Reflective Tool" in this chapter.

The midterm reflection (see the appendix at the end of this lesson exemplar) is an important exercise in metacognition. Although students engage in class discussion about their learning, the in-depth process of thinking, reflecting, and writing is invaluable. A written reflection requires students to consider the practices, procedures, and dispositions toward learning that go into developing their reading and writing skills. This prompt is assigned in the middle of the semester, so students are still trying to figure out their needs as a learner. I ask students to also include information on skills or areas they wish to develop in the remaining weeks of the semester. They have a chance to see what they are doing well, and where they need to metacognition turn their focus. This is midterm, after all, and time remains to work and in whatever areas they feel need more attention. Significantly, the responsibility success of the reflection lies in increased student metacognition and taking greater responsibility for their work. As I remind them, we are in class together for a few hours a week, but the rest of the time they are solely responsible for their own learning (see the appendix at the end of this lesson exemplar).

Student Response and Successes and Challenges

Student reaction ranges from anticipation to anxiety. Sometimes a few students are familiar with writing reflection essays. Often, they are not. Many are intrigued by a prompt that requires them to write about themselves. Most ask if it is okay to use personal pronouns and are unsure of how to begin. At this point we discuss the prompted information they want to include in their essay. Ultimately, students engage in the opportunity to metacognate over the length of the assignment. This also includes reflecting on and learning from what they have not done, or strategies that do not work for them. Students themselves often write about how they have transferred skills they learned, both in and from the class, to other courses. Another accomplishment is that students respond by writing about ~~adaptability~~ their responsibility in their learning.

A primary challenge is that as instructors we have to keep modeling the habits of mind and bringing them into the class focus. The habits are not part of class content, so they are brought in as a complement to the root of the class learning. Explicit discussion of the habits must be an ongoing classroom effort. I have found that initiating a short discussion at the beginning of a class meeting serves as a useful reminder and helps us to keep the habits in our consideration and dialogue. After the initial introduction, a few of these discussions throughout the semester should be plenty.

Quick Start Guide

1. Early in the semester, introduce habits of mind as integral to learning. Select the habits you want students to work with in your course. In this course, we use the eight habits identified in the *Framework for Success in Postsecondary Writing* (CWPA, NCTE, and NWP).
2. Continue to use this language throughout the semester to help students connect these habits with learning.
3. At midterm, pass out and review the habits of mind reflection prompt.
4. To familiarize students with the assignment, employ multiple activities. Class, small-group, and even pair discussion of the prompt is effective.

5. After discussion, ask students to freewrite or use any other pre-writing strategy to get their initial response to the assignment on paper. If time permits, another good activity is reading and assessing a sample reflection essay or two as a class. This is a good opportunity for students to read as writers, and see how previous students have approached the assignment.

6. After students develop a complete draft of their essay, have the class complete peer reading of reflections.

Work Cited

CWPA, NCTE, and NWP (Council of Writing Program Administrators, National Council of Teachers of English, and National Writing Project). *Framework for Success in Postsecondary Writing*. Berkeley: National Writing Project, 2011. Web.

Appendix 6.C: Midterm Reflection

Midterm Reflection

Purpose: Your objective in this reflection is to clearly and thoughtfully explain how your reading and writing skills have progressed this semester. Remember that developing an understanding of one's literacy processes is one of the learning outcomes of this course. In this course we are trying to elevate not only reading skills and essays, but also self-awareness of these skills.

Directions: Write a three- to four-page self-evaluative essay focusing on the overall reading and writing processes and habits of mind you have developed and used in this course. You may also wish to state what future steps you will take to continue your evolution as a college-level reader and writer.

1. Discuss the strategies you use when reading for this class. Describe what you do to ensure you comprehend and analyze texts. Explain any new strategies you use and why they are helpful.

2. Explain your writing process, from prewriting to polished draft. Describe what you do to ensure you follow directions, begin with a clear thesis, write complete paragraphs, and finish your essays

on time. Explain all of the strategies you use and why they work for you.

3. Specifically introduce and discuss the revised papers you are turning in. For these essays,

   a. Discuss the strengths and things you would like to continue working on in the final version you are turning in. <u>Highlight all the changes you make directly on the revised essay.</u>

   b. Cite specific evidence from your work to show how you have edited and revised your coursework both after peer review and after instructor evaluation.

   c. Explain how you have edited and revised the essay through multiple drafts, specifically based on the assignment prompt, evaluation sheet, course outcomes, and shared criteria for assessing formal writing.

4. Explain which habits of mind have helped you most in this course. Also discuss if you need to focus on developing and using any other habits in the remainder of the semester.

Work Cited

Keillor, Garrison. "How to Write a Letter." *The Norton Reader: An Anthology of Nonfiction*. 13th ed. Eds. Linda Peterson, John Brereton, Joseph Bizup, Anne Fernald, and Melissa Goldthwaite. New York: W.W. Norton, 2011.

Twain, Mark. "Advice to Youth." *The Norton Reader: An Anthology of Nonfiction*. 13th ed. Eds. Linda Peterson, John Brereton, Joseph Bizup, Anne Fernald, and Melissa Goldthwaite. New York: W.W. Norton, 2011.

Words of Advice by Jennifer McGuire

Activity: writing advice for the next semester

Learning Outcomes: self-awareness, self-management, and critical thinking

Habits of Mind: transfer of learning and persistence

Okay, you're done. This is the last class, and this is your final. Look around the room. Are we all here? Is this the same group as we had at the beginning? Are we missing a couple of people? Now look at your seat. Look who's in it. You are. And it's the last time. What got your butt in that seat all semester?

At the end of the semester, it's hard to put a finger on everything students have learned. We can ask them to take out their first essays, look at how far they've come, and compare their skills now to the skills they had four months prior. Yes, there will be a difference. But what did students really take in? What they take with them and what got them through the semester will be widely different. The semester is over, the students are all ready for the next step, and, most important, they have the skills they need to make that step with confidence. But the semester-long process has been a lot like learning the alphabet; they learned it gradually—built a foundation, went letter by letter, and somehow learned the whole thing. Moving on to the next class is one more step on that same journey. We all started with the alphabet—learned the letters, strung them into words, made sentences, paragraphs, essays, communicated whole ideas and thought processes——and we just kept going. At the end of the semester, students are ready to go into their next class and their next encounter with learning.

But what gets us through? How do we learn anything? What motivates us? What stops some students from going to class? A class may be compulsory or elective, but the question remains the same: What makes a student stick to it? Whether it is a community college pretransfer class or a senior seminar, students learn something aside from mastering course objectives in the classroom. Depending on their life circumstance, students bring unique assets to their educational experience while developing and fortifying habits of mind that generate success. These habits of mind can be shared with others in the class, with future classes, and are what students take with them as they proceed in their educational journey. Their success at the end of the semester is a testament to persistence, and students can help each other learn what it takes to make it through.

persistence
and
motivation

Tell It Like It Is

When students ask about the final day, I don't need to prepare them. I tell them the final will be cumulative, but they don't need to study for it. When the last day comes, the final is simple. I ask them to think for a moment about what they learned this semester from class. Then I have the students take turns orally giving their answer. The responses are usually really simple and the process goes quickly. I mostly hear one-word or one-sentence answers that include things such as sentence structure, how to start an essay, or how to do citations. I say, "Great" and nod my head. It is great. But . . .

reflection

Then we talk about those skills and how they are going to be used in their futures. This part takes a little bit longer because it turns out more like a discussion. We throw around ideas, how skills we learned in class have been applied to our real lives, and how they may be used in our chosen careers, jobs, school, and life. I veer the conversation to how the semester went and all the things that happened in the four months since we started class. I hand out letters that I had them write to themselves at the beginning of the semester. At that time I had told them, "You will not be the same person you are now by the time this class is over. Write to yourself, and tell it like it is." When they read over their letter, they are often taken aback. We share what has changed, what we expected then, and how much has happened both personally and academically since the start of the term.

spirit of transfer

This is when I tell them their final prompt: "You have made it through a semester. Not everyone could. You had to deal with making the choice to attend, finding the money to pay for it, attending, doing the homework, maybe raising kids, maybe with a job, usually with some goal in mind, personal stuff going on, family, friends, everything. And you made it. How did you do it? If you could give advice to students just starting out their semester or to someone who is having a hard time in the middle of the semester, what advice would you give them? What got you through the semester?"

self-efficacy

They can address this topic however they like. Completely informal. They are not evaluated on this task: They get full points just for being there. This will be read by others. I will collect their letters, and they will not get them back. They know this because I passed around folders containing old student letters at the beginning of the semester. Now is the time they remember reading those letters. Some students saw them again midsemester, when I brought the letters out and shared them with the class again, especially if they were having a hard time just making it through.

I give the students time to think about and write down their ideas. I tell them not to worry about spelling, grammar, or anything. I ask them to just get what they want to say down on paper. It doesn't take long to write these reflections, maybe half an hour at most, and they usually run about a page. Generally the students finish at about the same time. Then they share their responses if they want to. They usually do, and there are many more nods and "greats" than just mine! Through their letters they are able to reflect and share a whole other set of skills that they learned, taught each other, and will carry on, that will help future students.

The types of letters they end up writing range from personal to academic. Sometimes the students tell a little about what they went through as a story, and sometimes they write a list. Because their final is something that they, and only they, know, there is an absolute confidence in their words. They have made it through the semester, they know how they did it, and there is no guessing about what they know.

The reaction from students is in their writing. Here are a few common gems:

- "Ask questions! The teacher is here to help. If you don't know something, let them know!"
- "Get support from your friends. Having my friend in class with me made me want to go to class, and helped when we did homework together."
- "Don't take class with friends since it can be distracting if you're like me. Plus you make friends with the other people in class and that's another thing college is good for."
- "Do your homework. Keep caught up."
- "Don't party the night before a morning class."

And here's my personal favorite:

- "Eat a good breakfast."

I've never come across a one-sentence letter from this activity. It's the only challenge I think could arise, but students don't even ask me the "required" amount that they need to write. They just do it. If you did come across such a request, you could give a time and page limit.

If you want to give this assignment more of a grade, instead of assigning points for showing up, the essay could be stretched into a more formal paper with more specific boundaries—for instance, a reading-based argument essay defining *college success*. There are many wonderful essays about letters out there that can offer students inspiration, such as Garrison Keillor's "How to Write a Letter" and Mark Twain's "Advice to Youth." There are also innumerable letters of advice to find (e.g., in newspapers and magazines), and the topic of advice is easy to research. This activity doesn't need to be the final; it can just be an activity for the final day, or a close to the final day. It's a great way to wrap up by having students create a transfer of learning for themselves and the next group of students.

Quick Start Guide

1. Assign participation points for attending the final in your syllabus.
2. During the first week of class have students write a letter to themselves about what they hope to learn in class that describes why they are taking the class and what they think the class will be like. (After two semesters, you will have a set of letters to show current students and in that way help motivate students to make it through the course successfully.)
3. Keep those letters!
4. At the final, pass out the letters written in the first week of class and have students write the final letter.

Works Cited

Keillor, Garrison. "How to Write a Letter." *The Norton Reader: An Anthology of Nonfiction*. 13th ed. Eds. Linda Peterson, John Brereton, Joseph Bizup, Anne Fernald, and Melissa Goldthwaite. New York: W.W. Norton, 2011. Print.

Twain, Mark. "Advice to Youth." *The Norton Reader: An Anthology of Nonfiction*. 13th ed. Eds. Linda Peterson, John Brereton, Joseph Bizup, Anne Fernald, and Melissa Goldthwaite. New York: W.W. Norton, 2011. Print.

Negotiating Transfer within Sustainability: From Consumer to Policy Maker by Rebecca Kersnar

Activity: Personal Sustainability Indicators Essay

Learning Outcomes: understand sustainability and sustainability indicators; clarify how they measure them; clarify measurements of indicators; and analyze student motivations, choices, and opportunities for making choices as a consumer and enacting policies as a policy maker at California State University Monterey Bay

Habits of Mind: transfer of learning, curiosity, engagement, openness, and persistence

Some assignments provide a strong enough challenge to push students to the edge of their abilities, and the process can feel messy and, at times, disorienting to both students and teachers. In these moments, it's easy to wonder if the challenge is too much—that is, until students begin to take ownership of the process, build satisfying depth and thoughtful reflection, and express pride in their own growth. Such is the common sequence of events when my lower-division university students develop the Personal Sustainability Indicators Essay, an early to midsemester assignment within my environmental studies and communication course (Introduction to Science and Environmental Policy: The Sustainable Campus) at California State University Monterey Bay (CSUMB) (see the appendix at the end of this lesson exemplar). Within this assignment, one primary reason why the process can be especially challenging and rewarding is that students practice the habit of mind of transfer, or the ability to apply past knowledge to new situations, not only when viewing their choice between two indicators through different lenses as a consumer, but also when using that earlier context as an upcoming sustainability policy maker at CSUMB.

spirit of
transfer

The Course, the Assignment, and the Process

The Personal Sustainability Indicators Essay (aka Sustainability Indicators Essay) begins after students have completed the Sustainability Position Paper during the first month of the semester. Through the initial Sustainability Position Paper assignment they investigate the meaning of sustainability, take an ecological footprint quiz, read about the connection between consumer culture and ecological degradation, and then use all of that context to take a position on the extent to which they feel they could lighten their ecological impact and whether or not they feel they should. In effect, at this stage the students gain an introductory understanding of sustainability and their orientation to it, providing an excellent means for students to warm up to one another and our content. Within this introductory assignment, I find that students especially enjoy determining and comparing their ecological footprint results and making choices related to their lifestyles. Thereafter, within the Sustainability Indicators Essay, students fulfill a central aim of this second major assignment: to make the concept of sustainability more concrete. Students build this deeper understanding by choosing two sustainability indicators—or markers that show how well we are meeting the needs of current and future generations (e.g., the gallons of water they use, the volume of trash and recycling they accumulate, the ounces of meat they consume)—to measure within a short-term personal study. They then reason through their decision making between these indicators based on their values, a published consumer impacts study, and their own personal studies. Students next fulfill the second central aim of the Sustainability Indicators Essay: to judge the extent to which those earlier considerations (their values, the published study, and their own personal study) are relevant as they transfer from consumer to policy maker, and to settle on a sustainability policy area to plan within at CSUMB (e.g., a campus water policy). Participants have more than four weeks to develop the Sustainability Indicators Essay, and they do so in stages, using a number of smaller assignments to guide their understanding of some associated readings, their own measurements, and the drafted sections within the essay. Students commonly use the policy area focus chosen at the end of the Sustainability Indicators Essay as the basis for their upcoming Campus Sustainability Policy Essay, although they are allowed to shift focus later on, if desired. The demands of this assignment are substantial and require thoughtful facilitation, but most students seem to enjoy the related challenges and changing purposes within our process.

integrative thinking

intellectual stamina

Within the four-week-plus sequence for the Sustainability Indicators Essay, students spend the first week going over life cycle impacts associated with some standard industry consumer products compared with some sustainable consumer products. This initial week provides a useful bridge between the Sustainability Position Paper and the Sustainability Indicators Essay, concretizes some connections between consumer behaviors and sustainability impacts, and aids students in selecting their sustainability indicators. During the second week, students plan their methods for their personal sustainability indicator studies, begin to measure both indicators, and start to research environmental issues associated with both of their indicators (background for the value section). During the third week, students continue to measure their indicators, read and discuss the published consumer impacts study (see, e.g., M. Brower and W. Leon's *The Consumer's Guide to Effective Environmental Choices: Practical Advice from the Union of Concerned Scientists* and/or a related update study), and discuss drafts of their value and environmental impacts sections. During the fourth week, students discuss the results of their personal sustainability studies, consider a draft of the personal sustainability study section, and plan the global analysis section (i.e., when they

reflection   shift from a consumer to a policy maker). Students then conduct a peer review of the entire essay, including a deconstruction of a past student product, leaving the weekend to finalize the essay, which is due on the following Tuesday (week five in the essay sequence). The sequencing within this complex assignment is a bit of a marathon endeavor. I therefore find that students can execute the product most successfully if I start with a general overview, and then provide more context and instructions as I move through the sections over time. In this way, students gain clarity and confidence as they are exposed to digestible chunks along the way.

Student Responses to the Assignment

Orchestrating such an intricately scaffolded assignment requires strong organization and focus, and the students do not always view the process and rewards in the same way I do, but the learning and growth that emerge are often remarkable. The end-of-semester survey and supplemental evaluation responses from my fall 2013 students (14 of 20 responses collected for the survey and 20 of 20 responses collected for the supplemental evaluation) included some enlightening and surprising patterns.

With few exceptions, these students—possessing little prior knowledge of environmental science content—strongly enjoyed the learning environment, felt highly motivated to complete the tasks within the assignment, indicated that the tasks were clear, and expressed strong interest in the focus of the assignment. For example, most described the learning environment as "personal," "positive," and "welcoming," while one student expressed that there was "a lot of discussion over similar topics." In reflecting on the source of their motivation within the assignment, students most commonly expressed that they were "curious about their own habits," "interested in the topic and materials," and "interested in the environment." One student asserted that it was "sometimes hard to get engaged" while another said he "didn't like the subject." Given the challenge of explaining the unique and shifting sections of this assignment, most students nevertheless felt the tasks were "very clear," "well detailed . . . online," and clear because "the teacher was very thorough in explaining." The few students who mentioned that parts of the guidelines were confusing also indicated that e-mail clarification was helpful. In reflecting on their interest in the topic, many students cited an initial curiosity about their habits, followed by a growing interest in sustainability issues through their review of source information and personal studies. Some students also asserted that their classmates' excitement fueled their interest, while a number of individuals identified their strong concern for the environment as the source of their interest. A handful of students professed some mixed interest in the topic, such as one student who asserted, "Sustainability is not high on my list of priorities, but it should be." These generally positive outcomes suggest that many students engaged with a number of habits of mind. For example, students demonstrated curiosity in wanting to know more about our ecological challenges and their own habits, openness in their positive orientation toward classmates' perceptions, engagement by involving themselves thoughtfully in their personal studies, and persistence by sustaining interest in our complex and detailed process.

engagement and motivation

curiosity, openness, and persistence

My aim within this assignment was for students to expand their communication skills while thinking more concretely about their sustainability-related habits, choices, and decision making, from the vantage point of a consumer and of an upcoming policy maker. While doing so, I also hoped that they would become more agile in using transfer skills. I found that students gained many things related to these aims, but they largely did not reflect on their decision-making skills or ability to shift between contexts. Most commonly, students expressed that they gained a deeper understanding of sustainability, sustainability indicators, and environmental challenges; learned how to reduce their impact and improve their habits; understood themselves better; and expanded their writing skills. Students also seemed to be thinking in more nuanced ways about the issues they researched and the challenge in progressing from caring to making smaller lifestyle changes to making a substantial difference. By far, students were most excited about the hands-on components of this assignment—the opportunity to collect their own data and investigate their own habits. For example, one student asserted, "The Sustainability Indicators Essay was my favorite essay [for] this class. It was the most challenging and the task I dedicated the most time to. I enjoyed measuring my indicators and discovering the number of calories consumed and the amounts of trash produced." Students' research of source information also seemed highly important to them—a means to gain expertise within and a reason for caring about their indicator areas. As one student explained, "I really enjoyed the Brower and Leon readings because they gave you concrete facts about . . . all the negative effects . . . from your bad habits." Through both of these components, I observed and many students shared that they began to take stronger ownership of their projects. Concurrently, most individuals expressed a related increase in their confidence through completing this assignment, because they felt the knowledge they gained was "practical and useful," relevant to other contexts, and helpful in advancing their writing skills.

responsibility

If students were not generally focused on the decision-making and transfer components within their reflections, did they nevertheless successfully meet these outcomes? Through my assessment of their products, I assert that on the whole students were able to demonstrate very strong decision-making and transfer skills in composing their essays. A basic requirement for passing this assignment is that students understand each unique decision-making lens (e.g., values, environmental impact, personal study, global analysis) and exhibit appropriate focus and sound reasoning in explaining the basis for their choices within each section, including their final selection of an upcoming policy area at CSUMB. This group of individuals received an average of 89% on their final essays, ranging from 85% to 97%. In other words, within my assessments all students were able to communicate their decision making successfully across a range of contexts. The global analysis section tends to be the most challenging section for students, so it requires a good amount of in-class support, likely a bit more than I currently provide. Nevertheless, even with the current level of support, students composed generally successful global analysis sections. For example, here is part of one student's submission within this section, showing her application of elements from earlier sections when making a CSUMB policy area choice:

> My decision to focus on food policy at CSUMB is due to adherence to my values as well as data collected by the Brower and Leon

(1999) study. The issue of food production struck deeply with my value for animals and their environment, and serves as a motivational factor for my decision. The Brower and Leon (1999) study is broad and provides the hard facts I needed to appeal to my logical senses. It also pins food as one of the most harmful consumer activities. The campus houses thousands of students and provides food resources to them through various dining halls. What types of food CSUMB decides to serve, as well as what organizations/food producers it decides to support can have a significant impact on the environment.

In other words, this student and most other students in the group were able to communicate successfully the extent to which the earlier considerations were relevant, not only within their personal lives but also within their decision to focus on improving CSUMB.

Strengths and Challenges of the Sustainability Indicators Essay

The Sustainability Indicators Essay is an assignment I've been tinkering with for years. It creates an athletic experience for the students and for me. Most students appreciate that stretch ("I liked . . . the opportunity to explore within [the Sustainability Indicators Essay]"), but some are not as enthusiastic ("Sometimes the amount of writing and in-depth research became tedious"). In spite of the hesitation of a few, I continue to be convinced that the uphill climb of the Sustainability Indicators Essay pays off immensely in student learning and personal growth. Here are some of the strongest strengths and challenges of this assignment:

persistence

Strengths
- Students are allowed flexibility, choices, and the opportunity to explore their own reasoning (selecting indicators, deciding between indicators, selecting a policy area).
- Hands-on components and engaging opportunities for discussion are provided.
- Students are introduced to peer-reviewed research and their own rudimentary original research.
- The skill of transfer—applying parallel decision making when moving between contexts—is incorporated.

- Excellent opportunities for critical thinking and introspection (asserting why and how beyond what, requiring evidence, reasoning through value hierarchies, creating a hierarchy within the earlier sections, etc.) are provided.
- Nuanced thinking is increased as students realize that priorities can change depending on the lens utilized.

Challenges
- Students can become somewhat fatigued with all of the details and shifting purposes.
- Substantial instructor explanation and facilitation are required.
- Students who are not as interested in sustainability and environmental science content may not be as engaged with the process (to be fair, however, this is an environmental studies communications course housed within Science and Environmental Policy).
- Assessment of the partial draft (a thought piece in the middle) and the final essay may involve considerable instructor feedback.

In response to the challenges identified here, I've provided revised Sustainability Indicators Essay guidelines (see the appendix at the end of this lesson exemplar). The newer version retains the primary components identified, but some sections are more confined, which should reduce fatigue for everyone.

Quick Start Guide

1. Provide an overview of the entire assignment early on, but don't overwhelm students with the particulars until soon before the information is needed. In effect, following the initial overview, introduce the particulars within individual sections as you go, and have students draft and discuss the sections along the way.
2. Ask students to provide cited evidence in their value sections to show they understand some key environmental issues surrounding their indicators. Provide a few sources per sustainability indicator that they can use for this purpose as part of a smaller journal assignment to make the workload a bit more reasonable for students.

3. Provide support in deconstructing the published research, particularly for early stage lower-division students. Students have to read between the lines to decide how their indicators relate to the consumer behaviors in the study, so it's important to guide this process.

4. Provide guidance about effective methods for their own research as a means of increasing the quality of students' personal studies. I let students brainstorm their approach, and then we decide together on effective approaches before they start collecting data. I emphasize that I'm looking for them to design a reasonable process that will yield the most accurate data possible.

5. Instruct students to draft the global analysis section, and then walk through one of their examples together. The global analysis section can be somewhat tricky for students, because it is distinct compared to the other sections. In future semesters, my aim is to spend a bit more time on this section to see if I can increase the quality of their responses.

6. Remind students about context needed In the Introduction to guide an uninitiated reader. Encourage students to make thoughtful use of transitions to create a smooth pathway among the assignment's various sections.

7. Share and discuss at least one past student exemplar, so the class can see how the entire product looks fully realized.

Appendix 6.D: Personal Sustainability Indicators Essay Guidelines

The Personal Sustainability Indicators Essay: Choosing a CSUMB Policy Area through an Investigation of Sustainability Indicators

1st Draft Due:

Final Draft Due:

Purpose: The purpose of the Personal Sustainability Indicators Essay (aka, Sustainability Indicators Essay) is to deepen your understanding of sustainability; clarify how you measure it; and allow you to analyze your motivations, choices, and opportunities more deeply before you settle on a university policy area to plan within for our next essay. This last point is primary, as it will help you consider—through a careful analysis of multiple categories (detailed in the following section)—which one university sustainability policy areas you would like to choose overall as your focus for our final essay, the Campus Policy Essay. Note that you are using the skill of transfer in many ways within this essay, first in shifting between three categories as a consumer (i.e., choosing between your two sustainability indicators in all three categories—your values, environmental impact, and your personal study sustainability opportunity) and then in making one final choice as a policy maker (i.e., choosing between two policy areas).

The Sustainability Indicators Essay data collection requirement: The Sustainability Indicators Essay will require you to conduct a personal sustainability indicator study. That is, you will measure your personal use of <u>two</u> environmental resources (or waste products) for a minimum of one week each (i.e., collect at least seven consecutive days of data for two personal sustainability indicators, e.g., your gallons of gas, gallons or pounds of waste/recycling, etc.) to get a better sense of your habits and opportunities.

See the Personal Sustainability Indicator Study section and appendices description for additional details.

Difference between a sustainability indicator and a sustainability policy area: A sustainability indicator (the focus of the three earlier body sections in the Sustainability Indicators Essay) is a marker that allows us to measure how well we are meeting the needs of Earth's current and future members (environmentally, socially, and economically). For example, one might measure the gallons of gasoline they consume. A policy area (your choice within the Global Analysis section of the Sustainability Indicators Essay and focus of your upcoming essay) is a subgroup you will plan within when proposing one or more sustainability improvements at our university. For example, the policy area that corresponds with gas use is transportation.

The Sustainability Indicators Essay sections—In an essay of approximately five (5) double-spaced pages, please respond to the following:

A. Introduction (one paragraph):
  a. Justify humanity's focus on the environmental challenges we face.
  b. Provide a cited definition of *sustainability* and *sustainability indicator*.
  c. Assert which two indicators you selected, and why.

    d. Introduce some context for the decision-making process in the investigation (walk the reader through the upcoming process).

    e. Thesis—Introduce your final choice for one university sustainability policy area at the end of your investigation, and assert one primary reason for your choice.

B. Values (the first sustainability indicator category; two paragraphs):

    a. Values Paragraph 1:

        i. Provide a combined transition/topic sentence that introduces the values focus.

        ii. Introduce a prominent environmental issue unique to one indicator (i.e., a major associated environmental challenge—not largely shared by the other indicator—that arises when many of us overuse the resource or overproduce the waste).

        iii. Provide a specific, cited empirical claim to detail and illustrate that issue.

        iv. Reflect on your primary value related to that issue/claim (why you care, the nature of your concern).

        v. Repeat the process for your other indicator (introduce a prominent, unique environmental issue; provide a cited empirical claim to detail/illustrate; reflect on your primary related value).

    b. Values Paragraph 2:

        i. Provide a transition/topic sentence to assert your choice between the indicators based on your values (i.e., which issue engages your higher concern).

        ii. Reason through which problem and associated value discussion engages your higher concern, not only by asserting why you have higher concern for one associated environmental issue, but also why you have a lower concern for the other (example lines of reasoning: the more challenging and far-reaching problem connects better with your professional aims/interests/passions/childhood experiences, matters more for our future, feel more hopeful about tackling, feel more concerned about what might happen if we don't focus on this area, a more tangible issue [you can better picture it, so you are more concerned], a less tangible issue [many don't think about it, so it's a hidden and therefore more insidious problem], connects more with a physical ailment you have or someone you love has, or might someday have, etc.).

Values section notes: In the values section, do not relate to the upcoming study by Brower and Leon or the associated update by the Union of Concerned Scientists. Your cited source information should come from elsewhere, and your discussion in this section should primarily focus on your value leanings.

C. Environmental Impact (the second sustainability indicator category; one paragraph):

   a. Provide a transition to redirect the focus to environmental impact, and provide a topic sentence to assert which indicator creates the higher environmental impact according to the results of one of the two studies.
   b. Cite and discuss the most prominent environmental problems associated with each of your indicators according to this study (you may need to search to find your indicators, e.g., consumer waste production = "household solid waste" and consumer water use = "household water use"). To do so, cite and discuss some claims within the chapter.
   c. Provide a comparison of percentages within parallel environmental problems (i.e., % contributions to those problems) for both indicators to reason through and establish why one indicator creates a higher environmental impact compared to the other according to one of the studies. To do so, you will likely need to cite the appendix (required for any indicator that is part of Household Operations).

Environmental Impact section note: All information in this section should come directly from the Brower and Leon (1999) study or the Union of Concerned Scientists' (2012) update. Your task in this section is to report the comparison between your two indicators based on the results of one of these studies alone (i.e., leave your perspective out of this discussion to maintain the focus of the section, knowing you will later get a chance to share your reaction to the study in the upcoming Global Analysis section). See the Thought Piece 2 assignment guidelines for more information on both studies.

Brower, M. & Leon, W. (1999). *The consumer's guide to effective environmental choices: Practical advice from the union of concerned scientists.* New York: Random House.

Shulman, S., Deyette, J., Ekwurzel, B., Friedman, D., Mellon, M., Rogers, J. & Shaw, S. (2012). *Cooler smarter: Practical steps for low-carbon living. Expert advice from the union of concerned scientists.* Washington: Island Press.

D. Personal Sustainability Indicator Study (the third sustainability indicator category; two paragraphs)

   a. Personal Study Paragraph 1 (narrowing indicators and methods):

   i. Provide a combined transition/topic sentence that introduces your personal sustainability indicator study.

   ii. Describe exactly what you measured (how you narrowed, if you did, and why) and identify the units for both indicators. Note that I am allowing you to narrow your indicator focus within this study—if you wish—simply to make your personal study more manageable, but you should not similarly narrow your focus in other sections of this essay.

   iii. Describe the particular methods you used to measure each indicator (explain how you determined any rates or other values; cite any sources used; describe how you kept track of times, miles, gallons, etc.; explain your calculations to get the required units).

   b. Personal Study Paragraph 2 (results and sustainability opportunity):

   i. Provide a combined transition/topic sentence to assert which one provides you the better opportunity to improve your habits.

   ii. Describe your results for each indicator: average daily use, total for the week, and a description of patterns throughout the week for both indicators (cite your attached data; label tables when you share your data from them).

   iii. Reflect on which indicator provided the better opportunity to improve your sustainability by asserting why the opportunity seemed higher in one area and weaker in the other (important basis for deciding—how did your results inform your decision about sustainability opportunity?).

   Personal Sustainability Indicator Study note: See specifications for your data in the appendices section.

E. Global Analysis (one paragraph)
   a. Provide a combined transition/topic sentence that reminds the reader of your shifting focus in this section (i.e., to reflect back on values, environmental impact, and personal study opportunities when choosing one CSUMB policy area for Essay 3), and assert which one policy area you will plan within at CSUMB for Essay 3, and why.
   b. Reflect on one to two of the earlier category discussions (values, environmental impact, personal study/sustainability opportunity) to reason through which of those discussions <u>did not</u> strongly influence your final CSUMB policy area choice, and why.
   c. Reflect on the remaining earlier category discussions (values, environmental impact, personal study/sustainability opportunity) to reason through which of those discussions <u>most</u> strongly influenced your final CSUMB policy area choice, and why.

   Global Analysis section note: For this section you need to use the skill of transfer to apply your learning in one context (i.e., you as a consumer) to a new context (i.e., you as a policy maker). In other words, which earlier discussions are most and least instructive to you as a sustainability policy maker at CSUMB: your values (e.g., "I'm passionate about waste issues and the Pacific Garbage Patch, so I'll be able to plan more creatively within this area."), and/or the environmental impact (e.g., "The study revealed that the environmental impacts within food are very high, so it's important to concentrate CSUMB efforts in this area."), and/or the sustainability opportunity within your personal study ("I discovered I frequently waste gas, and I've noticed that many other students have a similar problem; it would be wise for me to take advantage of this opportunity by encouraging alternatives to single-occupancy car use on campus.")? Be sure to connect back to your reasoning and conclusions in your three earlier sections when transferring to this new context!

F. Conclusion (one paragraph)
   a. Transition
   b. Conclude your essay by revealing one major insight you gained through the process of your investigation, and reflect on the importance of your upcoming CSUMB policymaking

within your chosen policy area. Why does this upcoming project matter (to you, to the university, to our surrounding community, to the planet)?

G. Appendices—Data for the Personal Sustainability Indicator Study
Your personal study data will need to be organized into two separate, labeled tables (labeled as Appendix A and Appendix B). Place your labeled tables at the end of your essay, and be sure to summarize and cite this information in the results discussion of your personal study.
Information to Provide in Your Tables.

a. A title for each table—Identify the indicator and units (e.g., "Appendix A: Gallons of Water")
b. Units for your data:
   i. Water = gallons
   ii. Gas = gallons
   iii. Electricity – kilowatt hours (kWh)
   iv. Food = ounces or servings (or food carbon points) and describe the contents (e.g., hamburger, broccoli, organic apple, etc.)
   v. Waste/recycling—gallons or pounds, and describe the contents (e.g., water bottle, soda can, plastic wrapper, paper, etc.)
c. These values (i.e., what you need to measure, calculate, and describe for each indicator):
   i. Daily measurements (at least seven consecutive days; indicate dates)
   ii. Total (sum of the daily measurements)
   iii. Average (total divided by seven)
   iv. Description of contents (for food and waste only!)

Writing in the Math Class by Ken Rand

> Activity: a variety of writing homework assignments that are adaptable to any course and discipline

> Learning Outcomes: self-management and self-awareness

> Habits of Mind: metacognition, critical thinking, engagement, motivation, and confidence

One of the latest and more important movements in education is "transfer of learning." In 1970, when I was teaching math in a Bronx junior high school, I remember our attempt to organize all of our classes into "clusters"—the purpose of which was to allow the possibility of "transfer of learning" from one course to another and to keep the class rosters the same for each of these courses regardless of discipline. For example, a typical cluster would have four courses (math, biology, English, and history) and each class in that cluster would have the same 30 students. The concept, which was thought to be unique for its time, made sense. What we learned in mathematics might have applications in biology and what we learned in English might have applications in mathematics (e.g., word problems). This type of organization also helped the cluster instructors share not only curriculum but also the progress (or lack of progress) of particular students in that cluster. The concept still makes sense.

spirit of transfer

For quite a few years now I have been giving a number of writing assignments in my community college math classes. When I first came up with these assignments I didn't consciously think, "How do I link math and English?" or "How do I instill 'habits of mind' in my students?"; I simply wanted to know what my students were "thinking." I wanted to stimulate thought about some topics that I felt were important, not only in learning mathematics, but also "learning" in general, and I wanted my students to reflect upon the consequences of their choices.

curiosity and reflection

All of the writing assignments except for one are homework assignments, and I do not give these assignments a grade. I simply give the students credit for doing the assignment. I do, however, make corrections in spelling and grammar, and I am continually surprised by how clearly my students are able to express themselves, especially when they know that they are not being graded on the assignment. Most of the assignments are 25–100 words and I do not ask them to type them, but many students do exceed the word limit and quite a few do type them. My guess is that in the near future I will begin to ask all students to type their short essays (my eyes are not getting better). At my college, almost every math classroom is a smart classroom with projectors, desktop computers, and electronic overheads. We also have a great audiovisual department that will bring the necessary equipment in case the classroom does not have it. As a result, I am able to show movie video clips as well as YouTube videos and display some of the assignments on the electronic overhead projector.

Activity #1: Math Is a Four-Letter Word!

In the first week of my Beginning Algebra classes (and in the Summer Math Academy) I show a short (20-minute) movie called *MATH! A Four Letter Word*. In this movie a number of college students are interviewed about their "negative" feelings about learning mathematics. The movie also shows interviews with college instructors and counselors who try to explain math anxiety on a very basic and understandable level.

The Assignment

After showing the movie, I give a homework assignment that asks the students to answer questions where they need to reflect upon their own feelings and experiences about learning mathematics (minimum 100 words):

1. Did you identify with any of the students in the movie? Which one(s)? Why?
2. Do you have "math anxiety"? How much? Write a number from 0 to 10 that best shows your level of anxiety (0 means no anxiety and 10 means you never ever want to see a number again).
3. Do you recall an early experience when you knew that you did not like math or knew you were not good at math? When and where did this happen? Please describe this incident. Also, if you have no or very little math anxiety, please explain how and when you first knew you were really good at math.
4. Do you think it is possible that you will actually enjoy doing math or that you may even be good at it?
5. Do you think that being good at math is important? Why or why not?

reflection, self-confidence, and self-efficacy

What's Next?

The next day in class I ask students to share with their table mates their answer to question #3. After about 10 minutes I ask for volunteers to read their personal stories to the class about the origin of their math anxiety. Next I relate to the students good and bad experiences that I personally had while learning math and also tell them about the incredible anxiety that I have toward anything electronic including lightbulbs and computers. Anxiety that is ignored leads to fear and failure. Anxiety that is addressed leads to new possibilities.

Results

By having the opportunity to reflect and to share and collaborate, many students realize that they are not the only ones who have had past difficulties with math. Hearing from classmates who like math also helps these students see that math can be enjoyable.

Activity #2: Test Corrections

This is probably my favorite writing assignment even though it causes the most work on my part. In this two-part assignment students get the opportunity to increase their test scores. It doesn't seem to make a difference which course you teach to have had the experience of students disregarding their low test scores by quickly putting away their exam or, even worse, tossing it into the garbage. I firmly believe that we can turn our students' mistakes on their tests into a learning activity. I also believe that given enough time and effort, all the students in my class have the ability to learn everything I teach them.

The Assignment

After I pass back the first exam to my students, I hand out a detailed answer sheet that includes all the steps to obtain the correct answer. I tell my students to go over their tests to try to figure out what they did wrong by comparing their work with that of other students who have the same exam and by reviewing the answer sheet. (I always give two different forms of the same exam to prevent cheating.) I also ask the students who receive 95% or higher on the exam to walk around the classroom and act as tutors during this process to help those who are confused.

After about 15 minutes I make this announcement to the class: "How many of you feel that you could have and should have done better?" The response is always unanimous (with the exception, of course, of those who received 100%). I then tell them that if they complete a two-part assignment I will increase their test scores.

I hand out a paper (see the handout at the end of this lesson exemplar) that has a complete description of both parts of the assignment and go over the directions on the overhead projector. Part I of the assignment tells the students to write an essay in which they answer about five questions relating to their test experience including how they prepared for the exam, how they feel about their score, and what they will do differently on the next test. I also make it clear that I do not accept "one-word" answers and that all answers must be in a complete sentence. This is a mandatory assignment for all students, even the students who received a score of 100%. Part II of the assignment has six steps:

1. Rewrite the problem they got wrong exactly the way they did it on the test.
2. Do that problem over again correctly (using the answer sheet).
3. Write down how many points they lost on that problem.
4. Write down exactly "what" they did wrong (I am looking for the mathematical mistake they made).
5. Write down "why" they got it wrong (I am looking for "I didn't study it enough").
6. Create a new problem that is exactly like the one they got wrong and do it correctly.

Students need to do these six steps for each and every problem that they got wrong (no matter how many points they lost on that problem).

The reward for both my students and me is phenomenal. I tell them that if they complete this assignment correctly, I will give them back "half the points they lost" on the test. I go to the board and write the following examples: "If a student received 80% that means they lost 20 points and by completing this assignment they can get back 10 points, which changes their 80% (a B) to 90% (an A). Likewise, a student who receives 60% on the test can get back 20 points, changing their D to a B." Basically, I make them an offer they cannot refuse.

self-efficacy and metacognition

This assignment is mandatory for the first test. After subsequent tests I allow students the option of doing the test corrections. At this point I feel they need to care more about their grade than I do.

Results

Students who do the assignment correctly not only increase their grade but also their confidence. This is not an easy assignment, especially for students who received a low grade. They have to work very hard to get back half of the points they lost. But, it is well worth it. During the essay part of the assignment students definitely need to reflect on their study skills and their test-taking skills. I often get student comments such as, "Next time I will not spend 15 minutes on one problem." These students have obviously learned something about time management.

self-
management

Challenges

I have had other instructors tell me that I am allowing students to get a "false" and higher grade than they deserve. This argument that their new grade is really a false one doesn't make sense to me. All that makes sense to me is that students have proven that they know their mistake and can now do the problems correctly. Learning from mistakes shows a true growth of knowledge.

I need to point out that this is an extremely difficult assignment for students and almost half of them do not do it correctly on their first attempt. Many students have a difficult time understanding, distinguishing, and articulating what they got wrong and why they got a problem wrong, and they also have a difficult time creating a new problem and then doing it correctly. With time and patience I work with the students who continue to make mistakes or do not do the assignment correctly with the hope that on the next test they will—to

persistence   use their own comments—"actually study" or "go slower."

A word of caution: Grading these test corrections often takes more time for me than grading the actual test. But it is well worth my time and their effort. As mentioned, too many students have a difficult time distinguishing the difference between what they did wrong and why they got it wrong.

Another challenge is that some students still get the new problem wrong. I usually write, "see me" next to the error and I announce in class that this does not mean "look at me," but, rather, they need to make an appointment with me to go over their continued mistake(s).

The good news is that I have gotten better at explaining the difference between "what" and "why" by doing examples on the board, and recently more and more students are doing this assignment the way it is intended to be done.

Summary

All of these assignments and activities (including videos and links) can be found on my college website (No1professor.webs.com). Just click on the file that says "Engagement Conference."

Quick Start Guide

1. Let students know they'll be doing some low-stakes writing in your class as a way to deepen their content learning and foster their habits of mind. Tell students you won't be grading these assignments, just checking for completion.
2. Find or create a variety of writing-to-learn prompts, such as those described in this exemplar, that you can use throughout the course. Try a mix of reflective prompts that target metacognition and self-efficacy and content-based prompts that help students process their understanding of disciplinary concepts and skills.
3. Encourage students to apply these writing-to-learn strategies to other classes and assignments.

Test Corrections: Part I

Essay Questions:
1. What was your immediate reaction when you saw your test score?

2. How did you prepare for the test?
    a. Where?
    b. Study group?
    c. What did you study?

3. Does TIME = SCORE?
    a. How much time did you spend preparing for this test?
    b. Does your test score indicate the amount of time you spent?

4. In your opinion, was the test fair?
    a. Did you have enough time to take the test?
    b. Were there any surprises on the test?

5. What will you do differently next time?
   a. In preparing for the test?
   b. In "taking" the test?

Test Corrections: Part II

Steps:

1. Copy the original problem with your original mistake showing my corrections.

2. Copy the original problem with the correct solution and answer.

3. Write down how many points you lost on that problem (e.g., –3 points).

4. What? Explain "what" you did wrong. Be specific about your error. Use arrows if necessary. Do not say, "I got it wrong." I already know that.

5. Why? Please explain "why" you got the problem wrong.
   a. I got it wrong because I did not practice it enough.
   b. I got it wrong because I never understood it and I should have asked for help.
   c. I went too fast. I was in a rush to get it done. :(

6. Create a "new" problem exactly like the one you got wrong and "do it" correctly. Your new problem cannot be easier than the one you got wrong. (Don't change signs.)

Work Cited

MATH! A four letter word. Public Films, 1990. VHS.

CONCLUSION

Jennifer Fletcher

In "10 Rules for Going to College When Nobody Really Expected You To," *San Jose Mercury News* columnist Joe Rodriguez offers first-generation students some pointed advice: "Study what you love. Campuses are delightful villages of practical and heart's delight learning. Embrace and expand there, even if the job market says you're an idiot." The value of "heart's delight learning" is implicit in the instructional approach we've described in this book. By fostering habits of mind in our students, we've targeted more than just basic skills or retention or career readiness. While we, of course, want our students to graduate and get good jobs, the real prize we're after is passionate intellectual engagement. We want *all* our students to fully benefit from the transformative learning experiences offered by a college education.

As we hope this collection of lessons shows, an instructional focus on habits of mind is ultimately a focus on joy, on learning for its own sake, and on the intellectual and emotional lives and identities of the students we are privileged to serve in our classes. It's an approach both compassionate and rigorous. Because so many of the students we meet in our developmental education courses face significant obstacles to degree completion, these classes present a critical opportunity for welcoming and supporting underrepresented students while nurturing the dispositions that will help them thrive in college.

What is it, then, that we hope our students will be disposed to do?

We hope our students will be more inclined to appreciate their assets, embrace the value of community and collaboration, cultivate curiosity and creativity, fully engage with their educational opportunities, persist in the face of difficulties, trust their efforts, and sustain an ongoing practice of metacognition and spirit of transfer.

This is the goal we're pursuing. Here's what we've learned from trying to reach it:

- For our most vulnerable students, the cultivation of habits of mind needs to be more than merely incidental. We need to make the invisible visible.
- Students need extended opportunities to develop habits of mind. We can foster internalized, routine ways of thinking by repeatedly asking our students the following kinds of questions:
  - How can you use what you learned in the future?
  - Which habits of mind are you exemplifying right now?
  - Which habits of mind could help you with this task?
  - Which habits of mind could you show more of?
- Instruction based on habits of mind is relationship intensive. This isn't an approach that can be scaled up and automated. We're inviting students to join us in sharing the high-quality learning experiences that drive our own intellectual passions.
- Students need access to rigorous academic content from the moment they enter college. A narrow emphasis on "fixing" or "remediating" students' deficits stifles the development of habits of mind. It's hard to feel engaged, invested, and curious without intellectually challenging subject matter.
- Students have different needs at different moments in the academic term. An instructional cycle that progresses through increasing levels of emotional and intellectual risk encourages students to rely on strategic habits of mind as the situation demands. This whole-term approach also orients students toward a growth mindset.
- Our colleagues, administrators, and policy makers need to know we value our students and the programs that support them. Developmental education is not a problem to be solved or a burden to be outsourced. It's an opportunity to welcome, honor, and challenge students who are a critical part of a diverse, flourishing academic community.
- Following our heart isn't always easy or fun; a critical part of success is learning to dig deep and have faith in ourselves and the process when the stage of learning or living we're experiencing isn't so joyful.
- We need to prioritize the long view of learning. Students who start college in effective developmental education courses do

as well as, or better than, students who start with college-level writing and math courses. We're teaching students who will excel in general education, their major, graduate school, and their career.

Ultimately, we've learned that cultivating our students' habits of mind is a powerful way to promote high-quality higher education for *all* students. The life of the mind shouldn't be a luxury enjoyed only by students at elite institutions or in accelerated programs while less privileged or "prepared" students must prioritize more practical concerns. Degree attainment is important, but retaining and graduating more underrepresented students will do little to reduce the class divide if we don't examine the kind of education those students receive. When we cultivate students' habits of mind, we develop their passion for brain work—and that disposition has social and personal benefits that long outlast the college experience itself.

Work Cited

Rodriguez, Joe. "10 Rules for Going to College When Nobody Really Expected You To." *San Jose Mercury News.* Web. 3 June 2012.

APPENDIX A: MAKING CROSS-DISCIPLINARY, INTERSEGMENTAL COLLABORATION WORK

The Story behind the Exemplars

Jennifer Fletcher and Becky Reed Rosenberg

ooking back, we're tempted to say it was easy—that the close relationships we now enjoy with our partner institutions were a matter of luck or chemistry. We visit each other's classrooms and department meetings, share student work, write curricula and assessments together, attend conferences together, present together, and write together. Some of us have even hosted gatherings in our homes and arranged playdates for our children.

Serendipity did play a role: Several people on the California State University at Monterey Bay (CSUMB) campus came across Lumina Foundation's call for applications to the Minority-Serving Institutions–Models of Success program. Those of us who came across the call almost didn't find each other. But thanks to happenstance, we were able to get together to talk about what we might propose. The provost, two deans, and the faculty development director sat down together and hammered out a plan for collaborating with two of our local community colleges (from which many of our transfer students come) to improve the success rate of students in developmental writing and mathematics courses and to align those courses across our three institutions. We developed a plan for the project that enabled us to create a leadership group representing the two disciplinary areas and faculty from the three campuses. We'd hold five-day summer institutes for two summers and then share our work and invite others to share theirs at a regional conference in the third summer. In a period of extraordinary budget constraints (the grant began October 2009), we'd be able to provide some summer funding to faculty to engage in activities we were confident would benefit students and provide faculty with renewed energy for their work. A fine plan as far as it went, but time was short and the intercampus collaboration that went into the proposal extended only as far as CSUMB's provost asking her equivalents at the community colleges if they wanted to be included. They agreed and we submitted. Given the odds against funding, we didn't give a great deal of thought to how to actually build the collaboration. And then, much to our surprise, we learned that we were receiving the $500,000 we requested.

Less surprisingly, it turns out that the grant getting was the easy part. At CSUMB, because our campus had initiated the proposal, we at least knew who was going to participate on the leadership team: Hongde Hu, professor and chair of mathematics and statistics; Jennifer Fletcher, associate professor of humanities and communication; and Becky Rosenberg, director of faculty development and project manager for the grant.

Now we had to reach out to the other campuses and begin to build our team and our collaboration. Not so easy. Some of the early obstacles we faced were pretty daunting, and we learned that the multicampus, interdisciplinary alliance we proposed was fraught with challenges, not the least because it would involve both adjunct and full-time faculty at all three institutions. With patience, planning, and careful facilitating, however, we've created a successful collaboration that continues to have a positive impact on both student and faculty learning. We have seen changes in attitude, motivation, and self-concept in not only our students but also ourselves. Here's how we've made it work.

First Contact

It's one of the most ancient and enduring rituals of cultural contact—the giving of gifts. With the foundation gift in hand, we next made an offering: We'll host a catered meeting on our campus and pay participants to explore the value of this potential partnership.

This first meeting was marked by curiosity and doubt. The mix of faculty from different disciplines and segments of higher education revealed the challenges inherent in our project; we had different ways of thinking and talking about our work, yet the grant required us to design and implement two five-day summer institutes and a regional conference that addressed academic preparation issues common to both content areas and both college systems.

Math faculty were concerned that sessions would feel like English department meetings. Writing faculty were concerned that they wouldn't understand math content. Two-year college faculty were concerned that four-year college faculty would try to pull rank. Part-time faculty were concerned that they wouldn't be equal participants. And though we weren't exactly from different worlds, each campus had its own unique infrastructure, faculty culture, and student population. There would be no shortcuts to trust building.

Although our initial contact generated interest among potential participants, our efforts to cross disciplinary and institutional lines soon met with several obstacles. Conflicts in teaching loads and schedules, different institutional missions, distances between campuses, and incongruent campus leadership structures presented early challenges. One of the first campuses we had approached rejected our offer as being "too top-down," because our initial development of the proposal had involved consultation only with administration, and the faculty we hoped to bring in doubted the sincerity of our promise that the real content of the project was still open to their input.

We made overtures to another community college in our area and worked to reassure faculty at all three institutions that this would be an open-ended process, that our initial steps would be to identify and share effective practices at each campus *before* determining the goals of the newly formed collaboration. We successfully drew Hartnell College, with Hetty Yelland and Ken Rand leading writing and mathematics, respectively, and Cabrillo College, with Adela Najarro and Ed Braunhut leading writing and mathematics, respectively. The membership of our leadership team was not complete until well into the spring, leaving a short time to clarify goals, design the first summer institute, and recruit faculty.

A Team Is More Than a List of Members

The work began in earnest as we started meeting face-to-face, with food. Like gift giving, breaking bread is an ancient and enduring ritual of cultural contact. These face-to-face meetings were difficult to arrange, but we immediately became convinced that they were critical to starting the process. We needed to get to know each other—our shared values and our differences, the needs and concerns of our colleagues and our students—to fill in the spaces in the vague proposal that had won us the grant. We discovered that we all thought we were doing a lot right in developmental education. So we began by, in a sense, downsizing from a proposal that called for "revision of the curriculum" to a project that would enhance the dual role of our courses as socialization to college and skill development by designing new assignments and activities. The themes we adopted to guide those changes were habits of mind and transfer of learning.

Time pressure required us to work efficiently, methodically, and quickly. Every meeting had a set of goals that had to be achieved, and everyone left with homework and deadlines that had to be met. And we were fortunate that the team was up to the challenge.

The team met, set the schedule for the first summer institute, selected readings to be shared with participants, framed activities, invited speakers to address our themes and demonstrate pedagogical approaches that support learning, and recruited on our campuses.

Finally, by late spring of 2010, we had our full complement of grant participants from all three institutions and both academic areas: five writing faculty and five mathematics faculty from each campus, for a total of 30 instructors, and we were ready to go.

Building Trust

Following the model we used to develop our leadership team, from the first day of our first summer institute, we worked hard to create a climate of mutual respect and trust. Knowing that some of our faculty had never collaborated outside of their disciplines before and that many of our adjunct faculty had not previously been included in their campus's professional development activities, we sought ways to showcase the various strengths and experiences of our diverse group. We wanted to cultivate an assets-based approach to learning—in terms of both students and instructors. We thus facilitated several activities that prominently featured the rich personal resources of our multicampus, cross-disciplinary community. These included the following:

- *Collective CV*: Mixed-campus groups answered questions about their collective experiences in education, including the degrees they held, institutions they'd attended, their number of years in the profession, faculty development experiences, and hopes for their students. Some groups had more than 150 years of combined experience in higher education—a clear sign of the leadership potential in the room.

- *Icebreakers*: One activity asked participants to list favorite books, movies, and food on large posters around the room. Another asked a series of provocative questions, such as whether we would like to "travel to the moon or the bottom of the ocean," "lose 10 pounds or gain 10 IQ points," and "win the lottery or find true love." Each activity functioned to build community and identify the interests and experiences of the individuals who had joined our partnership.

- *The Name Game*: We entered the project without a name for it. Finding a name became a group activity during our early meetings. Ideas were generated by small groups and individuals and we went through rounds of voting and revising. We played with acronyms, alliterations, and a variety of other approaches. The final choice was selected in a landslide vote because it combined ideas we valued with an acronym that resonated with the group. We became thenceforth the Collaborative Alliance for Postsecondary Success (CAPS).

- *Demonstration Lessons*: Representatives from both content areas and all three campuses presented minilessons showcasing best practices. These demonstration lessons further enhanced our assets-based approach by featuring participants as local experts in their fields.

- *Program Presentations*: Participants shared information on a wide range of effective and innovative practices, assessments, and programs already in place. Clearly, it made sense for us to learn from each of our successes before initiating any changes.

- *Shared Study of Professional Resources*: We read and discussed literature on academic success and college readiness, including California's Basic Skills Initiative (Fulks and Alancraig), the *Framework for Success in Postsecondary Writing* (CWPA, NCTE, and NWP), David Conley's work on college readiness, and John Bean's *Engaging Ideas*.

- *Learning Community Norms*: We set and monitored positive learning community norms for our institute days, such as "communicating with others in mind," "withholding judgment," and "minimizing multitasking."

- *Daily Raffles*: We combated afternoon sluggishness by coaxing participants back from lunch with raffles of books, candles, and miscellaneous goodies.

Crossing Institutional Boundaries

To ensure that new relationships could form across departments and campuses, participants were seated in mixed groups and had frequent opportunities for movement and interaction. We also worked to keep the tone invitational; this was an opportunity, not a mandate.

Sometimes facilitators had to field tricky questions about our institutional differences. Why do you use *that* placement test? What's the logic behind your course numbering system? How do you *know* when your students are ready to move on? What do you mean you don't have an English department?[1] We tried to prevent the information-sharing portion of our first meetings from turning critical or defensive—not an easy task.

We were aided in our efforts by the outstanding professionalism and collegiality of our participants. Because this was a self-selected group, we had a significant advantage; these faculty already believed in the value of learning from and with their colleagues from other campuses and disciplines. That's why they were willing to give up 10 days of summer vacation over the next two years to participate.

Wanting to honor this impressive dedication, we tried to reward faculty for their time and to keep them coming back; we made sure we had door prizes, engaging keynote speakers, good food, comfortable rooms, and interactive activities for each institute day.

Discovering Assets

Perhaps the greatest contributor to our success was our assets-based approach to student and faculty learning. As Ken Rand, the math lead from Hartnell College, put it, "Because the conversations were positive, they were productive." We deliberately stayed away from the blame game, focusing instead on the rich experiences and intellectual gifts that our students bring to our classrooms and that we ourselves brought to this collaboration. One leadership team member had described the "oogie" feeling she gets when she hears faculty criticizing colleagues or other institutions for students' perceived shortcomings—a mistake we wanted to avoid.

Activities such as the Collective CV were a good start because they made clear the wealth of practitioner knowledge our participants brought to this partnership. The Collective CV was also an important introductory activity for us because it demonstrated that what we knew as a group was far greater than what we knew as individuals.

While we did provide some redirection when individuals began to lament the deficits of their students or administrations ("But they're so underprepared and there's no support!"), we assured participants that there would be a space for addressing needs later in the institute. We would gently remind faculty of our focus on assets and our own learning community norms, which included listening with the purpose of understanding and postponing judgment. This way, we began by building faculty's trust and confidence and reserved the more challenging conversations until after our relationships had been established.

By and large, we believe we succeeded in creating a positive professional learning environment. Leticia Bustillos, codirector of Policy Research on Preparation, Access and Remedial Education (PRePARE) and our consultant on this project, commended our "insatiable appetite for wanting to learn more and to learn from [our] colleagues," adding that "no one's pointing fingers . . . that deficit model of thinking doesn't exist." Tina Gridiron Smith, program officer for the Lumina Foundation, also praised CSUMB's partnership with Hartnell and Cabrillo as an exemplar of effective collaboration in her remarks at the 2012 Institute for Higher Education Policy MSI Models of Success Grantee Meeting.

Building Consensus

During the second part of our first summer institute, we began the more arduous work of identifying program needs that could be addressed through the collaborative grant. Math faculty reached agreement on essential topics for pretransfer-level mathematics instruction. Writing faculty proposed developing a collection of lesson exemplars that target key habits of mind necessary for college success, including motivation and engagement.

To accommodate the need for all faculty to share a common vision of student success while still completing disciplinary tasks, we divided the institute days between plenary sessions in the morning and break-out sessions for each content area in the afternoon. Structured lunchtime discussions—for example, a conversation about how habits of mind relate to student success—helped us develop shared language and values.

Addressing Challenges

As our work progressed over the course of the first academic year following the inaugural institute, we encountered additional challenges. Some participants dropped out of the grant while others joined. Teaching assignments changed. Securing administrative support proved fairly easy on two campuses but more difficult on the third. Institutional data collection at the community colleges stalled, due to funding and staffing cuts.

Some "mistakes" turned out to be blessings in disguise. We didn't start out with clear goals or outcomes. We weren't sure of all the data we would be collecting. We didn't protect our control groups. However, not having a clearly defined intervention to be implemented through the grant allowed our purpose and plans to evolve from our interactions. Our foggy focus ultimately resulted in greater faculty investment and consensus. And although the lack of control groups resulted in "dirty data," it ensured our work had a more immediate and widespread institutional impact because grant participants readily shared their learning with colleagues.

We also experienced a post-honeymoon period when we had to accomplish real tasks together—such as planning a conference and writing a book. Meetings became more candid although no less collegial. And, to be sure, drafting documents by committee is never easy.

Sustaining and Assessing Our Collaboration

As our partnership matures, we've been able to move from shared practices toward shared artifacts. A follow-up grant from "Give Students a Compass," part of the Association of American Colleges and Universities' Liberal Education and America's Promise (LEAP) initiative, enabled the CAPS project to move attention to habits of mind and transfer of learning to introductory college-level courses. The 11-member task force we created for this part of the project has utilized ePortfolios in linked math and writing courses at all three institutions to measure transfer of learning across disciplines.

At the conclusion of the second summer institute, we conducted a faculty survey, seeking feedback on all aspects of the project. Here are highlights of the responses:

- Nearly half identified John Bean's *Engaging Ideas*, which we provided to all participants, as the single most useful resource.
- Participants were overwhelmingly positive about the role of the leadership team in building a collaborative, assets-based community and a learning environment that was motivating, helpful, well informed, and well organized.
- Participants found the consultants we had brought in "great," "fabulous," "excellent," and "informative." They included Sugie Goen-Salter of San Francisco State University, Marcy Alancraig of Cabrillo, Dale Oliver of Humboldt State University, and Emily Lardner of the Washington Center for Improving the Quality of Undergraduate Education.
- Institute goals were productive.
- Team building was universally reviewed positively—even enthusiastically—with comments about the value of cross-disciplinary and cross-institutional sharing, the benefits of understanding how the different colleges operate, and the sense of community that developed.
- Demonstration lessons were rated very positively, with comments about the many ideas that participants have incorporated into their teaching, the technologies with which participants were able to experiment, and the high quality of the presentations.
- Research provided on habits of mind was received positively to enthusiastically by nearly 90% of respondents, with comments describing it as "fantastic" and "excellent" and crediting it with "revolutionizing" their teaching. Several respondents (about 12%), however, found it distracting or, as one wrote, "old ideas with new labels."
- Research on transfer of learning received universally positive reviews, even from those for whom it was familiar.
- Assets-based instruction, too, received positive to enthusiastic responses, with many faculty indicating that they are using it in their instruction and one commenting that "to me it was the credo of our collaboration."

Asked if they were interested in continuing with the project beyond the period of the grant, 68% replied yes and the rest were uncertain. Of those who said yes, most (62%) wanted to continue to meet to share classroom practices and develop new ones, 14% wanted to visit each other's classrooms, and 24% wanted to complete their contributions to the very volume you are reading (!) and undertake more collaborative publications and presentations.

Going Public

As promised in our grant proposal, we concluded our project with a multiday professional conference, "Teaching 21st Century Students: Fostering Postsecondary Success for All Learners." Its design was one outcome of our second summer institute, with collaboration naming the conference; developing the description and call for proposals; and, once proposals were received, reviewing the proposals. In the end, we had 35 sessions, eight posters, and three keynotes. Including CSUMB, presenters represented 14 of the 23 colleges in the CSU system, with additional presenters from six middle and high schools, one University of California campus, an additional California community college, and three out-of-state universities. The response was extraordinarily positive, with innumerable calls to offer the conference annually. Connections were made that have produced continuing professional collaborations.

If We Knew Then . . .

As the engagement and responses reported here indicate, the project was a great success for our faculty. What we know about student engagement and responses is not as clearly demonstrable. Our faculty are convinced that the student experience was improved by the changes they've made in their teaching. We have anecdotal evidence from students that they value the attention to habits of mind and transfer of learning and take those approaches with them after they complete their developmental courses. What we don't have are good measures of the impact on student persistence and success. There are a variety of reasons for that.

For one, we haven't found, and were not, within the time frame of the project, able to create, instruments for determining growth in habits of mind and transfer of learning. Because we didn't anticipate when we wrote the grant application that these would be our focus, we didn't address the need for such an instrument in the proposal. As habits of mind, soft skills, and the range of manifestations of these concepts are advanced, it is important that we be able to assess their development, and we are actively seeking opportunities to create and pilot such instruments.

A second challenge was the short period we examined. After our initial planning and exploration year, we had only two years to implement and refine the activities we developed.

A third challenge was specific to the years we had the grant, 2009–2012. The impact of the economic crisis on the staffing of institutional research offices made data collection almost impossible, and we had not factored funding for data collection and analysis into the grant adequately.

Affirming the Value of Developmental Education

When we wrote the first CAPS annual report, we included an excerpt from an item in the *Chronicle of Higher Education* (Kelderman), citing comments by Jamie Merisotis, president of Lumina Foundation (our funder), to the annual meeting of State Higher Education Executive Officers:

> While Mr. Merisotis praised state higher-education leaders, he urged them to accept a changing higher-education landscape that will include a much more diverse student body requiring more remedial education.
>
> "Higher education needs to remove the stigma for students who arrive at college without the academic preparation they need to succeed," Mr. Merisotis said. "Higher education needs to be more focused on the needs of students and less focused on the needs of the institution," he said.

We were heartened by this statement, at a time when universities throughout the country were looking for ways to offload "remediation" and/or pointing fingers at secondary educators.

Recently, however, we have seen assaults on development education. Some of that is due to credible research on the impact multiple levels of developmental prerequisites have on progress to college-level work and the impact of those delays on student retention. But we need to be cautious in our generalizing, lest we tar successful programs with the same brush as unsuccessful programs. Much can be done to improve developmental education, including current efforts to accelerate the development process and to offer "stretch" programs that embed pre-paratory work in college-level courses. We and our institutions have a responsibility to ensure that our students' assets are valued and that their needs are inclusively and adequately served by our institutions.

Why Collaboration Matters

On one of our final institute days, Emily Lardner, director of the Washington Center for Improving the Quality of Undergraduate Education, asked us the following question: What aspects of the collaboration had the greatest impact on participants? These are the answers we gave:

- *The opportunity to talk with colleagues.* Regardless of whether the conversations took place in mixed groups or in campus or disciplinary teams, sharing our stories with other educators was a profoundly reassuring act.
- *The motivation to learn something new.* And while we did indeed learn important content (e.g., models of successful summer programs or effective learning communities), the real magic was in the *increased* sense of energy and openness we felt and our *decreased* sense of isolation.
- *The shared study of resources.* Discussing key research and position statements together enhanced our credibility and solidarity as a community of educators.
- *The Demonstration Lessons.* Seeing the successful practices of colleagues was inspiring.
- *The opportunity to build leadership capacity.* The collaboration gave participants—including the many adjunct faculty—more "airtime" at their own campuses as they reported what they learned and accomplished through the grant.
- *The sharing of student stories.* After talking with colleagues in other disciplines and types of institutions, we had a better sense of our students' academic lives; of the different schedules, workloads, and discourses they had to negotiate; of where they had been and where they were going.

As gratifying as these outcomes are for our faculty, the ultimate hope was to have an impact on our students. While we have con-fessed to the limited quantitative data, we have seen and heard the benefits to our students. We close with a reflection written by Liliana

Castrellon, who served as the student assistant for CAPS while she was an undergraduate at CSUMB. Lily, a first-generation college student whose journey has taken her from developmental education courses at CSUMB to graduate study at the University of Utah, gave us an eloquent reminder of why collaboration matters:

> Prior to working with CAPS, I never thought about what went on behind the scenes to ensure student success. Students often are so overwhelmed with academics, work, and life that we do not see how hard someone is working to make sure that we do well. When I first saw that CAPS was formed by faculty members from three different institutions and funded by an organization to help students of color succeed, I was really taken aback. All of a sudden I was making connections about programs that have been available to students on campus and that behind that program were individuals who truly cared about the student. More importantly, these were not just our own faculty, but from other institutions, and national programs.
>
> Seeing the collaboration between the faculty members, and how hard they are working for their students is extremely supportive to the student. It showed me that the professors do not take only academics into account, but the whole student as a person. . . . This in itself is inspiration and motivation. This gave me a goal—to one day work in higher education and join the advocates who promote student success.

We'll welcome her with open arms.

Note

1. CSUMB has an interdisciplinary Humanities and Communication Division and a campuswide, distributive writing program but does not offer a traditional English major.

Works Cited

Bean, John. *Engaging Ideas: The Professor's Guide to Integrating Writing, Critical Thinking, and Active Learning in the Classroom.* San Francisco: Jossey-Bass, 2001. Print.

Bustillos, Leticia. Institute for Higher Education Policy MSI Models of Success Grantee Meeting. Lansdowne Resort, Leesburg, VA. 21 July 2012. Remarks.

CWPA, NCTE, and NWP (Council of Writing Program Administrators, National Council of Teachers of English, and National Writing Project). *Framework for Success in Postsecondary Writing*. Berkeley: National Writing Project, 2011. Web.

Fulks, Janet, and Marcy Alancraig, eds. *Constructing a Framework for Success: A Holistic Approach to Basic Skills*. Sacramento: Academic Senate for California Community Colleges. 2008. Web. 28 May 2010. <http://www.cccbsi.org/basic-skills-handbook>

Gridiron Smith, Tina. Institute for Higher Education Policy MSI Models of Success Grantee Meeting. Leesburg, VA. 2012. Remarks.

Kelderman, Eric. "Lumina Foundation Will Shift Away from New Projects, State Leaders Are Told." *Chronicle of Higher Education* 14 July 2010. Web. 1 May 2014.

APPENDIX B: CONNECTIVE LEARNING LOG

Questions for Reflecting on
Transfer of Learning

Directions: Choose ONE of the following prompts to respond to in a freewrite after completing each course assignment.

1. How is this assignment similar to work you've done in other classes? How is it different?
2. To what extent did your prior knowledge contribute to your success on this assignment?
3. Where do you see yourself using this knowledge and these skills again?
4. How might you need to adapt what you've learned for another genre or discipline?
5. Which habits of mind most contributed to your success on this assignment? Why?
6. What are the key principles, or "big ideas," behind this text/task/lesson?
7. What generalizations can you make about what you learned?
8. What did you most enjoy about this work? What would you like to do again?

APPENDIX C: HABITS OF MIND
LESSON STUDENT FEEDBACK FORM

Directions: Please respond to each of the following questions. Your purpose is to provide thoughtful feedback on today's lesson.

1. Were you interested in the lesson? Why or why not? What did you do to stay focused?

2. How motivated were you to learn the new material?

3. What did you learn?

4. How did the lesson make you feel?

5. Was anything confusing? If so, how did you deal with your confusion?

6. How can you use what you learned for other assignments and classes?

7. In what ways did the lesson support—or not support—your personal learning style?

8. What did you like best?

9. What would you change?

10. How confident do you feel applying what you learned in this lesson?

APPENDIX D: PRESURVEY OF MATH

Presurvey of students (stats/precalculus)

I. Current information

   A. Name: _____ _____
   B. Course: _____
   C. Section: _____
   D. Number of units you are currently taking (including this class): _____
   E. Work hours per week (on average): _____
   F. Other time commitments/week (e.g., caring for family, volunteering).

Type of commitment	Hours/week
_____	_____
_____	_____
_____	_____

II. Past experiences

   A. Last math class: _____
   B. When taken: _____
   C. Where taken: _____
   D. Grade received: _____
   E. Hours per week outside of class you spent on your last math course: _____
   F. Did your grade reflect the time you invested in the course? _____
   G. What one thing would you change in your approach to the last class? _____

III. Habits of mind inventory: "Habits of mind" refers to ways of approaching learning that are intellectual and practical and that will support students' success in a variety of fields and disciplines. The eight habits of mind listed here have been identified as critical for success in college.

How would you rate yourself on the following habits of mind? Circle one number for each.

A. Curiosity: I am intrigued and have a sense of curiosity about the world. I enjoy finding problems to solve.
   Not yet but   I usually
   I'm learning –1—2—3—4—5—6—7—8—9—10– behave this way

B. Openness: I listen to others with understanding and empathy.
   Not yet but   I usually
   I'm learning –1—2—3—4—5—6—7—8—9—10– behave this way

C. Engagement: I ask questions, search for data to support conclusions, and am curious to learn new things.
   Not yet but   I usually
   I'm learning –1—2—3—4—5—6—7—8—9—10– behave this way

D. Creativity: I am a creative person and know how to generate different ideas and processes to complete a task.
   Not yet but   I usually
   I'm learning –1—2—3—4—5—6—7—8—9—10– behave this way

E. Persistence: I am a persistent person. If I don't succeed on the first try, I keep trying until I do succeed.
   Not yet but   I usually
   I'm learning –1—2—3—4—5—6—7—8—9—10– behave this way

F. Responsibility: I check my work for quality and try to be accurate and precise in everything I do.
   Not yet but   I usually
   I'm learning –1—2—3—4—5—6—7—8—9—10– behave this way

G. Flexibility: I am a flexible thinker. I look for new and different perspectives and can change my mind. I am willing to try different ways of completing a task.
   Not yet but   I usually
   I'm learning –1—2—3—4—5—6—7—8—9—10– behave this way

H. Metacognition: I am always learning. I reflect on and learn from my experiences and can discuss what I don't know.
   Not yet but   I usually
   I'm learning –1—2—3—4—5—6—7—8—9—10– behave this way

IV. Content/skill inventory: Circle one number for each.

   A. I am confident with my math skills.
       Extremely –1—2—3—4—5—6—7—8—9—10– Not at all

   B. I am confident with my writing skills.
       Extremely –1—2—3—4—5—6—7—8—9—10– Not at all

   C. I am good at math.
       Extremely –1—2—3—4—5—6—7—8—9—10– Not at all

   D. I am good at writing.
       Extremely 1   2—3—4—5—6—/—8—9—10– Not at all

   E. Writing makes math easier to learn.
       Extremely –1—2—3—4—5—6—7—8—9—10– Not at all

V.   Future (self-efficacy/reflection)

   A. What do you believe is the greatest obstacle to your success in this class? _____

   B. Describe your study environment (i.e., Where do you study, when, with whom, with what distractions?) _____

   C. What are you willing to do to be successful? Pick your top three (3).
       ____ Ask more questions in class
       ____ Go to instructor office hours
       ____ Attend regular tutoring
       ____ E-mail instructor with questions/concerns
       ____ Take better notes
       ____ Attend/create review sessions
       ____ Review notes
       ____ Read textbook/complete daily assignments
       ____ Attend/join/create study groups
       ____ Allow 2–3 hours outside of class for every hour in class
       ____ Other: _____

APPENDIX E: PRESURVEY OF WRITING

Presurvey of students (composition/English)

I. Current information

    A. Name: _____

    B. Course: _____

    C. Section: _____

    D. Number of units you are currently taking (including this class): _____

    E. Work hours per week (on average): _____

    F. Other time commitments/week (e.g., caring for family, volunteering):

Type of commitment   Hours/week

_____   _____

_____   _____

_____   _____

II. Past experiences

    A. Last composition/English class: _____

_____

    B. When taken: _____

    C. Where taken: _____

    D. Grade received: _____

    E. Hours per week outside of class you spent on your last comp/English course:_____

    F. Did your grade reflect the time you invested in the course? _____

    G. What one thing would you change in your approach to the last class? _____

III. Habits of mind inventory: "Habits of mind" refers to ways of approaching learning that are intellectual and practical and that will support students' success in a variety of fields and disciplines.

The eight habits of mind listed here have been identified as critical for success in college.

How would you rate yourself on the following habits of mind? Circle one number for each.

A. Curiosity: I am intrigued and have a sense of curiosity about the world. I enjoy finding problems to solve.
Not yet but   I usually
I'm learning –1—2—3—4—5—6—7—8—9—10– behave this way

B. Openness: I listen to others with understanding and empathy.
Not yet but   I usually
I'm learning –1—2—3—4—5—6—7—8—9—10– behave this way

C. Engagement: I ask questions, search for data to support conclusions, and am curious to learn new things.
Not yet but   I usually
I'm learning –1—2—3—4—5—6—7—8—9—10– behave this way

D. Creativity: I am a creative person and know how to generate different ideas and processes to complete a task.
Not yet but   I usually
I'm learning –1—2—3—4—5—6—7—8—9—10– behave this way

E. Persistence: I am a persistent person. If I don't succeed on the first try, I keep trying until I do succeed.
Not yet but   I usually
I'm learning –1—2—3—4—5—6—7—8—9—10– behave this way

F. Responsibility: I check my work for quality and try to be accurate and precise in everything I do.
Not yet but   I usually
I'm learning –1—2—3—4—5—6—7—8—9—10– behave this way

G. Flexibility: I am a flexible thinker. I look for new and different perspectives and can change my mind. I am willing to try different ways of completing a task.
Not yet but   I usually
I'm learning –1—2—3—4—5—6—7—8—9—10– behave this way

H. Metacognition: I am always learning. I reflect on and learn from my experiences and can discuss what I don't know.
Not yet but   I usually
I'm learning –1—2—3—4—5—6—7—8—9—10– behave this way

IV. Content/skill inventory: circle one number for each.

    A. I am confident with my math skills.
        Extremely –1—2—3—4—5—6—7—8—9—10– Not at all

    B. I am confident with my writing skills.
        Extremely –1—2—3—4—5—6—7—8—9—10– Not at all

    C. I am good at math.
        Extremely –1—2—3—4—5—6—7—8—9—10– Not at all

    D. I am good at writing.
        Extremely –1—2—3—4—5—6—7—8—9—10– Not at all

    E. Writing makes math easier to learn.
        Extremely –1—2—3—4—5—6—7—8—9—10– Not at all

V. Future (self-efficacy/reflection)

    A. What do you believe is the greatest obstacle to your success in this class? _____

_____

    B. Describe your study environment (i.e., Where do you study, when, with whom, with what distractions?) _____

_____

    C. What are you willing to do to be successful? Pick your top three (3).
        ____ Ask more questions in class
        ____ Go to instructor office hours
        ____ Attend regular tutoring
        ____ E-mail instructor with questions/concerns
        ____ Take better notes
        ____ Attend/create review sessions
        ____ Review notes
        ____ Read textbook/complete daily assignments
        ____ Attend/join/create study groups
        ____ Allow 2–3 hours outside of class for every hour in class
        ____ Other: _____

APPENDIX F: POSTSURVEY OF MATH

Exit survey of students (stats/precalculus)

I. Current information

   A Name: _____

   B. Course: _____

   C. Section: _____

   D. Based on the work you've completed so far, approximate grade you're receiving in this course: _____

   E. Average hours per week outside of class spent on this course: _____

   F. Does your current grade reflect the time you invested in the course? _____

   G. What one thing would you change in your approach to this class if you were starting over? _____
   _____

   H. Has the integration of writing in this course benefited your learning statistics/precalculus?

Not at all			A great deal
1	2	3	4

   Please explain your response: _____
   _____

II. Habits of mind inventory: "Habits of mind" refers to ways of approaching learning that are intellectual and practical and that will support students' success in a variety of fields and disciplines. The eight habits of mind listed here have been identified as critical for success in college.

How would you rate yourself on the following habits of mind at the start of the semester and now that you've reached the end of the semester? Circle one number for each.

A. Curiosity: I am intrigued and have a sense of curiosity about the world. I enjoy finding problems to solve.

	Not yet but I'm learning		I usually behave this way
Start of semester	−1—2—3—4—5—6—7—8—9—10−
End of semester	−1—2—3—4—5—6—7—8—9—10−

B. Openness: I listen to others with understanding and empathy.

	Not yet but I'm learning		I usually behave this way
Start of semester	−1—2—3—4—5—6—7—8—9—10−
End of semester	−1—2—3—4—5—6—7—8—9—10−

C. Engagement: I ask questions, search for data to support conclusions, and am curious to learn new things.

	Not yet but I'm learning		I usually behave this way
Start of semester	−1—2—3—4—5—6—7—8—9—10−
End of semester	−1—2—3—4—5—6—7—8—9—10−

D. Creativity: I am a creative person and know how to generate different ideas and processes to complete a task.

	Not yet but I'm learning		I usually behave this way
Start of semester	−1—2—3—4—5—6—7—8—9—10−
End of semester	−1—2—3—4—5—6—7—8—9—10−

E. Persistence: I am a persistent person. If I don't succeed on the first try, I keep trying until I do succeed.

	Not yet but I'm learning		I usually behave this way
Start of semester	−1—2—3—4—5—6—7—8—9—10−
End of semester	−1—2—3—4—5—6—7—8—9—10−

F. Responsibility: I check my work for quality and try to be accurate and precise in everything I do.

	Not yet but I'm learning		I usually behave this way
Start of semester	−1—2—3—4—5—6—7—8—9—10−
End of semester	−1—2—3—4—5—6—7—8—9—10−

G. Flexibility: I am a flexible thinker. I look for new and different perspectives and can change my mind. I am willing to try different ways of completing a task.

Not yet but   I usually
I'm learning   behave this way
Start of semester   –1—2—3—4—5—6—7—8—9—10–
End of semester   –1—2—3—4—5—6—7—8—9—10–

H. Metacognition: I am always learning. I reflect on and learn from my experiences and can discuss what I don't know.

Not yet but   I usually
I'm learning   behave this way
Start of semester   –1—2—3—4—5—6—7—8—9—10–
End of semester   –1—2—3—4—5—6—7—8—9—10–

III. Content/skill inventory: circle one number for each for the start of the semester and one now.

A. I am confident with my math skills.

Extremely   Not at all
Start of semester   –1—2—3—4—5—6—7 8—9—10–
End of semester   –1—2—3—4—5—6—7—8—9—10–

B. I am confident with my writing skills.

Extremely   Not at all
Start of semester   –1—2—3—4—5—6—7—8—9—10–
End of semester   –1—2—3 4 5—6—7—8—9—10–

C. I am good at math.

Extremely   Not at all
Start of semester   –1 2—3—4—5—6—7—8—9—10–
End of semester   –1—2—3—4 5—6—7—8—9—10–

D. I am good at writing.

Extremely   Not at all
Start of semester   –1—2—3—4—5—6—7—8—9—10–
End of semester   –1—2—3—4—5—6—7—8—9—10–

E. Writing makes math easier to learn.

Extremely   Not at all
Start of semester   –1—2—3—4—5—6—7—8—9—10–
End of semester   –1—2—3—4—5—6—7—8—9—10–

IV. Future (self-efficacy/reflection): How do you see yourself using the skills and knowledge you learned in this class in other classes?

APPENDIX G: POSTSURVEY OF WRITING

Exit survey of students (composition/English)

I. Current information

    A. Name: _____

    B. Course: _____

    C. Section: _____

    D. Based on the work you've completed so far, approximate grade you're receiving in this course: _____

    E. Average hours per week outside of class spent on this course: _____

    F. Does your current grade reflect the time you invested in the course? _____

    G. What one thing would you change in your approach to this class if you were starting over? _____ _____

    H. Has the integration of math in this course benefited your writing?

Not at all			A great deal
1	2	3	4

    Please explain your response: _____ _____

II. Habits of mind inventory: "Habits of mind" refers to ways of approaching learning that are intellectual and practical and that will support students' success in a variety of fields and disciplines. The eight habits of mind listed here have been identified as critical for success in college.

How would you rate yourself on the following habits of mind at the start of the semester and now that you've reached the end of the semester? Circle one number for each.

A. Curiosity: I am intrigued and have a sense of curiosity about the world. I enjoy finding problems to solve.

	Not yet but I'm learning		I usually behave this way
Start of semester	–1—2—3—4—5—6—7—8—9—10–
End of semester	–1—2—3—4—5—6—7—8—9—10–

B. Openness: I listen to others with understanding and empathy.

Not yet but
I'm learning   I usually
behave this way

	Not yet but I'm learning		I usually behave this way
Start of semester	–1 2 3 4 5 6 7—8—9—10–
End of semester	–1—2—3—4—5—6—7—8—9—10–

C. Engagement: I ask questions, search for data to support conclusions, and am curious to learn new things.

	Not yet but I'm learning		I usually behave this way
Start of semester	1 2 3 4 5 6 7 8 9 10
End of semester	–1—2—3—4—5—6—7—8—9—10–

D. Creativity: I am a creative person and know how to generate different ideas and processes to complete a task.

	Not yet but I'm learning		I usually behave this way
Start of semester	–1—2—3—4—5—6—7—8—9—10
End of semester	–1—2—3—4—5—6—7—8—9—10–

E. Persistence: I am a persistent person. If I don't succeed on the first try, I keep trying until I do succeed.

	Not yet but I'm learning		I usually behave this way
Start of semester	–1—2—3—4—5—6—7—8—9—10–
End of semester	–1—2—3—4—5—6—7—8—9—10–

F. Responsibility: I check my work for quality and try to be accurate and precise in everything I do.

	Not yet but I'm learning		I usually behave this way
Start of semester	–1—2—3—4—5—6—7—8—9—10–
End of semester	–1—2—3—4—5—6—7—8—9—10–

G. Flexibility: I am a flexible thinker. I look for new and different perspectives and can change my mind. I am willing to try different ways of completing a task.

	Not yet but I'm learning		I usually behave this way
Start of semester	–1—2—3—4—5—6—7—8—9—10–
End of semester	–1—2—3—4—5—6—7—8—9—10–

H. Metacognition: I am always learning. I reflect on and learn from my experiences and can discuss what I don't know.

	Not yet but I'm learning		I usually behave this way
Start of semester	–1—2—3—4—5—6—7—8—9—10–
End of semester	–1—2—3—4—5—6—7—8—9—10–

III. Content/skill inventory: circle one number for each for the start of the semester and one now.

A. I am confident with my math skills.

	Extremely		Not at all
Start of semester	–1—2—3—4—5—6—7—8—9—10–
End of semester	–1—2—3—4—5—6—7—8—9—10–

B. I am confident with my writing skills.

	Extremely		Not at all
Start of semester	–1—2—3—4—5—6—7—8—9—10–
End of semester	–1—2—3—4—5—6—7—8—9—10–

C. I am good at math.

	Extremely		Not at all
Start of semester	–1—2—3—4—5—6—7—8—9—10–
End of semester	–1—2—3—4—5—6—7—8—9—10–

D. I am good at writing.

	Extremely		Not at all
Start of semester	–1—2—3—4—5—6—7—8—9—10–
End of semester	–1—2—3—4—5—6—7—8—9—10–

E. Writing makes math easier to learn.

	Extremely		Not at all
Start of semester	–1—2—3—4—5—6—7—8—9—10–
End of semester	–1—2—3—4—5—6—7—8—9—10–

IV. Future (self-efficacy/reflection): How do you see yourself using the skills and knowledge you learned in this class in other classes?

ABOUT THE EDITORS AND CONTRIBUTORS

Editors

Jennifer Fletcher is an associate professor of English in the Division of Humanities and Communication at California State University at Monterey Bay (CSUMB). Before joining the faculty at CSUMB, she taught high school English for 10 years in Southern California. She currently assists with the statewide implementation of the CSU Expository Reading and Writing Course (ERWC). She earned an MA in English from the University of California, Irvine and a PhD in English from the University of California, Riverside.

Adela Najarro teaches at Cabrillo College as the English instructor for the Puente Project, a program designed to support Latinidad in all its aspects, while preparing community college students to transfer to four-year colleges and universities. Her extended family's emigration from Nicaragua to San Francisco began in the 1940s and concluded in the 1980s, when the last of the family settled in the Los Angeles area. She holds a PhD in literature and creative writing from Western Michigan University, as well as an MFA from Vermont College.

Hetty Yelland earned her BA in comparative literature from University of California, Davis; her MA in English from the University of the Pacific; and her PhD in English from the University of Tulsa. She has been teaching at the college level for 20 years and is a tenured English instructor at Hartnell College in Salinas, California.

Contributors

Olga Blomgren works to create in all of her classes a community where the students understand that they are each responsible for one another's learning. She earned a BA from the University of California, Berkeley, and an MA from San Francisco State University; both degrees are in comparative literature. She has taught ethnic studies, college-level and developmental composition, and literature. She is a native of Salinas, California, and teaches English there at Hartnell College. She likes to make sure her students have fun.

María Boza was born in Havana, Cuba, and grew up in Miami, Florida. She earned her AB at Barnard College and her MFA in creative writing at the University of Maryland, College Park. Since fall 2007 she has been teaching composition at California State University at Monterey Bay, both at the developmental level and at the sophomore level. She has also taught a developmental English course at Hartnell College.

Lydia Graecyn has a BA in literature from the University of California at Santa Cruz. From Cal Poly, San Luis Obispo, she earned an MA in English and an English Single Subject Teaching Credential and a Technical Writing Certificate. Since 2003, she has been an English instructor teaching and learning at Cabrillo College.

Rebecca Kersnar has an MA in TESOL (Teaching English to Speakers of Other Languages) with a focus on academic writing and reading from the Monterey Institute of International Studies, a certificate in language program administration, and a BS in biology with a concentration in botany from San Francisco State University. Rebecca teaches science and environmental policy communication courses and offers writing support within the environmental studies major at California State University at Monterey Bay (CSUMB). On this campus, she has participated in a range of learning communities, committees, and initiatives, such as the Campus Sustainability Committee, the Focus the Region Steering Committee, some critical thinking collectives, and a math-writing initiative through a Compass grant. Rebecca is also the faculty adviser for the CSUMB Garden Club, a student-run sustainable garden on campus.

Sunita Lanka teaches English at Hartnell College. She has also been teaching at California State University at Monterey Bay since fall 2004. She has two postgraduate degrees (MA and MPhil) and a PhD in English literature from Osmania University, India. In the master's program at Osmania, she was awarded three gold medals for her proficiency in English literature. She has been teaching at the university level, in India and the United States, for about 25 years. She enjoys teaching world literature, critical thinking, and English, the latter especially to nonnative speakers.

Emily Lardner is the director of the Washington Center for Improving Undergraduate Education at The Evergreen State College, where she teaches various forms of academic writing. Before moving to Washington, she taught in the writing program at the University of Michigan. She holds a BA from Augustana College and an MA and PhD from the University of Michigan. Her research interests lie in two areas—how people become more confident and competent writers in their chosen fields, and how campuses use learning community programs to promote student success. She is coeditor for the peer-reviewed journal *Learning Communities Research and Practice,* and serves on the editorial boards of *The Journal of Faculty Development and Numeracy.*

Kathleen Leonard is currently an English instructor at Monterey Peninsula College. She has been teaching English and writing letters to the editor for more than 30 years. In 2012, she published *Dueling with Dementia: Not the Love Story We Planned,* a book about her family's experience with her husband's dementia. She earned her BA and MA in English from San Jose State University.

Jennifer McGuire has an MFA in creative writing and has held numerous diverse jobs, from a horse stall cleaner and envelope stuffer to a screenwriter and teacher. She is lucky to be able to translate her varied background to make English and the writing process relatable and relevant to the goals and interests of a wide demographic of students at Cabrillo College, where she currently teaches.

Rhea Mendoza-Lewis has been teaching in the English department at Hartnell Community College for 12 years. She has a BA from University of California, Santa Barbara, and an MA from San Francisco State University.

Natasha Oehlman has an MA in English composition from San Francisco State University. She has been an instructor of writing and professional communication at California State University at Monterey Bay (CSUMB) for more than 10 years. Her scholarly interests include peer review in the classroom, transfer of learning in integrated reading and writing environments, and the use of digital environments (i.e., blogging, ePortfolios, multimedia) in ways that deepen and enhance student learning experiences, both professionally and personally. She enjoys fostering confidence in students through their discovery and development of voice as academic and professional writers. She works with undergraduate students in the Undergraduate Research Opportunities Center (UROC) at CSUMB, an accelerated research and scholars program with educational pathways leading to graduate and doctoral programs.

Ken Rand is a community college math instructor at Hartnell College in Salinas, California. He has been teaching there for 27 years and has taught math on a variety of educational levels for more than 45 years. He has also authored his own beginning algebra textbook (*Elementary Algebra: Solving the Mystery*) as well as numerous math activity workbooks for Creative Publications. In addition, he has invented strategy and word games that have been sold on the retail market. He earned his BS in mathematics at Fairleigh Dickinson University and his master's degree in math education at City University in New York.

Becky Reed Rosenberg received her PhD in history from the University of Michigan, where she also worked closely with the English Composition Board, studying rhetoric and composition. She has focused most of her professional career on faculty development and student support services, with particular attention to underserved, underrepresented students. She was founding director of the faculty development center at University of Washington, Bothell, and directed the Center for Teaching, Learning, and Assessment at California State University at Monterey Bay, which provided the extraordinary opportunity to serve as program manager of the Collaborative Alliance for Postsecondary Success (CAPS) project.

Tina Sander received her BA in biology from the University of California at Santa Cruz and her MA in English with a concentration in TESOL (Teaching English to Speakers of Other Languages) from San Francisco State University in 2003. Tina has also been teaching English at Cabrillo College since 2004.

Daphne Young earned a BA in English from University of California, Berkeley, and an MFA in fiction from Mills College in Oakland. She has been teaching literature and college composition since 1999. She is an engaging and well-liked instructor at Cabrillo College, Hartnell College, and California State University at Monterey Bay.

INDEX

one-shot but, rather, a structured opportunity for a faculty member to examine and adapt practice over time and to assess the impact of changes on student learning.

The faculty members who have participated in the *Taking College Teaching Seriously* experience—full-time and adjunct teachers conducting developmental math and English classes—have found it to be transformative.

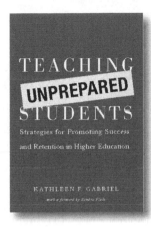

Teaching Unprepared Students
FosteringStrategies for Promoting Success and Retention in Higher Education
Kathleen F. Gabriel
Foreword by Sandra M. Flake

"Teaching is a tough job, especially when your pupil is under prepared. *Teaching Unprepared Students* is a guide for this all too common situation where a student is dangerously in over his or her head in the class they are in. Aiming for students to get the resources they need to turn a subpar student into a superb one, *Teaching Unprepared Students* is an invaluable manual for when traditional methods just aren't good enough."

—*Midwest Book Review*

Sty/us

22883 Quicksilver Drive
Sterling, VA 20166-2102

Subscribe to our e-mail alerts: www.Styluspub.com

Also available from Stylus

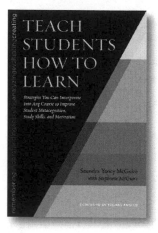

Teach Students How to Learn
Strategies You Can Incorporate Into Any Course to Improve Student Metacognition, Study Skills, and Motivation
Saundra Yancy McGuire
With Stephanie McGuire
Foreword by Thomas Angelo

"If you are already convinced—or are at least willing to consider the possibility—that your students could learn more deeply and achieve more success than they are at present, this book is for you. If you are frustrated by students who seem unmotivated and disengaged, this book is for you. If you find it challenging to teach underprepared students, this book is for you. And if you care about educational equity and fairness, this book is for you.

The not-so-familiar good news is that these same students can both survive and thrive in higher education. The message from relevant research is quite clear: What students *do* in college matters more than who they are or which institution they attend. What these underprepared students need most to do is to *learn how to learn.*

Saundra McGuire provides specific, practical, research-based strategies to teach students how to learn, focusing on the three key M's—mindset, motivation, and metacognition."

—*Thomas A. Angelo,*
Clinical Professor of Educational Innovation & Research,
Eshelman School of Pharmacy, University of North Carolina–Chapel Hill, and
coauthor of Classroom Assessment Techniques

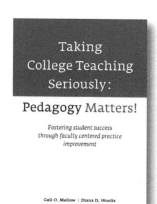

Taking College Teaching Seriously: Pedagogy Matters!
Fostering Student Success Through Faculty-Centered Practice Improvement
Gail O. Mellow, Diana D. Woolis, Marisa Klages-Bombich, and Susan Restler
Foreword by Rosemary Arca

This book presents a model of embedded professional development, which capitalizes on the affordances of technology to enable groups of faculty to examine their practice in a non-evaluative context, but with a clear focus on improvement. The core of the work involves individual reflection and the design provides for an accessible way to "see" into the classrooms of discipline peers. Most importantly, the *Taking College Teaching Seriously* experience is not an intense